TURNING
POINTS a memoir

For our dear, dear friend Phyllis—
for almost forty years
she has been our loving
neighbor at the lake —
We wish her all of the best —

Bud Sinner

TURNING POINTS a memoir

by George A. "Bud" Sinner and Bob Jansen
Foreword by Clay S. Jenkinson

The Dakota Institute Press
of the Lewis & Clark Fort Mandan Foundation

*Library of Congress Control Number: 2010939179
ISNB-13 987-0-9825597-4-1 (Hardcover)
ISBN-13 978-0-9825597-5-8 (Paperback)*

*Distributed by The University of Oklahoma Press
Created, produced, and designed in the United States of America
Printed in Canada*

*Book layout and design by:
Margaret McCullough corvusdesignstudio.com*

*The paper in this book meets the guidelines for permanence
and durability of the Committee of Production Guidelines for
Book Longevity of the Council on Library Resources.
10 9 8 7 6 5 4 3 2 1*

Cover Image: *Governor Sinner delivers his State of the State
address to a joint session of the North Dakota Senate and House of
Representatives at the 50th Legislative Assembly on January 6, 1987.
The speech was titled "To Greater Goals."* Photo by Garry Redmann.

Frontispiece: *George Sinner checks the soybean crop at the
Sinner-Bresnahan farm in 1964.* Photo courtesy George and Jane Sinner.

The Dakota Institute Press
of the Lewis & Clark Fort Mandan Foundation
2576 8th Street South West . Post Office Box 607
Washburn, North Dakota 58577
www.fortmandan.com
1.877.462.8535

MIX
Paper from
responsible sources
FSC® C016245

I DEDICATE THIS BOOK TO:

My wife Janie. Thank you for your love, your support, counsel, advice and strong leadership, your infinite patience and forgiveness, and for your superb management of the residence and staff, to say nothing of your handling of family matters when I wasn't there to help.

My children. You have always been there to reassure and encourage me. You and Janie are the source of huge pride and gratitude for me. You are my best friends and the focus of my greatest love.

My brother Bill who was stricken with terminal cancer, and brother-in-law Ellery Bresnahan, both brilliant and ever-patient business partners, who along with the younger partners always gave me encouragement and wide berth and support for my public activities.

Lieutenant Governor Ruth Meiers, for her extraordinary role in our first election and first term. As lieutenant governor she developed, without question, the most forward-looking program for coordination of youth services in the nation. Her patience in her gallant fight to live when she fell victim to cancer was an inspiration to all of us.

Lieutenant Governor Lloyd Omdahl, who came to help when Ruth Meiers died. Lloyd's and my friendship and mutual respect go back a long way, so it was easy to have Lloyd cover critical areas of government in addition to playing a key role in our group discussion of critical issues. His historical perspective was an invaluable asset.

My Governor's Office staff, for the total commitment of their brilliant minds. Of like mind, they were dedicated to making service the key part of our joint leadership. Without this amazingly close-knit group who wanted most of all to make our office a place that tried to do what was right, life would have been very different indeed.

State agency heads, a group of true professionals, a large number of whom were first appointed by my predecessor Governor Olson. They were the ones who literally ran the place with pride and with remarkable class, and with my earnest blessing and profound and eternal gratitude.

State employees, who are to this day under-appreciated by the public. They work with integrity and patience day after day to serve the public. When a new governor comes in everything goes on without missing a beat.

Our congressional delegation members, who were always powerful allies in any effort to improve the lives of the people of North Dakota. They were always great friends and wonderful to work with.

Elected officials and legislators of both parties, who were as interested as I was in solving problems and with whom it was always rewarding to find solutions together.

The citizens of North Dakota who, even when they did not always agree with my efforts, were always gracious and kind to Janie and me. It was always a joy to be among them.

I am eternally grateful to all of these fine people and to all previous governors who have each in their own time and in their own way contributed to building the state into this wonderful place that we all, lovingly, call "home."

—*George Sinner*

CONTENTS

FOREWORD

George A. "Bud" Sinner was governor of North Dakota during one of the most difficult decades in the state's history. He served two four-year terms between 1984 and 1992. A protracted drought, the worst in decades, and a severe farm credit crisis combined to put more pressure on North Dakota agriculture than at any time since the 1930s. It was a period of farm foreclosures and accelerated rural outmigration, which helped to inspire a series of radical farm movements across the Great Plains. Some of that radical populism found voice in North Dakota. The state treasury was severely constricted throughout the decade. And in 1989, in a statewide referral, the people of North Dakota rejected a modest tax increase passed by a conservative legislature and signed by Governor Sinner.

The population of North Dakota in 1980 was 652,717. By 1990 the population had diminished to 638,800, a loss of 2.1%. The decline felt worse than the statistics indicated, perhaps because the population decline was dramatically more severe in rural than in urban North Dakota. At the time, nobody knew where this sad trend would end. In 1970 there were 45,000 farmers in North Dakota. In 1980 the number of farms had diminished to 40,000. By 1990 only 33,000 farms remained. The average farm acreage was 752 acres in 1970, 921 acres by 1980, and 1,224 acres in 1990. Thus approximately 7,000 North Dakota farms went out of business during the Sinner years. On September 22, 1985, the first of Willie Nelson's Farm Aid concerts was staged at Champaign, Illinois. Throughout the Great Plains, including

North Dakota, suicide hotlines were established and the rural clergy worked tirelessly to provide counsel to farmers in danger of bankruptcy or foreclosure.

In the midst of all this rural pain, North Dakota managed somehow to celebrate its centennial in style, in what planners called "The Party of the Century." North Dakota had become the 39th state on November 2, 1889. On that day, President Benjamin Harrison shuffled and then signed the statehood bills of North and South Dakota to avoid the appearance of preference. North Dakota (39th state) and South Dakota (40th state) were admitted simultaneously. Montana followed on November 8, 1889, and Washington on November 11. With this flurry of railroad-inspired western expansion, 1889 was the year of the largest number of state admissions since 1788, when eight states joined the union following the adoption of the U.S. Constitution.

Governor Sinner named former Governor Arthur A. Link to chair the eighteen-member Centennial Commission. President George H. W. Bush visited North Dakota to celebrate the centennial. He was the first sitting president to visit the state in three decades. He planted a tree on the capitol grounds. North Dakotans were encouraged to plant 100 million trees in North Dakota by the year 2000. This did not occur. As Governor Sinner acknowledges in his memoir, co-authored with his long time press secretary Bob Jansen, the tree planted by President Bush subsequently died. David Solheim of Dickinson was chosen as the state's Centennial Poet. Chuck Suchy of rural Morton County was named Centennial Troubadour. Bobby Vee (a North Dakotan), Myron Floren, Roy Clark, and the comedy team of Williams and Ree performed on the capitol grounds on July 4, 1989. A crowd of 100,000 sat on the capitol lawn to watch the centennial fireworks.

In spite of the centennial celebration, the 1980s were a period of pessimism in North Dakota history. There was a widespread view then that North Dakota's progress had stalled. Some believed that the state was in decline, and that the decline would continue indefinitely. Commentators wondered what North Dakota's bicentennial celebration would bring; a few wondered if North Dakota would be around to celebrate its 200th birthday in 2089. The future was that uncertain.

In 1987 a pair of professors from Rutgers University, Frank and Deborah Popper, published an infamous essay in which they predicted radical depopulation of the Great Plains. The time may come, they argued, when it would be best to let the plains revert to native grass, to permit Native Americans to reclaim lands lost to white conquest in the 19th Century, and to re-introduce large herds of buffalo on the emptied prairie. The Poppers were not the first to make this radical suggestion. As far back as 1833, the artist George Catlin argued that the Great Plains could never successfully be cultivated, that the region should be preserved by the United States government as "A Nations Park, containing man and beast, in all the wild and freshness of their nature's beauty!"

Although the *Buffalo Commons* thesis was more predictive than prescriptive, it provoked widespread anger and outrage on the Great Plains. North Dakotans shouted the Poppers' thesis down and denounced the mild-mannered authors, insisting that the state's coal and oil resources made it unlikely that the economy and population of North Dakota would collapse altogether. So far, the people of North Dakota have been vindicated in their baseline hopefulness about the future. Times were difficult on the northern plains, but the people of the region adamantly refused to give up.

The 1980s would seem to have been an unpropitious time to try to govern North Dakota. The voters of North Dakota, traditionally Republican, turned emphatically towards Democrats as the crisis deepened. Democrat Byron Dorgan was repeatedly re-elected to his position as the sole North Dakota member of the U.S. House of Representatives. Democrat Quentin Burdick continued to serve in the U.S. Senate. Although he was 80 years old, he easily defeated Grand Forks Republican Earl Strinden to hold his senate seat in 1988. Democrat Kent Conrad unseated Republican incumbent Senator Mark Andrews in 1986 by 2,100 votes. Even the North Dakota Senate was controlled by the Democrats between 1986 and 1993, the first time that had ever happened in North Dakota history. Democrat Sinner was elected Governor in years when Republicans dominated the presidential elections in North Dakota In 1984, incumbent President Ronald Reagan defeated Walter Mondale 65-34% in North Dakota. In 1988 George H. W. Bush defeated Michael Dukakis in North Dakota by a 56–43% margin.

In the face of these problems, and because of the severe belt-tightening that characterized his tenure, George Sinner was regarded by some observers as "Governor Gloom and Doom," a title he acknowledges and disputes in his memoir (page 100). Sinner remembers himself as an upbeat executive who often entered the Capitol singing, surrounded by a happy and energetic staff, the best, he says, in North Dakota history. He declares many times that he thoroughly enjoyed his time as governor and looked upon North Dakota's difficulties as problems to be solved rather than indications of state decline. Quoting his remarkable wife Jane he calls himself a "feedlot carpenter," willing to take a stab at problems even when he was unsure how his intervention might play out.

Turning Points is not even slightly pessimistic. It is the story of a hard working and principled governor, who had forged his character on a North Dakota farm, studied philosophy at an elite Minnesota university, considered becoming a priest, served in the United States military, married a woman of extraordinary intelligence, character, and strength, returned to Cass County, North Dakota, formed a farm partnership with his brother and his best friend, and prospered during difficult decades in North Dakota agriculture. He was, he says, unfazed by the crisis of the 1980s. Governing the state when the budget was constrained was strangely easier than presiding over good times, he writes. "If you have lots of extra money everyone and his half-sister wants to get a piece of it and are mad at you if you can't cut a big enough piece for them. We didn't have that problem because we never had any money. All we had to do was cut."

Sinner was preceded in office by Republican former Attorney General Allen Olson, who served a single, troubled term (1980-1984), and succeeded by Republican Ed Schafer, who served two terms (1992-2000).

Sinner was committed to the rights and opportunities of women. Ruth Meiers of Ross in Montrail County became North Dakota's first woman lieutenant governor in 1985. She died in office in 1987. On January 17, 1985, Governor Sinner appointed Beryl Levine to be the first woman to serve on the North Dakota Supreme Court. During his tenure 20 women served in the North Dakota State Legislature. He credits some of his sensitivity to women's issues to his marriage to his strong and often outspoken wife Jane. The memoir contains several moving tributes to Jane. Sinner tells the story of deciding in 1992 not to stand for a third term and seeking out his spouse to inform her of his decision, only to be preempted by spouse, who informed *him* that she had decided they would not run again! The Sinners were close friends of Bill and Hillary Clinton before, during, and after Clinton's presidency. During the darkest days of the Monica Lewinski scandal, the Sinners reached out to the Clinton's, particularly the First Lady, and advised forgiveness and reconciliation.

• • •

In the first paragraphs of the book, Sinner makes sure that the reader knows he is not writing an autobiography: "This is a memoir, thus it is more selective than comprehensive. These are highlights, as recorded in my memory."

Because *Turning Points* is not an autobiography or a chronological review of his life, it may be useful to provide a brief outline of George Sinner's life here. He was born in Fargo, North Dakota, on May 29, 1928. He grew up on a farm near Casselton. He was the son of Albert Francis Sinner and Katherine Augusta Wild. By his own account, his father was stern and increasingly conservative, a member of the John Birch Society. His mother was able to combine hard work with a generous and loving manner. He was the youngest of four children. His childhood, he says, was happy.

Sinner attended St. John's Preparatory School at Collegeville, Minnesota. He graduated in 1946. Thereafter he attended St. John's University at Collegeville, from which he graduated in 1950 with a B.A. in philosophy. He began to study for the priesthood, but left the seminary when a friendly monk advised him that he was sufficiently interested in women to make the priesthood a problematic vocation.

Sinner served in the North Dakota Air National Guard 1950-1953. His unit, the 178th Fighter Squadron, was activated for duty during the Korean War. Sinner was stationed at Moody Air Force Base, Valdosta, Georgia, and George Air Force Base at Adelanto, California. He was not engaged in combat activities.

George Sinner married Elizabeth Jane Baute of Lebanon, Kentucky, on August 10, 1951. The ceremony took place in Valdosta, Georgia. They met on a blind date in September 1950 while Sinner was attending a conference in St. Louis. Together the Sinners had ten children: Robert, George, Elizabeth, Martha, Paula, Mary Jo, James, Gerard, Joseph, and Eric.

Sinner served one four-year term in the North Dakota Senate from 1962-1966. In 1964 he challenged Republican incumbent Mark Andrews for a seat in the U.S. House of Representatives. He lost that race by 6,307 votes.

After this defeat, Governor William L. Guy appointed Sinner to a seven-year term on the North Dakota Board of Higher Education. During his tenure on the state board, Sinner championed freedom of the student press at the state's colleges and universities, helped save the career of UND President Tom Clifford, and voted to close Ellendale College after its main buildings burned in 1970. He also helped to create the Tri-College University Consortium of North Dakota State University, Concordia College, and the University of Minnesota Moorhead. The consortium shares library collections, outreach programming, and permits students to take courses at any of the three institutions. Sinner served as President of the State Board of Higher Education in 1970.

He was one of 98 delegates to the North Dakota Constitutional Convention 1971-1972. The Convention sat formally from January 3 to February 17, 1972. In a special election held on April 28, 1972, the voters of North Dakota overwhelmingly rejected the proposed new constitution. At the convention, among other things, Sinner championed separation of church and state in North Dakota.

In 1982 he was elected to the North Dakota House of Representatives. In 1984 he was nominated by the Democratic-NPL Party as its candidate for governor, over rival candidates Arthur A. Link, S. F. "Buckshot" Hoffner, and Walt Hjelle. Sinner won the election with 55.3% of the vote. The incumbent Allen Olson received 44.7%. Four years later, in 1988, Sinner defeated Republican challenger Leon Mallberg, of Dickinson, 59.9%–40.1%.

Sinner's tenure as governor began with a constitutional crisis that seems trivial in retrospect but produced considerable legal and political consternation at the time. Although he defeated Allen

Olson handily, Sinner was unable to move into the governor's office on January 1, 1985, the day traditionally regarded as the starting date of a new term. Olson's partisans challenged the January 1st transition date, arguing that the North Dakota Constitution did not specify the date of a governor's term, and that precedent, therefore, should be the deciding factor. Sinner's lawyers argued that the governor's term began on January 1, 1985. Olson's lawyers insisted that he could continue in office until January 6, 1985, a full four years since he had filed his oath of office with the North Dakota Secretary of State on January 6, 1981.

The North Dakota Supreme Court agreed to take original jurisdiction of the case. On January 4, 1985, the Court unanimously decided that Sinner had legally been governor since January 1, 1985 and, by implication, that Olson had been occupying the office extra-constitutionally for four days. The opinion, written by Chief Justice Ralph Erickstad, declared, "...the term of office for which Olson was elected in 1980 commenced on January 1, 1981, and terminated on December 31, 1984." The court enjoined Olson from "exercising the powers and duties of the office of Governor of the State of North Dakota." In spite of the ruling, Olson did not vacate his office until the January 6, the day *he* regarded as the date of transfer.

The crisis did not affect the domestic arrangements of the Sinners, since Governor Olson—to the consternation of the people of North Dakota—had declined to live in the Governor's Residence.

In *Turning Points*, Sinner argues that these political machinations were not the work of Allen Olson himself, but of Republican partisans who were bitter about the results of the election and bent on keeping Olson in office long enough to fill empty seats in the North Dakota court system. Sinner reports later conversations with Olson which indicated that Olson was as much a victim of these maneuvers as Sinner. Historians are less certain of this assessment.

Once Sinner was safely seated, things settled down quickly into a budget crisis that lasted for most of ensuing eight years. His work as governor consisted principally of cutting the state budget, not just fat but often enough muscle too, particularly in K-12 and university education. Sinner began his tenure by calling for $73 million in additional cuts to the lean budget that outgoing Governor Olson had submitted. Sinner's attempts to balance the budget by reducing expenditures and raising taxes were hamstrung by a series of referral drives, some of them led by Leon Mallberg of Dickinson.

In July 1991, near the end of his second term, Sinner was attending a Western Governors Conference in Rapid City, when he suffered heart pains sufficient to send him to a local hospital. The attending physicians recommended immediate surgery. The operation was conducted in Rapid City, South Dakota. Sinner returned to work in a couple of weeks, on a limited basis, and eventually made a complete recovery.

Sinner gave four North Dakotans the coveted Rough Rider Award during his tenure. Ronald N. Davies, the federal judge who in 1957 ordered the integration of Little Rock Central High School in Little Rock, Arkansas (1987); athlete and coach Phil Jackson (1992); actress Angie Dickinson (1992); and man of letters Larry Woiwode (1992).

Sinner left office voluntarily, on the new constitutionally-mandated terminus, on December 14, 1992. In the election of 1992, Republican Ed Schafer, an entrepreneur and son of the legendary Harold Schafer, defeated Democrat Attorney General Nicholas Spaeth 58.2-40.9%.

Sinner has had a long association with the sugar beet industry. From 1975-1979, he was the president of the Red River Valley Sugarbeet Growers Association. During his tenure, he chaired a farm commodity group that was responsible for creating the Northern Crops Institute at North Dakota State University in Fargo. That institute became the model for the Lignite Energy Research Council, created during Sinner's term as governor. Following his two terms as governor, Sinner served as Vice President of Public and Governmental Relations for the Crystal Sugar Company in Moorhead, Minnesota. He has been fully retired since 1996. He was the last Democratic governor of North Dakota. He remains active in North Dakota life—particularly in Fargo, where he and Jane now live.

The story Sinner tells in *Turning Points* is of a political career in which "doing the right thing" took precedence over political expediency. At the 1964 Democratic National Convention in Atlanta, then state senator Sinner took the lead to find a place for uncredentialed African-American delegates from Mississippi to sit. The black delegates, positioned alphabetically near to the North Dakota delegation, had been suffering on their feet in the aisle next to the "official" (all white) Mississippi delegates. Sinner won national attention for his leadership at the convention, and for the way he explained his actions in terms of human decency rather than in the tense context of race and politics.

In 1968, he supported the principled but quixotic presidential campaign of Minnesota Senator Eugene McCarthy rather than the Democratic Party's establishment candidate Hubert Humphrey, and, at the disastrous Democratic National Convention in Chicago, he pressed for a more radical platform plank on Vietnam. This struggle pitted him briefly against his political mentor Bill Guy. "I was at odds with my highly respected and beloved friend Bill Guy over the language. Bill supported and had been involved in writing the pre-convention draft, which was patently evasive of the real issues. However close Bill and I were—and we were close—I stood up at our delegation meeting and ardently opposed it. ... He was offended, but he got over it."

In 1990, Governor Sinner banned smoking from the North Dakota State Capitol by executive order. Sinner believes that that controversial decision may have cost him appointment as President Clinton's U.S. Secretary of Agriculture (see page 166).

In 1991, Governor Sinner, a devout Catholic, vetoed the anti-abortion statute passed by the North Dakota State Legislature. The law would have been one of the most restrictive in the United States. His accompanying veto message provided a historical survey of Christian theologians' positions on when life begins, dating back to St. Thomas Aquinas—and beyond. Twenty years later, Sinner remains proud of the veto and proud of his veto message, which is reprinted as an appendix to this memoir. Of the veto, which the North Dakota House of Representatives failed to override by a 63-43 vote, Sinner wrote, "What was ironic, I've never believed that abortion was a good thing—it wasn't that at all—but when you get into the area of public policy you have to be scrupulously careful to not ever give credence to the idea that the state can impose church opinions, even when they are the opinions of the majority."

• • •

Among other things, *Turning Points* is a beautiful paean to family farm life in North Dakota. Sinner provides lovely, whimsical, sometimes sad accounts of the hired men who worked on the farm, and recreates their Norwegian and German-Russian dialects beautifully. His portrait of his father, with whom he engaged in epic quarrels over national politics and the management of the family farm, is loving and forgiving. He provides a beautiful portrait of his brother Father Richard (Dick) Sinner, a man who took Christ's message so seriously that his life constituted a sustained challenge to the everyday world. Sinner explains how Dick's involvement in the sanctuary movement in the 1980s threatened to become an issue in his political career, but was disarmed by the governor's ready wit, which he ascribes to grace.

Most political memoirs pay lip service to the writer's religious experience, and move on emphatically to secular affairs. This is not the approach of *Turning Points*, which could be classified not as a political memoir but rather as the spiritual autobiography of a man who happened also to have enjoyed a successful political career. Although Sinner is a firm advocate of Jefferson's "wall of separation" between church and state, he was never afraid to let it be known that his serious religious education and his spiritual life informed his work in the public arena. Without often making it overt, it may be said that Sinner brought a spiritual dimension to every decision he made in the course of his public career. His policies, his political decisions, and his life have been informed by Christian principles of brotherhood, sympathy for the poor, the weak, and the unprotected, and forgiveness. Sinner's memoir reflects a deep devotion to integrity in himself, his staff, fellow North Dakotans, and those who sought the help of the North Dakota government. When others exhibited human frailty, Sinner was quick to forgive. When they exhibited dishonesty and an unrepentant attitude, he was unafraid to express his anger. In a few cases, he admits, that anger has not waned over time.

Sinner informs the reader that his life and work were guided by two great insights, offered to him by his spiritual mentors. The first came early in his life during a stay at a Trappist Monastery called New Melleray. An old priest told Sinner that while man has free will and God does not direct his actions in a specific way, God nevertheless makes things work out. "That's who God is," the priest said, "and that's what salvation is. God is all love and will make it all work out. He doesn't control our lives." The other lesson was offered decades later by Sinner's personal physician Ralph Dunnigan. When he was dying in 2002, asked by Sinner if he was ready to face the end of his life, Dunnigan said, "I've been fine ever since I learned that God's love is all about forgiveness. I've been praying a lot and studying scripture a lot, and I've discovered that every reference in scripture to salvation is about forgiveness." Dunnigan suggested that Sinner should take the lesson of forgiveness, including self-forgiveness, to heart.

Even so, Sinner admits that it was his political style to "lead with my chin." He is fond of the coincidence that his mother's maiden name was Wild and his family name is Sinner, thus making him a Wild-Sinner.

Sinner's memoir is not a breezy book of gubernatorial anecdotes or an attempt to paper over the qualities in his leadership style that made him sometimes a man of controversy. This is a book of serious spiritual and philosophical reflection written by a man who is nevertheless not afraid to relive old battles, to settle some scores, to opinionate about some things that a former governor might easily have left alone. *Turning Points* is easily the most unusual political memoir in North Dakota history and quite possibly the most valuable, because it takes us inside the decision making process and reminds us that politics—at least for Bud Sinner—is more about people and personalities and ideas than it is about the decisions themselves. Above all, *Turning Points* is a memoir by a public servant who intends to be taken seriously, then and now, and who developed a national consciousness and a national range of association, while trying to hold North Dakota together during one of the most difficult periods of its history.

"How would I like to be remembered as governor?" he asks at the end of the book. "I wasn't perfect, but was open and honestly trying to be a good servant. I didn't put a lot of stock in prestige. I wanted people to know that I was just like they were, somebody who laughed at his own mistakes, and someone who understood human need and human suffering and had a good human sense of humor."

Clay S. Jenkinson
Editor-in-Chief
The Dakota Institute Press

MAJOR MILESTONES

May 29, 1928—George Albert "Bud" Sinner
is born in Fargo, North Dakota

1946–1950—At St. John's University, earns bachelor
of arts in philosophy; scraps priesthood plans

1951–1952—Active duty with Air National Guard during
Korean War

August 10, 1951—Marries Elizabeth Jane Baute

Fall 1952—Returns to Casselton farm

November 1962—Elected to North Dakota Senate

Summer 1964—Delegate to Democratic
National Convention in Atlantic City

Summer/Fall 1964—Loses close race for US
Congress to incumbent Mark Andrews

November 1966—Defeated for re-election to State Senate

July 1, 1967—Begins seven-year term on North
Dakota Board of Higher Education

Summer 1968—Supports Eugene McCarthy at
Democratic National Convention in Chicago

Winter 1972—Delegate to North Dakota
Constitutional Convention

April 1972—Loses Democratic-NPL Party
gubernatorial endorsement to Arthur Link

November 1982—Elected to State House of
Representatives; chairs Finance and Tax Committee

April 1984—Wins Democratic-NPL Party
endorsement for governor

November 1984—Upsets Republican
incumbent Governor Allen Olson

January 1, 1985—Takes office as governor

March 1987—Appoints Lloyd Omdahl lieutenant governor after
death of Ruth Meiers, the state's first woman to hold that post

July 1988—Convenes drought-assistance meeting in Chicago

November 1988—Re-elected governor by large
margin over challenger Leon Mallberg

Fall 1989—Travels around the state to support
state sales tax and other revenue sources

December 1989—Voters reject tax measures in special election

July 1991—Undergoes heart bypass surgery in Rapid City

October 1991—Decides against running
for re-election to a third term

November 1992—President-Elect Bill Clinton
consults on appointments to cabinet

December 15, 1992—Moves to south Fargo
home after second term ends

PREFACE

"The past is prologue." William Shakespeare said that, and the famed phrase appears often in my speeches. It fits then that this preface serves as something of a prologue that introduces you to my past and the review of my past on the pages to follow.

Many people in recent years urged me to compile my memoirs. The kids began to press, and my wife Janie started some years ago to do her own compilation, again at the children's insistence, and then she kind of joined the chorus. I don't mind telling my story orally because it leaves my mind a little freer, but you can hardly read my scribbling in long hand because my concentration is never on the pen or the words—it's more on the thoughts. One day a woman named Gloria Larson called and said she wanted to compile my memoirs. That's what finally pushed me into it. But when Gloria moved away, the project stopped. Janie and I ran into Bob Jansen, who was my press secretary during my eight years in the Governor's Office and for several months with the campaign before that. He is a close friend and I asked him if he would consider working with me. I have relied on Bob to put my memories into publishable form. He has also provided historical settings and context for many of my memories. We collaborated to write my stories and perspective from his interviews with me, along with additional research and documentation. Without him, this book would not have happened.

This is a memoir, thus it is more selective than comprehensive. These are highlights, as recorded in my memory. What we present here is neither an academic paper nor a literary work of art.

Neither is it a definitive or scholarly history of my life and times. Except where they were recorded in news accounts or printed in official documents, most of the quotations included here are reconstructed from my memory. I have tried to best reflect those statements and conversations as I remember them.

Memory, particularly distant memory, is usually incomplete. So, we have inserted the perspectives of a few others to provide additional context and clarity and confirm accuracy. Janie has a more complete awareness and also has sharper memories concerning our home and family life and some other experiences and events that we've shared. So, we've excerpted portions of her writing about those areas. We've also included some of Lloyd Omdahl's insights, taken from a videotaped interview by historian Tracy Potter when Lloyd was finishing up his time as lieutenant governor.

You will find that my lifelong passion for issues dominates the perspectives and the memories incorporated in this memoir. I've tried to avoid getting too carried away with that, but for anyone who is really interested we have also highlighted some of those issues in a separate section at the end of this book.

Some humorous incidents lighten and balance the serious stuff. For example, we laughed a great deal about an episode related to my appointment of a broad state Committee of 100, which we put together in consultation with the Greater North Dakota Association to study the best ways to create economic development. I announced the committee at a press conference the day before, left early the following morning for Washington, and returned that night. As I got off the plane and came up the ramp, there were all the cameras and reporters. Something was up.

A reporter said House Republican Leader Earl Strinden had ridiculed our 100-member committee as being totally unwieldy and an exercise in futility. Did I have any comment?

The irony of Strinden's remarks hit me instantly. An angel of light flashed through my mind and I quipped: "It's a little bit smaller than the House of Representatives," which of course Earl prided himself in being the head of in all its great achievements. The whole group en masse immediately turned and ran for the door to get to their stations and to where they could put it in print.

That retort wasn't really mine—it just came out of the blue—but it was sure fun.

Obviously I love humor (as almost everyone who knows me is aware of) and telling stories; usually they are old stories, and some people get to hear them more than once.

Gerard Manley Hopkins is one of my favorite poets. He was a Jesuit who died more than a century ago and on his tombstone is the epitaph *Esse Quam Videri*, a motto of his family. It's a Latin phrase that means "to be, rather than to seem." Although in the crazy world of politics we are often told that perception is reality, perception is rarely reality. Even though the memories recorded here in my writing are my perception, it is my hope they also reflect reality. I hope they portray what I have been and what I am, not merely what I have seemed to be.

—George "Bud" Sinner, Fargo, North Dakota

CHAPTER ONE: early political impact

Northern Hospitality

It is my great belief that the Holy Spirit provides guidance in important situations, as the ensuing encounter illustrates.

Following my first session in the State Senate, I was a delegate from the North Dakota Democratic-NPL Party at the 1964 Democratic National Convention in Atlantic City.[1] As a member of the Platform Committee, I helped draft the section on agriculture. Georgia House Representative Julian Bond, a civil rights activist who was later elected to the Georgia Legislature, worked to get blacks included in the southern Democrats' delegations. The all-white Mississippi delegation was supposed to be seated right behind our North Dakota group. A white minister named Ed King led the alternative Mississippi Freedom Democratic Party (MFDP), which Bond had helped organize. King had terrible scars on his body from being beaten several times. We had gotten acquainted and I found him to be an outstanding man. MFDP filed a protest with the Rules Committee of the convention, as I remember it. The committee ruled the official Mississippi party delegation invalid because it refused to allow African-American participation. Others have written that the segregated Mississippi delegation refused to support Lyndon Johnson because of his support for civil rights legislation.

The convention's credentials committee declined to seat the Mississippi delegation, and also declared that the Mississippi

Freedom Democratic Party was not chosen by any appropriate structure either. The MFDP rejected a compromise offer of including two of its members as at-large delegates, so neither party was seated.

On that first night, the Freedom Party delegates were there in some numbers and they demonstrated silently on the floor by standing in the area of the Mississippi delegation. Late in the session they had started to move into the delegation seats. After standing for a long time, they finally just decided to sit down. Suddenly somebody gave an order to the sergeant at arms and to the bevy of security people on the floor to remove these black people from the seats of the Mississippi delegation. It was nonsense and it was pretty obvious that we were going to have bedlam on the floor. It was a crazy move.

Cliff Carter, Lyndon Johnson's chief of staff (or aide de camp), was running things, so I called him at convention headquarters: "This is Senator Sinner and I am the leader of the North Dakota delegation. You're risking a riot, a full-fledged riot down here. Your security people are trying to physically remove the Mississippi Freedom Party from the seats of the Mississippi delegation in front of the world's television cameras.

"I don't know why they are being removed," I continued. "They can't vote, they can't do any damage by sitting there—they are tired from standing all evening. I think you are doing a stupid thing by risking a riot here on the floor of the convention. I spoke to one of the security people and he agreed it was nonsense. Why not just let them sit?"

"Senator, give me a couple of minutes and I will get back to you," Carter said.

After about two minutes he came back. "Tell them to let the people sit."

So I rushed back to tell the security people and by this time there were fistfights and grappling and everything else going on. "I just had instructions from Cliff Carter to tell you to let them sit. The directive is to not try to evict them." They immediately backed off and practically hugged me in gratitude.

Later on that evening, John Chancellor of NBC News asked me on camera what I had done to stop the eviction. "It seemed to me to be silly to try and push these people away and cause all sorts of turmoil when it really didn't make any difference," I said. "So I called Cliff Carter and he agreed, and I went and told the sergeant at arms."

"The sergeant at arms said you were the one that gave the order to stop."

"I didn't *give* the order, just passed it on."

Of course, the Mississippi people were grateful. The next day Ed King asked me to come and speak to their delegation. They were meeting at a church not far from our hotel. I went and talked to them briefly. "If my opinion is worth anything, I think you've made your case eloquently and you ought to let it rest." I said. "Just let it go, don't push it any further."

But that second night the Freedom Party people, despite my suggestion, were there in a four-foot aisle between the Mississippi section and our seats. The chairs had been roped off. It was extremely hot and this was late into the night, probably midnight. They stood patiently for two hours or more. There was no central air conditioning and they were visibly exhausted. I finally asked our delegation whether they'd mind if these people came and sat with us. Our group all said, "Good heavens, let's do it!" And they moved over to make room.

I went back and told the tired Mississippi people that we'd like them to share our seats. Of course they were grateful. One man there, a newsman who was also a political activist and was acting as a security person, apparently told Frank McGee, a floor correspondent with NBC News, that I had been the one who stopped the eviction the night before and had now invited the people to sit with the North Dakota delegates. Then, when the convention broke up about 1:30 AM, McGee came over and asked for a live interview there on the convention floor.

Chet Huntley was the lead guy up in the booth. McGee said in the two-way radio, "Huntley, I've got Senator Sinner down here."

Back came Huntley's voice saying, "Get somebody else, we had him last night."

Then McGee said, "God damn it, Huntley, you run it in the booth and I'll run it on the floor, I'm going to interview Sinner." Huntley didn't respond.

McGee then turned with his camera and microphone. Noting that we had been offering seats to the integrated Mississippi delegation, he said, "Senator, many people in the South, and I think you're aware if this, would say you can have a different feeling on this problem because you don't have many Negroes there [in North Dakota]. You simply don't understand what life is like, you don't understand. What is your response?"

I remember looking at him and saying, "I spent a lot of months in the South in the Air Force. I think most of the people in the South are the most hospitable people I've ever known. In this particular situation, this atmosphere, they would have shown the same kindness to these people that we did. Regardless of your disposition on the mechanics and the particular facts on this issue, kindness didn't seem to be out of order in any circumstances."[2]

Well that just shut McGee up—defused the loaded question. He walked away.

Looking back, I don't know how I came up with that answer. It seems a mind greater than mine had taken over and was whispering to me, providing the inspiration to point out the kindness of the southern people without condemning them. It was a time of learning for me during a period of dramatic change in the country.

Afterward, mail started coming in from all over the country, expressing thanks to our North Dakota group for brushing aside the attempt to inflame the situation. My large file containing all that correspondence has disappeared, but a man named John Sherman from Providence, Rhode Island, provided one perspective in a letter to the editor of *The Fargo Forum*. He wrote:

High praise is due the delegation from North Dakota for its exemplary conduct at the Aug. 26th session of the Democratic National Convention. The delegates' patience in putting up with the tumultuous, exasperating conditions in the neighboring Mississippi delegates' section and their friendliness and courtesy in offering their seats to Mississippi Freedom Party delegates are a credit to the state.

From Whence This Comes

Let's back up and further set the stage.

Looking back at my life, at my past, it seems I've pretty much just walked along. I've always tried to do the job at hand the best I possibly could and not worry about what came next. But a motivational speaker in Wahpeton, ND, had an inspiring message: "When you see a social problem that needs solutions, you have to ask yourself: if *I* don't do it, *who* will? And then you have to ask yourself: if I don't do it *now*, then *when* will I do it?"

That hit me hard. It used to give me all kinds of trouble because I transferred the concept to other things too. I'm forever getting halfway through a project, coming to something that needs to be fixed, and stopping and fixing that. Often I put away my tools before remembering I was originally doing something else. That message was a piece of wisdom because most of the time it's pretty easy to say somebody else will take care of that. We rarely did that in the Governor's Office. We were ready to tackle issues that came before us and we were pretty faithful at making people our priority. That was something that never left me. I always saw that the things I *could* do as the things that I *should* do. Otherwise it probably wasn't going to get done.

I still love fixing things. Janie correctly thinks I'm a haywire repairman. That's even more enjoyable now that I have time to fix things. Fixing people's problems is the same. I don't know how to say, "No, I can't help you," because if you think about it enough there is always a way to help. It may be there's some pride involved because of the huge satisfaction we feel in helping somebody. And people are grateful for just little things. If you can do it, it's kind of cowardly to pretend you can't.

During the 1997 North Dakota flood in Fargo, maybe four days before the crest, about twenty homeowners in our Oakcreek cul-de-sac came and asked me to take charge of our area since we were below the city's line of defense. I agreed to do it because I know that someone had to take the lead. We protected about forty homes. People worked together and accomplished things that nobody else was doing. I went around and told everyone to invite the volunteers who were helping fill sandbags to come in and use our bathroom, even if they dragged mud in. "Mud will clean up," I said. "If you need a bathroom, come in." We've heard many comments about that, about how the volunteers seemed to appreciate it. It was the kind of stuff that often leaders are afraid to say to people, afraid to teach. We put down a half a million sandbags in the cul-de-sac and all of us stayed dry.

One of our neighbors didn't want to cooperate. He wanted to do his own thing. Members of his church came and helped him. Some people were upset that he wouldn't work with the rest of us, but I said it would be okay. I didn't want his disregard for the whole group to reduce us to his level. But I had to explain to him that his way wouldn't work for the rest of us because half our people couldn't do it themselves. They were alone and incapable of handling sandbags. It turned out just fine. We were able to match up the dike with his, and when it was over we helped him get his sandbags carried out. All in all it was just a good experience for almost everyone. Homeowners made sure volunteers had food and water and a bathroom. Oh God, it was a great show. The city actually told me afterward that this was one part of town they knew they didn't have to worry about because they knew we were coping.[3]

That's also how in 2006 I got involved with the fight for a half-cent sales tax in Fargo that would have replaced a portion of the property taxes revenues that go to schools.[4] I knew what to do. Whether it was a perfect solution or not was certainly debatable, but somebody had to do something and it had to be done quickly. We came up short of the required 60 percent vote but we generated important discussion about the problem of high property taxes in our state. My involvement with more recent efforts to find solutions to substance abuse in the community was a similar recognition of a problem followed by action to address that problem.

I've always loved learning about new issues—always finding out there was a lot more about them—and loved the debate when I knew the subject and felt comfortable with my position. Granted, some were pretty murky and there were a few where it seemed to me I understood it but later discovered I really didn't know it at all. George Starcher, the former University of North Dakota president, used to say that, "Education is the transition from cocksure ignorance to knowledgeable uncertainty." The lesson in his wonderful statement became more apparent to me over time. It helps to explain to people that we really have to learn to listen to each other.

A school superintendent in Casselton displayed another aphorism from Mark Twain that said the same thing in essence on a small poster he kept under glass on a table in the center of his office. It read: "When I was a boy of fourteen, my father was so ignorant I could hardly stand to have the old man around. But when I got to be twenty-one, I was astonished at how much he had learned in seven years."

One great lesson in public policy happened a few years ago when Dick Lamm, former governor of Colorado, asked me to speak to a gathering of western United States think tanks. Some of the brightest people in the West were there in Vail, Colorado, about sixty people in the room, seated around tables arranged in a large quadrangle.

In opening the conference, I talked about the larger national problems and the uniqueness of the West. The discussion had gone on for some three hours about waste, water, the history of the West; about wetlands, economics, trade, environmental concerns and military bases. It was a serious, enlightening discourse among serious, thoughtful people. Suddenly a man who was sitting sullenly across the square of tables—a man who had not spoken—virtually exploded on the meeting. His name was Arturo Madrid.[5] He led a think tank in Claremont, California, that worked to help the burgeoning brown population of the southwestern United States.

In an angry, yet pleading voice, he said: "Doesn't anyone care about people? No one has mentioned people. I represent millions of brown people who have no hope, whose lives are desperate. Their children grow up in poverty and drugs and crime and violence. All they want is a chance to have children who can be educated, and who have some hope. They don't give a damn about economics. They don't give a damn about military power, and that's all you've talked about. Does not anybody here care about people? Not one has mentioned people not once, in all these discussions."

He went on passionately about the festering fury that filled the people with whom he worked. It was a shocking statement and we were all stunned and duly chastised. We all knew what he knew, that all of these forces of economics and environment affect people. But we had not said so, nor had we even hinted at the awareness of the frightening human problems of which he spoke at length. And he was right, of course. We had spoken as if there were some sacredness to economic theories, to environmentalism, to many broad issues. No one had mentioned people. We sat in stunned silence and then, betraying the truth of his allegations, we clumsily went back to the same sanitized subjects—safe from human implication.

His admonition continued to trouble me deeply long afterward. I realized he had reminded us all of the fact that has to be fundamental to all governmental activities, indeed perhaps all societal actions: every issue is a human issue, or it is not an issue at all.

Certainly in the American governmental scheme it is people who matter, and even from a theological point of view, God is not served unless we serve the creatures God created. The American Constitution says nothing about capitalism or free trade, and it says nothing about environmentalism or spotted owls. Arturo Madrid warned us who are environmentalists to remember we are not neo-pantheists—we do not worship God in nature. We do not serve environmental causes for their own sake, but for people's sake. Neither should we be blind capitalists who worship development and profit.

We are constitutionally if not philosophically and morally bound to serve human beings. Arturo Madrid drove that home in a way I hadn't heard before when he asked the simple question: Doesn't anybody care about people? We have given in to issues and slogans and have forgotten that it is people who matter. We've forgotten that American government should work for the people—all people.

In the end, government has only one real function, which is to protect the rights of people. If it means that corporations are getting too big and are taking away peoples' right to income and livelihood, we have to be proactive and do something about it.

My Beginning In Politics

People who think we live in a *pure* democracy are incorrect. Ours isn't a pure democracy where people vote on every issue, or vote on many issues. We live in a *representative* democracy where people are elected to the job of studying issues and doing the best they can to find truth and find justice, and then fight for it and explain it to the people. A vote by the people on an issue is an exception.

We are not elected to do whatever the latest poll shows. That's absolutely the wrong basis for taking public positions. All issues are complicated and can't be left to a whimsical judgment. That is often what citizens are faced with, because they don't have all the facts—it isn't their job to study them.

My own earliest foray into the political scene was really weird. Janie and I remember a bit differently the specifics of how it actually happened. I recall that sometime in 1962 a man named Johnny Murphy, a friend of Janie's and mine, came to see her one day and asked, "Are you guys going to the district convention?"

"Probably not," she said.

He had an idea: "Why don't we see if the party would draft your husband to run?" She thought that sounded good, which was crazy because we had nine kids already and our time was already stretched. Janie conspired with him. I didn't know about it and wasn't at the convention in Casselton, but was drafted.[6] It was in the spring and we were busier than hell at the farm. I was running the day-to-day operation of the fieldwork, and there was a lot to do. It was a time when I couldn't get away, and wasn't that active in politics yet anyway. As I said, Janie's memory about how that all happened is a little different than mine, but certainly she blessed the effort.

The incumbent senator, John Yunker from Durbin, wasn't running for re-election. The district apparently wanted competition to generate interest so the delegates endorsed two candidates—a former House member, Milton Myhre of Kindred and me. They also endorsed three people for two House seats.

I came out ahead in the June primary election and then won the Senate seat in November when I beat a Republican incumbent House member, Don Otos, by a vote of 3,067 to 2,889. He was a nice man, a friend of my father.[7]

I was thirty-three years old at the time of the district convention and I don't recall now whether I had even attended a district convention before that. I did a lot of door-to door campaigning and liked it. People were good to me. I had learned some tricks about leaving notes when people weren't home, and recognized that it was far better to ask a voter for his or her consideration than to directly ask for their vote because that recognized the fact it would be up to them to make the decision. My sense that that's the correct approach—to just say, "I'd be grateful for your consideration"—has grown through the years. That campaign was probably my first significant organizational work; winning the election was a surprise.

When running for the State Senate, I observed Lieutenant Governor Charlie Tighe, who was good on issues. He was humanistic in his approach to government. By my judgment he had things pretty well straightened out in his mind. But one day Charlie decided to run for governor. The guy I knew vanished when he calibrated discussion on a topic to give it a good political tone. A good political tone is one thing, but he began waffling all over the place. It was a great lesson because it really drove it home to me how important it is to do your job—don't worry about the aftereffects, just do your job.

In 1964, during a moment of weakness, I agreed to run for Congress. A stupid idea. I didn't win but was doing well, gaining rapidly on Mark Andrews, the sitting congressman.[8] Even though my campaign had almost no money, Mark won by only about 6,300 votes. Just going around and talking about some of the national issues was gratifying—losing the race was okay. Someone who was following it closely told me my campaign would have been successful if there had been another week.

I have always disliked doing polls. How can anybody in government spend the time it takes to study an issue—and most of them are complex—and make a decision and then turn around and analyze it on how it's going to play with the public? When you do that and you're in front of an audience, you are stuttering and stammering and making excuses, all of which indicates there is no conviction in what you are saying. The people read that.

Acting according to polls isn't leadership. Important times and issues and decisions require leadership in its real sense, not the kind espoused by Alexandre Ledru-Rollin, the French Revolution politician who said: "There go the people. I must follow them for I am their leader."[9]

Daley Masses

The Democratic Party's 1968 national convention in Chicago turned into a traumatic time for candidates and attendees like me, largely due to anger over the Vietnam War.[10] This was also the year that both Dr. Martin Luther King, Jr. and Robert Kennedy were assassinated. Feelings were running really high against Lyndon Johnson, who was under pressure because of Vietnam and had declined to run for re-election. I was no longer a fan of LBJ. I had observed a lot of self-aggrandizement going on in the Johnson administration, and he was taking advantage of the political machinery that he controlled to unethically get himself a lot of things that were purely for personal gain, as far as I could see.

Johnson had toyed with Minnesota Senator Eugene McCarthy in the 1964 convention about who was going to be his vice presidential running mate. He knew all along who he was going to appoint and had already promised it to Hubert Humphrey. A lot of us who found out about it were really angry because McCarthy was our guy.

When 1968 came, it was pretty inflamed. Chasm-like differences had developed between people everywhere, especially between generations. In Chicago it was a generation gap between the people in the convention hall and those in Grant Park. McCarthy and Harold Hughes, the then governor of Iowa, were two of the people who were anti-war, outspoken. I watched in horror as the police riot squads beat up the young people protesting the convention, protesting against President Johnson, protesting against a war that to them seemed senseless. Of the many who were passionately leading the protests, comedian and civil rights activist Dick Gregory comes to mind. It was there in Grant Park that Gregory gave his infamous response to critics of young people and especially those who had long hair. Gregory reminded all of us who would listen that, "If Lyndon Johnson wore long hair, we'd go bald."

Inside, with his deep, booming voice, Hughes was giving a nominating speech for anti-war candidate McCarthy, as violent demonstrations erupted on the streets. Even though Johnson had clearly endorsed Humphrey long in advance of the convention, they played fast and loose with McCarthy, toyed with him again. I don't think McCarthy ever forgave him for what happened in 1968, on top of the snub four years earlier.

When Humphrey accepted the nomination for president he gave a long commendation of Lyndon Johnson. The whole audience got up and applauded except Hughes. During two or three standing ovations, Hughes sat solemnly in the middle of the world's television cameras in a big box right next to the speaker's podium. I became embarrassed that I had stood up. Hughes was impressive. Everyone saw him with his large, square jaw. I took a big chunk of that into my head because it told me that there was probably a lot more about Lyndon Johnson that people didn't like. It turned out there was in fact a lot more.

It was unfortunate that Hughes, after only serving one term in the US Senate [1969-1975], went sort of super religious and didn't engage in political life much after that. That was a real loss because he had a great deal to offer to make the world a better place for people. He had a unique ability to speak in simple, understandable, acceptable language. He was just a good guy. He had been a truck driver and was a recovered alcoholic and had all that strength besides.

McCarthy, who had also been a candidate for the presidency at the convention in Atlantic City four years earlier, was a man of great honor and great intelligence. I knew him personally and I will always admire the fact that he stood up to the forces of near-tyranny in Chicago. We were staying in a little hotel right down the street. McCarthy came down the big grandiose steps and saw a policeman beating up on one of the protesters. He yelled out at the top of his lungs, which was unusual for him. "Take your hands off that kid! Right now!" He went down and actually grabbed the officer.

I wasn't in the avant-garde movement of that effort to oppose the war—my wife was actually much more an activist and vocal against the war than I was. But I was certainly sympathetic and fought hard to get the peace plank straightened out in the party platform. I was at odds with my highly respected and beloved friend, then Governor William "Bill" Guy over the language. Bill, who chaired our North Dakota delegation, supported and had been involved in writing the pre-convention draft, which was patently evasive of the real issues. However close Bill and I were—and we were close—I stood up at our delegation meeting and ardently opposed it. I had arrived late. One woman was crying. She said Governor Guy convinced the caucus that the existing platform was much more dovish than the replacement one was. "That's what he told us," she said.

I went to him and said, "Bill, you're wrong about this, that's a bad plank and needs to be amended." He was offended, but he got over it. I can't remember all the platform language but it was pretty clear to me it was wrong, as it was to this other lady. We favored a provision that called for a unilateral de-escalation in Vietnam instead of wording about a negotiated resolution to the unpopular war.

It was a difficult time for me because I respected Governor Guy as much as anybody and I had to say, "Bill you're wrong about that." I had some alternate language from McCarthy and a group of core activity people who had drafted an amendment that was clearly better, in my judgment. Our delegation voted with Bill and the convention went on to defeat the peace plank language I favored.[11]

After Humphrey won the nomination, *The Fargo Forum* ran a front-page article about me at the Chicago convention with the headline:

A Defeated McCarthy Man, Tearful George Sinner Gives Sword to Gov. Guy

Staff writer and columnist Wayne Lubenow was pretty creative in his reporting. Here's some of what he wrote:

> With the four-letter obscenities ringing in the air from the mob in Grant Park across the street, a tearful George Sinner Thursday handed his sword over to Gov. Bill Guy.

Like U.S. Grant did for Robert E. Lee, Sinner and his six other McCarthy supporters in the North Dakota delegation were allowed to keep their horses.

For Sinner—a Casselton man and the acknowledged leader of the McCarthy people, it was a crushing defeat.

Because late until voting time, hope sprang eternal in the McCarthy breasts. They probably knew that they were beaten—but they kept expecting the miracle to happen. They were expecting to catch lightening in a bottle.

But when the North Dakota delegation caucused at 4 p.m. Thursday, it was Sinner—tears streaming down his face—who capitulated, more honorably probably than the Humphrey forces had a right to expect.

If it is true, as the TV experts claim, that this bloody convention has ripped the Democratic Party asunder, then it is for sure that George Sinner did more to patch it up than the rioters across the street who scream in the name of McCarthy.

George Sinner told the North Dakota delegation this: "I'm proud of the North Dakota delegation for helping us get rid of the unit rule.

"I'm sure some of you think we're kooks and hoodlums. I plead with you now to not damn us when you damn the hoodlums."

His voice broke as he said, "I don't blame Hubert Humphrey for a Vietnam position in which he was boxed in."

First he quoted the late Pope John: "We have to be good and kind to everybody all the time." And then he said the thing people were wondering about: "I am one McCarthy man who will vote for Hubert Humphrey."

Then George Sinner left the caucus room crying.

Lubenow concluded that the one thing that came clearly out of the caucus was this: patch up the party and we can win in November. He wrote, "It may take an awful lot of patchwork—but George Sinner took the first step Thursday afternoon."

But then, of course, Humphrey lost to Richard Nixon that fall while Republicans for other offices also won all across the country.

I left Chicago just sick to my stomach from all that took place. I have only been back once since then. It just seemed to me that the whole thing was overkill by about a thousand percent. Yet, many of the people I know in Chicago credit Mayor Richard Daley's ability to somehow extract some peace for the people who lived there during an earlier era when he was able to clean up some of the mob influence that was so strong, even though he may not have handled the demonstration at the convention properly. Then again, maybe no one could have handled it, as it was one difficult situation.

While I still don't have much respect for the senior Mayor Daley, it is easy to criticize from the outside. When you are in the arena fighting the bull you have to fight the way you know best.

Those were incredible times. To be in both Atlantic City and Chicago in the 1960s was to see the world changing, hopefully for the better. That whole decade was a time of great progress, but like a lot of other progress, it came with a good deal of pain and suffering.

CHAPTER TWO: philosophy of serving

Jock of All Trades

To use a baseball phrase, you might say I like to "swing away" at issues, like a batter stepping up to the plate. Years ago, Ralph Kiner, a Hall of Fame slugger and later broadcaster, wrote an article in *Look* magazine in which he explained the theory and mechanics of hitting a baseball. I think it was either the summer or fall of 1948 when Ellery Bresnahan (my close friend and future brother-in-law) brought the magazine clipping to St. John's University in Collegeville, Minnesota, where we were students.[12] As I recall, the first thing Kiner said was that the natural impulse is always to swing at the ball. Then if you make a decision to change that, that's the decision—to stop and *not* hit. If you wait and say, if there's a good pitch I'm going to hit it, you're dead. You could see this in Minnesota Twins slugger Kirby Puckett. When he was in a batting slump he'd get tentative. Ball players so often don't even get ready for the first pitch.

The second requirement of good hitting is to have your body cocked, ready to hit. And you must step into every pitch. That's the key: you step into every pitch. Those two requirements are really parts of one principle—being ready. Be ready to hit a ball or be ready to resolve issues.

The other advice Kiner gave was that regardless of the width of your stance, when you stride you generally end up in the same spot with your lead foot, and the back foot should be stationary. The stride ends in virtually the same spot regardless of where you start. If you start with too narrow a stance, when you stride you'll drop your eyes and arms and you'll swing under the pitch. Most batters, he said, start from too narrow a stance. Kiner pointed out that the great Ted Williams had a wide stance.

He also said pitchers differ. Some throw a rising fastball—for them you might not want to stride at all, you may want to stand straighter so you don't go under the pitch. Some throw a natural drop and for those, he said, you may want to narrow your stance. You have to pay attention to what you're doing—if you're popping up a lot, you need to widen out your stance. If you're hitting a lot of ground balls, you may need to narrow it a couple of inches. It was a great piece that Kiner wrote, and it taught me lessons I've never forgotten. I had been batting clean-up for the St. John's prep team and struck out a lot. My hitting improved dramatically as a result of Kiner's advice, which was so basic and instructional.

I considered myself a relatively good athlete and we started sandlot sports early. The kids from the two ends of town—the north side against the south side—made up games we played Saturday mornings. Then we had baseball and football from my earliest years in school. I remember several black eyes. My buddy Ellery gave me one of them in football—I tried to tackle him and got his knee in my face.

Dad didn't appreciate the love my brothers and I had for baseball but he tolerated it. He liked to play a little baseball with us, but it was pretty rare. Casselton had a pretty good team and sometimes we wanted to sneak away and play with them on Sunday when we had a major game. I was a good baseball player—a pretty fair shortstop—and in demand with the local team. Some people suggested I try for the majors, but I wasn't interested and didn't consider it. Dad complained about it sometimes if we had a game during harvest when we should be out driving a combine, but I don't remember that he ever interfered. For religious reasons, a lot of people, including my father, questioned back then whether we should really work or play sports on Sunday.

The two years before I went on active duty with the Air National Guard I played summer baseball two or three times a week and I never struck out. I was hitting against some pitchers who pitched in the Northern League. It was just amazing. One who comes to mind is Chuck Rohde, who played in the Northern League at the same time Roger Maris was with the Fargo-Moorhead Twins. He was good. I remember our Casselton team had six hits off him, including my two home runs, a triple, and a single.

The last game we played was against a good team in Fargo called the Red Sox. Our catcher had to go home for a funeral, so I caught. The Red Sox got a runner on third. He led off quite a bit and I threw down behind him. We had him by three or four feet twice but the umpire was looking the other way or didn't call it. I was furious and out of control. The next pitch this kid tried to steal home. I saw him coming and I stepped out and met the ball and the batter hit me across the back with the bat. I can't remember whether I caught the ball but it didn't make any difference because the runner came home and the batter reached first base and I got a sore back. I remember getting hit in both shoulder blades. He was able to slow down his swing so I wasn't badly hurt—there weren't any broken bones or anything.

Playing baseball was one of those fun times in my life. Later, I played baseball with my own kids. A lot of them have also been good hitters. Dad didn't come to my games. His life was so full then, but he probably regretted not seeing me play. I remember him attending only one athletic event I was in, a football game at St. John's.

As quarterback of St. John's prep school football team, it seems I was pretty fair at calling plays but I was so damn small. We ran a Notre Dame box, and the quarterback was essentially a blocking back.[13] At only 145 pounds soaking wet I wasn't big enough to block a light breeze.

In our senior year we only lost two games. In one of those we were ahead by a touchdown in the fourth quarter. We had fourth and long yardage on the forty-yard line. As we went into the huddle, the team's stud, Dick Shaughnessy, from Rice Street in St. Paul said, "George, let *me* punt." So I stupidly did—he shanked it and we lost two yards.

Our coach, former Minnesota Senator David Durenburger's father, George Durenburger, pulled me out of the game, grabbed me by the front of my shirt. "Who is the best punter out there?" he growled.

I was dumbstruck.

"God damn it," he demanded, "who is the best punter out there?"

"I am," I finally said. I had a thirty-seven-yard average as a high school punter.

And then he gave me a quick lecture. "You damn seminarians and your false humility," he said. "If you're going to be truly humble you've got to admit who can do it right, who's the best. Don't apologize to anybody." I never forgot that angry admonition.

I actually thought about that at length before deciding to run for governor. I had knowledge of state government and local government. And coach Durenburger's words came back to me: "You can do it, don't apologize." I remember that term *false humility*. Know thyself. It was a very important lesson.

Of course, this is perhaps a rather ironic story to draw any kind of deep meaning from, because when it comes to calling the signals or tackling issues, I rarely punt.

All About Service

I went to the seminary at St. John's University probably because even then I was sort of obsessed with helping others. My mother and father emphasized that service is the most gratifying work there is. My dad was a man who didn't tolerate fools easily. He expected honesty from other people and was absolutely, totally intolerant of compromises in that regard. He had no patience with deceitful people or deceit by itself. Both of my parents honored the truth with a passion. If you didn't tell the truth, it would be found out anyway.

As I said earlier, when it comes to service, I had learned somewhere along the line that you can't assume somebody else is going to do it. I think a lot of us too often are motivated by other motives than who can do it. But it became important to me throughout my life and it taught me, among other things, that if you don't know what you are doing, you had better look to somebody else who may know better.

It came up in the reworking of the executive budget in January 1985, that first month in the Governor's Office. We were undecided about whether to keep John Graham as head of the Department of Human Services. We were working on the human services budget trying to find anything to cut. We knew from the brilliant forecast by Dick Rayl, Office of Management and Budget director, that we had to reduce spending by 7 percent. During the conversation with

Rayl and Graham and my chief of staff, Chuck Fleming, standing around that round table in the office, I remember vividly that I made some stupid statement about where we could probably trim human services funding. John, who wanted to stay on in his job, just cut me off at the knees. He went on and on about how stupid my suggestion was. After John left that day and we finished the work, Chuck said, "There's one S-O-B we're going to get rid of."

"No," I said. "That's exactly the kind of people we must have and that's what everybody in here's got to do. We've got to have people around here to tell us we're idiots when we're idiots. When the rest of us are being stupid, somebody needs to wake us up."

It was part of that learning from Coach Durenberger, you've got to know who you are and go with what you believe.

My personal involvement was the only way to make sure human services and human needs were covered. Most people would be shocked to know the amount of time I spent on the budget. It was hundreds of hours, especially when we did the makeover when we first took office. Chuck Fleming was also huge in that. Chuck and I did hour after hour after hour of late afternoon work on the budget up in the Office of Management and Budget. Even with all the time Chuck and I put in, Rayl handled most of it and he really empowered his staff—man, they were good to work with. I had fairly good ideas about what programs were critical but there was so much I learned. "You have no idea how much it meant to Chuck and me in our appearances before the Appropriations Committee," Dick told me. "We knew exactly what you thought and it was always the merger of our ideas with yours so we never had to worry about coming back and wondering if we'd said the right thing." I had complete confidence in them and empowered them and they took care of it.

Admittedly there are many ways to serve the public. There are the Mother Teresas of the world who personally commit their lives to the poor. I've always believed that the commitment to service and public life is something worthy of Christian calling and I've always viewed it as that. In embracing service, I've always tried as ardently as I know how to avoid doing things out of any selfish goals or motives.

In that same light, I was careful not to favor relatives with appointments or special privileges. Doyle Schulz of the Highway Patrol, who is married to a close cousin of mine, Pat Wild, is an example. Doyle was held in high regard and clearly in line to become the new patrol superintendent. When I called him he said he knew I couldn't do that. There were some relatives who wanted jobs but I didn't consider them so their qualifications wouldn't fall under suspicion. Doyle felt the same way. I've always been grateful to him for his understanding and for his terrific recommendation for the appointment. "Brian Berg is by far the best, in my judgment," he said.

I immediately appointed Brian and have always been proud that I did.

Dick Gross, who was governor's counsel, picked up a series of three books on the leader as servant, which reinforced the belief that you can be both a leader and a servant. This writer, Robert Greenleaf, said any leader who doesn't understand that it's not about big cars and fancy parties and personal benefits, and doesn't understand that it's all about service, will never be a real leader. Leadership involves listening and intense commitment to the truth.[14] I think all of that goes back to my early training at St. John's and my early education there where that sort of philosophy was prevalent. Public service was heavily emphasized, particularly in the philosophy courses.

As governor, I told every state agency to understand that their operation wasn't about tyranny or control, it was about service.

Heidi Heitkamp, whom I appointed state tax commissioner, used to call me the "fire truck governor" because I moved pretty fast when there was a crisis. The first time she called me that was when a semi trailer load of radioactive uranium oxide hit a train at Bowdon, North Dakota.[15] As a former president of the fire department at Casselton, I knew that if you didn't go right away you might as well not go. So I grabbed the phone and called for a helicopter. I think they landed on the Capitol mall, picked me up, and we flew to Bowdon.

What was amazing to me when we got there, and still amazes me, was that the rural fire department volunteers from Bowdon not only had kept unnecessary people away, they had roped off the area, they had stopped and rerouted the traffic, and they had done an absolutely masterful, professional job of protecting the crew of the train. Everyone was taken right out of harm's way. They got people washed who were exposed, wonderfully demonstrating what ordinary people can do when they are serious public servants.

I went there intending to send National Guard people to help them. Turned out I didn't really accomplish much there, but if there had been a crisis I was ready to move. Another time, when range fires became a threat, I insisted the Guard buy aerial water buckets for firefighting. I had fought grass fires when I was with the fire department at home and it is a hellacious undertaking. People who try to do it better be in shape because it's fiercely difficult.

As was the case with those local volunteers, one thing that I learned in ways I had never realized before was how good our state employees are. Even though I probably knew as much about state government as any incoming governor, I discovered I really didn't know much at all. Operations and services carry on when a governor leaves office. Many times the other elected officials are changing at the same time. State employees are wonderful servants and if you don't listen to the agency people you won't understand anything. That was a highlight of my management style—I wanted professional people and I not only paid attention to what they said, I let them run the agencies.

Philosophical Lessons

My philosophy about service is illustrated in part by a set of profound declarations, or axioms, I will refer to as my Four Great Lessons of History. In public life and in corporate life these are good points to remember.

I have a special liking for the first lesson, which is by Euripides: *Those whom the gods would destroy, they first make drunk with power.*

That theme repeats itself in every walk of our lives, but clearly in politics. Politicians frequently get carried away with power and they do things that are completely out of line. Eventually their power leads them to do things that get them in trouble and they self-destroy. Historian Lord Acton warned that "power corrupts, and absolute power corrupts absolutely." A similar thought. Power leads people to lie and take advantage of others. It's a strange anomaly that really struck me as something I had to remember.

The second lesson is one you see so much: *The blossoms fall from the flower before it bears fruit.*

It all comes through aging and maturity. Like a plant, it takes us a certain amount of time before we accomplish things and see our actions bear fruit.

The third lesson is: *The stars shine brightest on the darkest night.*

I've told a lot of people that our group in the Governor's Office did a good job. We were there during challenging economic times. Sometimes it isn't as hard to solve problems as it is to go out and make things better when everything is going well: for example, if you have lots of extra money everyone and his half-sister wants to get a piece of it and are mad at you if you can't cut a big enough piece for them. We didn't have that problem because we never had any money. All we had to do was cut.

It seems to me as I've thought back that our whole group in that office really settled down when we had problems to solve. The PACE (Partnership in Assisting Community Expansion) program is a classic example. The program had been born out of the urgency of looking for an answer, a way to do economic development right. I won't ever forget passage of the program, which we were so sure was the right approach for economic development. Chuck Fleming and I got the idea for PACE when we were flying to Bowman one night. We went there to tell the Bowman people they needed to have an economic development tax to help new businesses, a process that was legalized and available but few counties or cities were using to help get businesses started.

The old system of approving loans for new businesses had no form or procedure that was well thought out, and we went through all sorts of efforts to get the PACE program adopted and provided to the business people. That was a huge satisfaction for me—I'm proud of the work we did on that.

The PACE Fund is designed to assist North Dakota communities in expanding their economic base by providing for new job development. This program has two major elements: (1) participation by the Bank of North Dakota with a local lender in a community based loan; and (2) participation by the PACE Fund with the local community in reducing the borrower's overall interest rate.

We went to Bowman to tell people they had to be proactive in this. When we talked about the concept of the PACE program that night, we didn't realize that it was the solution for getting people to start a local fund. When the PACE program details were finally finished—after the Committee of 100 had reviewed it and after Joe Lamb and Tim Moore at the Bank of North Dakota worked out the specifics—every economic development jurisdiction had to have an economic development plan of its own. They had to have a fund or they couldn't use the program.

The guy who eventually headed United States Department of Agriculture's (USDA) Rural Electrification Administration (now the Rural Utilities Service), our good friend Wally Beyer from Velva, said PACE was the best program in the United States. Others, too, have said the concept involved was the only one that really worked. Everyone had to be a player, all the interested parties had to put their money where their mouth is, and everyone had to behave—no passing the buck.

The greatest sense of achievement came many years later when one of the State Industrial Commission members noted that there had never been a business failure in the six or seven years the PACE program had been in place. None of the businesses funded in the first place by the PACE program had failed. The solution to the farm debt problem and how to save the banks and save as many farmers as possible was born out of the sheer urgency of the calamity.

The fourth lesson: *The mills of change grind slowly but exceedingly fine.*

In terms of history I think that's true. In the modern world it seems change comes pretty dramatically in some areas. But the adopting of societal change actually happens slowly. Even when voters bring huge changes in the country's power structure, it takes a long time to accomplish what's necessary to save the country.

A fifth axiom, which I always loved to quote, is one that someone brought in to me. Somebody asked the great Wayne Gretzky why he was such a great hockey player as he wasn't the fastest nor was he the toughest. "I'll tell you why," he said, "most people skate to where the puck is. I skate to where the puck is going!"

CHAPTER THREE: my childhood and family

My Ancestors Arrive

Let's look back a ways. My grandfather, John B. Sinner, came from Luxembourg, in the early 1880s. He worked first as a saloon bouncer and then was employed on Bonanza farms before later renting and then ultimately purchasing land. He was a great big man, a strong man. He came first to Blanchard, and later moved to Casselton, to the home place where my Uncle Leo Sinner later lived—about two miles east and a mile north of our farm. In 1889 he married Josephine Ries, who had also come from Luxembourg. They had twelve children.

The Wilds on my mother's side were Germans who came through Canada, from Edmonton, Alberta. Katherine Augusta Wild, who grew up to be my mother, was a bright lady. She had only a high school education but she was a tender, sensitive, wonderful teacher. My mother was an absolute saint—a Wild saint. After her marriage she became a Wild Sinner.

The Sinner name is German. When we were in Bismarck, the Mormon Church did a genealogical search and we learned that the Sinner name was originally Synnar. I jokingly told Mike Synar, the acerbic but liberal former congressman from Oklahoma, that we were cousins. He didn't care. Janie has visited Luxembourg, but I've never been there.

My father, Albert Francis Sinner, was an extremely intelligent man who overcame tons of debt and survived the Depression as one of very few farmers in Cass County who was able to keep his farm. He saved it from the banks when Governor Bill Langer declared a moratorium on farm loan foreclosures.[16] Getting through that era made my father a tightly wound person.

My grandfather had become ill and asked my father to take over management of the Sinner family farm, which includes some of the original Dalrymple Bonanza operation. Dad had a couple sessions of a special accounting course at St. John's. Other than that his education was just high school. He loved bookkeeping and he was good at it. He gave up his job as a bookkeeper at the Ford Motor Company in Fargo when his father got sick and then soon died. That was in 1920, when Dad was only twenty-one. He was the third oldest among ten siblings, but the heir apparent to the responsibilities of family finance. In the end, Dad was able to get one of his siblings through medical school and two through pharmacy. Two others became nurses and three received business majors.

He and my mother eventually moved from the farm into Casselton in 1948. About five years later, Bill, Ellery, and I formed the partnership called Sinner Brothers and Bresnahan. That arrangement was expanded in the early 1980s to include my oldest son Bob, the sons of Bill and his wife Jane, and Ellery and my sister Jeanne. Brother Bill died in 1984, and Ellery and I had sold our ownerships by 1990 to the family partners. Others among our descendants have since joined the operation, which is now known as SB&B.

Dad was considered probably the most knowledgeable cattle feeder in the region. He'd studied many things in nutrition. He argued constantly with the people at the university (North Dakota State University) who believed that beet pulp wasn't good feed and yet he had all the profits to prove that it was. His gospel was a book by Frank Morrison called *Feeds and Feeding*. Morrison had equated beet pulp in value to corn and that's the way we operated—if beet pulp was cheaper than corn, we added up to half the ration of beet pulp. He proved to be correct. Dad's rations were classically the lowest cost and generated the best gains of anyone in the region. He started feeding beet pulp to cattle in 1927 and eighty years later the farm is still using essentially the same rations as Dad did in the late 1920s and 1930s. We've always had wonderful cattle. And that all started with my father.

Dad's intensity in business dealings and business transactions was almost hard to imagine.

My father and I had an interesting relationship. He supported Democrat Franklin Roosevelt in the first two terms, but after the early Forties became very conservative, kind of led by my uncle Leo, who was an activist in the right-wing advocacy group, The John Birch Society. By the time I got involved in politics, Dad was already himself a Bircher. Dad tended to get exercised about economics and social issues, in the later years concerned that the liberals would run the country into debt. A good case can be made that the opposite is true when you look at Bill Clinton's experience and the success he had in getting the country's books balanced. Obviously Dad found my politics very difficult to accept.

Dad had been a close friend of Senator Bill Langer. In fact I remember Langer being at our home quite a bit when we were little. I don't know how Dad felt or voted during the World War I years, but later on during the Depression he became upset with government programs like the Civilian Conservation Corps. He began to have some financial security in the later Forties. Maybe that and the fact that he struggled so damn hard to get out of debt engendered a greater concern that his money might be taken in social programs he thought were doubtful.

The Birchers were critical of everything progressive so it was difficult for me to talk to Dad about anything except the nuts and bolts of farming. Discussions of things like benefits and salaries were difficult. After I came home from the service we had one pretty serious argument. I thought we should increase our workmen's pay. But Dad was pretty sensitive about how money should be spent. I remember saying to him, "Look, I spend more time with the employees than I do with my family. If you think I'm going to spend all that time with people that are unhappy, you've got another guess coming." That shook him up. He was passionate about his economics. But I'd spent six years studying to be a priest so I was nothing but passionate in my concern about employees.

Then, when I was elected to the State Senate in 1962, it was even tougher for him. Republican Don Otos, the man I defeated, was his friend. Dad said little, didn't try to interfere, but he was not happy. We had one particularly distasteful incident. Somewhere around

1964 we had built up some equity and Dad thought we should buy more land if we could find it. He and I had been out looking at farms and as we were heading back home he began ranting about civil disobedience by students on the campuses protesting the Vietnam War. Before I knew it he was just enraged. I was kind of getting the brunt of it because he knew I wasn't happy about the war either. Before long, he was blaming me and "my kind."

I was driving and we weren't far from home. Finally, unable to hold back, I looked at him and erupted: "Dad, as long as I can remember you have bragged to me about how you and your friends ran the sheriff out of Casselton with pitchforks when he came to foreclose on one of your neighbor's farms during the Thirties. What these kids are fighting for are their lives and the lives of their friends. Maybe that's just as important as your god-damn farms."

At first so shocked he didn't know what to say, Dad then went suddenly into a violent rage. He said he didn't ever want to see me again—didn't want me to ever come back. I was disgusted with myself for losing control. I don't know where the thought came from. I had never thought it before. I remember crying for hours, just couldn't get over it. What on earth had happened to me? I had always avoided this kind of controversy, but suddenly it bubbled out and I discovered I could be pretty destructive.

As a result of that incident, the love and support between my brother Bill and my brother-in-law Ellery and me became ever deeper. They commiserated with me because they knew my father's ability to work himself into a lather. Bill was even more distraught over Dad than I was. I blamed myself and Bill was angry at Dad, but eventually it went away. And the gentleness of my mother, who was supportive of both her husband and of me, became a bond of love that remained throughout her life and remains even since her death.

The lasting effects of that soul-disturbing experience taught me a lot. I learned that I too had a limit. Although I felt terrible about the mistake, I took comfort in realizing my outburst had been completely spontaneous and without a shred of premeditation. While humbled by my failure of control, I recognized my mind was capable of seeing inconsistencies and of responding in arguments and debates.

Some years later I was talking about Dad with a mutual friend of ours, State Senator Grant Trenbeath from Neche. "Bud," he said, "I don't know if you know this but your dad told me once how proud he was of you." So in the intervening years Dad apparently got over it. And I did too, but we never again could talk about anything political—I avoided that like the plague. I knew full well that my father was indeed a good man, albeit a tightly wound man.

Looking back, I'm amazed by my general feelings about my father's integrity and his business acumen. I always respected him and I now more fully understand how much he did in establishing my heritage on the farm and even to an extent my public life. Though we disagreed, particularly in his later years, his political activity played a part in the development of my interest in public affairs.

Growing in North Dakota

I was a child of the Great Depression, the youngest of four children born to a couple who had married quite late in life. In fact, my mother was over thirty-five when she was married and approaching forty-five when I was born.

Life was difficult then even in the rich Red River Valley. The Depression had taken a heavy toll and debt was everywhere. The struggle to keep from losing the farm was an omnipresent and pervasive threat. So, we grew up to be frugal, constantly being told to turn out the lights when you leave, don't use too much water in the bathtub, let me patch those pants and darn stockings. We always wore hand-me-downs, almost never had new clothes but we were always dressed pretty well. We used to hear a lot of moralistic sayings from Mom such as the proverb "a stitch in time saves nine." Yet life was not unpleasant, nor was the frugality in any way a detriment to our happiness.

My mother was one of those wonderfully sensitive, loving, always understanding, always attentive people who worked unbelievably hard. Patience was clearly her strength. Even in spite of her incredible busyness and never getting a vacation, my mother did not complain. She was long-suffering in fulfilling her obligations as she saw them to her family, her marriage, and her station in life. In addition to us, in those early years we often had eight to ten or more men whom she fed morning, noon, and night. She usually had someone there to help her, but it was a nightmarish amount of work. She and her help also had to clean the bunkhouses. She had a large garden and canned much of our produce. She saved all the leftovers from the meals and would never throw anything away.

Mother lived to be ninety-four and she put up with a life that was unbelievable. Her demanding husband would often be wound tighter than a fiddle string. He was sometimes unfair and impatient with my mother because of the horrible pressure he was under. Dad was preoccupied with the fierce battle he fought to retain his farm and achieve some sort of economic independence. He was an astute businessman who never missed a trick when it came to saving money. He was not the kind of person who was out running the tractors or driving the horses, though, because of the large crews we had in the early days. He was mostly a manager. Growing up, we boys became part of that big crew and worked under this rather hard taskmaster.

Dad was extremely tolerant of us children, but we spent only a limited amount of time with him. He only once said anything about whom I had as friends. Something like I should be careful whom I associated with. Aside from my politics, that's the only time he ever came close to questioning my ways. Certain episodes of teaching and assistance from him stand out, including the time he supported me after an embarrassing incident. When I was pretty young, but old enough to know better, a carnival came to town. I got sucked into a game and lost seventy-five dollars. That was a whole lot of money then. I was crushed beyond description, both because of my naiveté and because there was no way to hide my folly. But Dad helped me to get over it. "Don't worry about it," he said. "Maybe it was just a good lesson for you. All of us have gone through similar circumstances—we all had to learn how people can take advantage of us." I have never been able to gamble with abandon since then.

While my mother taught us softness, Dad's influence on us was confidence. He was a street fighter in many ways. The kindness and generosity of my parents is so memorable—it must have had an effect on me. Mother maintained a wonderful sense of humor, even in her final days on her deathbed. I was sitting with her in the hospital room when an old priest friend of mine popped in. He and I hadn't seen each other in many years. He looked at me. "Sinner, where's the gray hair?" he joked.

"He's got to have gray matter on the inside before there's gray on the outside," Mother whispered with her weakened voice.

It was Mother who started calling me "Buddy" the day I was born. I've been Bud since I was an infant. *Bud.* That's what I prefer.

Although we didn't engage in a lot of family activities, we did play cards at home. Whist was the family game. Also some euchre in the early years, but it was mostly whist that I remember. We didn't play that often, though, and Mother played more than Dad did. Despite all that she did she was the one that attended to us. That was the way it was—the old-school way—the father was the provider, the stern one who ruled the roost.

Christmas was always a pretty big deal. Those were lean years and I have one memory of coming down and walking into the living room and there was our first, brand new bicycle with lights and all the gear on it, fancy things. Extravagant gifts were unusual. We had this one bike for all of us kids to ride. Those were times not at all like today. We treasured things more than kids do now.

World War II so dominated everyone's thoughts. A lot of people from our community were involved. It seemed like every week someone we knew was killed or injured. We all accepted US policy and had a certain understanding of the American position. I don't think we sensed how close we were to losing the war. All serious public officials were acting as if we were in danger and history has borne that out. There were reports of submarine sightings near our shores and Pearl Harbor illustrated that we were far from secure. The Japanese won all the major engagements in the early months of the war until the tide turned in the summer of 1942 with the battle of Midway. Dad had a brother die in World War I, actually from influenza, in 1918. We also lost a couple other close relatives. A nephew, my cousin, was killed in World War II flying a P-38, I remember that rather vividly.

Mother and Dad were loyal to their traditions. Both were kind, and our family was very close. Despite the economic struggles, my life was blessed with a security and a freedom I don't often enough appreciate. I don't remember ever being questioned when I decided to go to St. John's to study for the priesthood. Just do it. They found the money somehow. That was in 1944. Never any questions about grades, never any questions about what I did in general. After I decided to leave the seminary and join the Air Guard, there were never any questions either.

For our parents, religion was more Christianity than Catholic. Dad rarely talked about controversies in the church. He wasn't trained in the arguments or the issues; nor was Mother. But they were profoundly Christian.

They Were True Partners

I had two wonderful farming partners, my older brother Bill and my brother-in-law Ellery Bresnahan. Ellery and I were closer than brothers since we were six. We started school the same year and became wonderful friends, even in grade school. Ellery played all the sports and owned the state football scoring record. He played six-man during the war, when so many of the older students had gone. Ellery was impossible to tackle. He's still a good golfer and routinely beats me at the game.

Bill was a genius at what he did. He was trained in accounting and good at it. He took business courses at St. John's but had to come home in 1943 after three years there because it was so difficult to get help on the farm. He was a man of incredible brains and a great manager who welcomed my brother-in-law Ellery and me home from the Air Force and took us into the farming operation.

Ellery and I were stationed together on active duty during the Korean War.[17] He and my sister Jeanne had been married four or five months before we were called up. Janie and I got married about a year later, in August of 1951. When the decision was made to get out of Korea, they started releasing us guardsmen and reservists. I got home a month ahead of Ellery and started right away at the farm once we got settled. But we didn't know what I was going to do, how it was going to work out. Ellery had absolutely no farming background either. His father was a grain dealer.

He and I were like twins, had been ever since we were six, so he decided he would help out on our farm until he got his feet on the ground and figured out what he was going to do in life.

One day in 1953, Bill said to us, "I'd really like it if you guys would join a farm partnership with me and stay together here." We were so grateful we couldn't say yes fast enough. Bill was willing to give us anything we wanted.

Unfortunately, Bill had a bit of a guilt complex because Dad had gotten a deferment for him during World War II so he could stay home and work on the farm. He and Jane Beron had gotten married in 1947. She was a nurse in Fargo and in the end they had twelve children—five boys and seven girls. Ellery and Jeanne had eight. And we had ten. So there were thirty children in this mix.

My sister-in-law Jane was as loving and generous to us as was her husband Bill. Their house was in the middle of the farm operations. Bill's office was in the house. The two-way radio was in the house, and it was just blaring a good deal of the time. The three women—his Jane, Ellery's Jeanne, and my Jane—were close. Never anything but kindness. Bill and Ellery were more than generous to me in my various meanderings and interests and departures for public office. When I was in the Senate (1963–1966), at the North Dakota Constitutional Convention in 1972, chairman of the sugar beet growers (1975–1979), later in the Legislature (1983–1984), and then running for governor (1983–1984), I drew full share compensation from the farm much of the time—in fact, most of the time. That was a huge luxury that few politicians have. They were so good to me. I can't ever possibly thank them enough, because they gave me such huge independence. They gave me the confidence to do the best I could regardless of consequences. I've often thought there were times I took advantage of their largesse. I have always thought they gave a huge strength to me all through my years in government particularly. They had always told me, "Do the best you can and if you get kicked out we want you back." That was so huge to me. Because of them I could honestly say to myself, "Do it right—full-speed ahead."

Those were great years—the three of us partners were close and discussed practically everything together. I don't remember a time when we had cross words. Things were said openly and candidly.

I ended up running the day-to-day operation and my brother and brother-in-law shared the marketing and business decisions except the operational part. Ellery took care of the cattle end of it. They, like my father and mother, did not compromise the truth, even when it was painful. Life was truly good in those years on the farm, nothing that I ever left easily. In fact, when I decided to run for governor, the sons of all three of us were getting in position to operate the place and it was time for one of us or two or all three to get out of the way. I was free to campaign. A funny thing happened on the way to the fair—I won.

With those dozen children, Bill usually had the patience of Job. But he could become angry and sometimes severe—not often but once in a while. A lesson I learned from him was he would never, ever let the day pass if he had done something he was not proud of. He served on the Casselton school board, which is by all the odds the toughest job there is. It is insanely difficult. He had gotten impatient with one of the other board members and said something he knew was offensive. I remember that incident clearly—he told me the next morning when I asked him why he looked so tired.

"I insulted one of the board members," he said. "I couldn't sleep so I called him and went in and talked to him."

It was a great lesson because while he knew how hard it was to say *I'm sorry*, he always did so. He was faithful to what he believed. He just couldn't ignore it and hope it would go away. Bill died just before I was elected governor in 1984.

Singing with My Sister

The other person I was close to all those years was my sister Jeanne, who is fifteen months older than I am. We have always been good friends and she ended up marrying my lifelong best friend, Ellery. We kids were pretty close together in age: Bill was born January 8, 1922, and then Dick on October 12, 1925. Jeanne was born March 5, 1927, and finally I came along May 29, 1928. Four siblings in six years. But my brothers were gone to St. John's during some of those early years, and I eventually followed them there.

Then the war overwhelmed our lives. Gas, tires, and sugar were rationed, and there wasn't much social life going on. One of the memories I have of that time is of Jeanne and me often sitting together at the piano—she would play popular songs and we would sing together. She could carry a tune. Whether I could or not is debatable. Another thing I remember about those particular instances was that my dad's office was right behind the wall where we sat at the piano. Even though he was a pretty irascible man, I remember hearing him humming and singing along in the other room while the two of us sang and played the piano.

Jeanne later went to the College of Saint Benedict and got her master's degree in dietetics at Ohio State. She was bright, and has become a thorough student of Vatican II.[18] She and my two brothers were all pretty good students. One or the other of them was class valedictorian or salutatorian. Our parents emphasized school. I was fairly high up in the scholastic rankings, but I wasn't the brightest of the bright in my class of thirty-five or forty kids. My grades at Lincoln High School in Casselton were probably a B average—a few Cs or Ds and probably not a lot of As. Math was always easy for me, though. In my freshman year I helped the senior girls with their math. In the two years I was in high school at Casselton I didn't date much. I don't remember Jeanne and Ellery dating then either—they started when I was a St. John's.

Along with Ellery and my siblings, my other really close friend was Tom Sinner, a cousin who was a classmate of Ellery and me. We had similar education and we discussed issues. At that time, which was before the Mass switched from Latin, we weren't as outspoken in criticizing the church bureaucracy as we became later. Tom also played football at St. John's.

Oh, Brother

My older brother Dick was a huge influence on me, and the time spent with him the last ten years before he died in early 2004 was invaluable. He had his faults but in him I saw spiritual honesty. He was a Catholic priest who embraced his feelings about Christianity and reached out to everyone. So many people were affected by his kindness and he taught so many to have concern for others. He also had a lot of very human instincts that he didn't deny, but the cravings of the world for power and wealth never affected him.

Although Dick was pious, no one ever thought he would turn out to be so passionately concerned about other human beings. The family didn't know what to make of that, and on occasion found him pretty embarrassing. I was supportive of Dick, but was also too righteous in my attitude about some of his activities. He was just way ahead of his time.

He was ordained in May 1952 at Fargo's St. Mary's Cathedral. In the early years of his priesthood, Dick was at the forefront of the movement away from Latin.[19] In fact, long before it was officially allowed he started saying Mass in English. Even the more progressive bishops didn't want to tolerate that. He also went against church rules in performing marriages for people who had been divorced. He also allowed a suspended, married priest to speak and administer communion. To his credit, Dick was constantly in trouble with the bishop—I learned to respect him for that early on.[20]

Dick played a large part in shaping my feelings toward church bureaucracies. He and some other close friends from the seminary saw the church pretty much as I did. I didn't always understand what Dick was teaching and what he was doing, but he lived Christianity the way he believed it should be lived, and broke rules that he thought were stupid rules.

In breakfasts with him during those last years, I learned how completely dedicated he was to giving of himself to help others who were in need, and how wrong it was to ever have judged him. I think if Dick learned anything from Dad, it was to think independently, and like Mother, Dick wasn't a vocalizer—he was a doer. He was a great human being who certainly affected a lot of people in his life. In many ways Dick was more a pacifist than the pacifists.

Dick went to St. John's Preparatory School in 1941, his sophomore year of high school. I was in eighth grade then. He graduated as valedictorian and president of the school council. Although Dick had some unique athletic talents, he didn't want to spend time on team sports at St. John's. He had an incredible batting eye, somewhat unorthodox, almost a little awkward. He rarely struck out, and would have had a great batting average had he wanted to compete. Another thing I remember that was amazing about him was that he was almost unbeatable in ping-pong and played strictly a defensive game. A competitor could hit kill shot after kill shot but the ball always came back. He had uncommon hand-eye coordination. I wasn't a bad ping-pong player, but rarely could get a shot past Dick.

Dick didn't like to kill anything and rarely went hunting. But I remember one Sunday in late summer we were out shooting gophers. The two of us were driving down the country roads with a .22-caliber rifle. About a hundred yards out in the field, two mallards swam about in a slough. When we shot at some gophers, a mallard drake got up. "Let's see if you can hit that," I said. Dick took aim and fired. The duck came tumbling down and Dick was just beside himself with guilt. I went out and picked up the bird—he'd shot it right through the eye. Dick cried because he felt so bad. It took a while for him to get over that; he didn't ever want to shoot again. He had great love for all living things.

Another memory about Dick's sensitivity was a time when I was ten years old. We were walking from the house to the barn. It was probably 150 yards. As we were going around the corner of a cattle yard fence, Dick snuck up from behind and tripped me. I fell and hit my head on the frozen ground—it knocked me out. I remember coming to and seeing Dick there on his knees, tears streaming down his face, praying, "Please God, don't let Buddy die."

He and I were really pretty close considering the small amount of time we spent together. I was a little more worldly and earthy in my growing up than he was, though, and Dick was not the savviest on the farm. One time he was raking hay with a dump rake and the team of horses ran away. He fell over the back and the team came in the yard with just parts of the rake dragging along behind. We all started to panic until we could see Dick walking down the road. I remember Eric Hanson, an elderly employee, saying, "Yah, Dick don't know how to svear at dem horses. Ya should da had Bill out dere."

I won't go into much detail about the Sanctuary Movement and Dick's many other humanitarian efforts as a Catholic priest, but the work he did in Honduras and El Salvador and the southern part of the United States to help immigrants was just unbelievable. In the end, he often jeopardized his own life helping to save a couple thousand people who were trying to run from the tyranny of government dictators. He first went to El Salvador and then came back to Tucson, Arizona, dismayed at what he had seen down in Central America.

At some point he started helping smuggle refugees into Canada. The first, while we were in Bismarck, he was in the newspaper more than I was because he was getting arrested all the time for taking illegal immigrants across the border. The feds took a couple of cars from him and I always wondered when I was going to get asked about it.

The media didn't bring up Dick to me, even when he was in the news or was arrested. I was pretty sure that was because they knew darn well he was doing what he believed was right. Finally after one time when Dick was in trouble, a broadcast reporter, Mike Kopp, asked me about him. His question came during a news conference in the latter part of 1987. That fall we had to slash the budget, and Dick Rayl and I were explaining the cuts to the press. We'd gone through all the numbers, explaining and fielding questions for over an hour. Looking at my watch and trying to bring it to close, I finally said to the reporters, "I need to get back to my office. People are waiting up there. Are there any more questions?"

Kopp, who was sitting on the left side of the conference room table, about three feet from me, jumped up with a hand-held recorder and blurted out, "What do you think about what your brother's into?"

Dick was far from my mind that day, even though I had sent him money to support his work. Fortunately, I always prayed to the Holy Spirit when I had major issues going on. I had prayed that day.

I looked at Kopp. I had no prepared answer. "Mike, let me tell you something about my brother. He is one of those people who believe that when Jesus said harbor the harborless, he meant harbor the harborless." I will never forget Mike Kopp with the microphone up to his mouth, starting to say something, and just standing there with his mouth open, and finally sitting back down.

I also remember Dale Wetzel, the Associated Press reporter, sitting at the table literally rubbing his hands, thinking I was going to bury Mike. But nothing more was said. It never came up again. I told Dick that story about three weeks before he died and he was so touched he cried almost uncontrollably over it. But that's who he was. He lived what he believed, sometimes in ways that were difficult to accept, but he had great courage.

How did he form those beliefs? Obviously it was an evolution. Dick's development probably started at St. John's. He suggests as much in a locally produced book about him titled *Striving for Justice: Reverend Sinner and the Sanctuary Movement.* Therein he noted that he and I both received strong doses of instruction in social philosophy and social economics, and he referred to lessons learned from good professors at St. John's who "taught us to be concerned about our fellow human beings, and who taught us that we had obligations of justice and even charity when it came to the poor or the less fortunate."

After two years in the seminary at St. John's, Dick received a scholarship to study philosophy at Catholic University and worked hard to earn master's degrees in philosophy and theology. No doubt his views and sensitivities were further shaped there. I think priest friends like Bob Hovda and Bill Durkin, and some of the people who were in the forefront of Christian thought, may have had some influence but, frankly, Dick was so dedicated to living Christianity that he pretty much reached his conclusions on his own.

He did something that I don't know how he pulled off—he put the same half section of his land up over and over again as bond to bail out refugees in Arizona. It never got picked up down there and, in fact, the statute of limitations had run out when an attorney who was a good friend of Dick's, Monty Strehlow, called for the creditors to come forth if they chose to claim rights to the land before it was sold. Nobody came forth. They cleared the slate. I was in the Governor's Office at the time and was ecstatic when I got the news.

Dick was generous to a fault. After he died, we went through his things and found a thick file of IOUs from people he had given money. One IOU was for ten thousand dollars and many of them were for over a thousand. In talking about it we realized Dick knew all along he wouldn't be repaid. He didn't want anybody to take money from him, or keep his money, because he wanted to give it away. Even in his early years when he didn't have much money, if he had any in his pocket and you said you needed it, he gave it instantly to you. But that's the way he lived his whole life. He did what he believed was right without a lot of thought about it. He just did it.

Right after I took office, my nephew convinced Dick he should sell his land ownership to the farming partners. They put the money into an annuity to guarantee him income, an annual payment for the rest of his life. Dick didn't feel good about that at first, but later became grateful. In the last ten years Dick probably told me fifty times how he couldn't get by without that annuity. The Diocese retirement money was not reliable and, in fact, they tried to take it away from him. He was terribly hurt about that and didn't want to tell me. I got his pension back for him but it was a nasty scene.

CHAPTER FOUR: fixing and discovering

Pass Me the Pliers, Please

I've always fixed things I was told could not be fixed. One example of that happened in the late 1960s or early 1970s. We had a huge rainstorm. The sugar processing plants had opened and they were crying for beets so we were encouraged to get out and start harvesting. We had a pusher tractor that went behind the truck, a twin-screw tandem truck. The tractor pushed the truck through the field as it was loaded. The truck hit a fairly firm spot and got going faster than the tractor could keep up with. The tractor fell behind, and suddenly the truck hit a low spot and down it went. The tractor couldn't push it out and the truck was sinking quickly. I knew if it went down fast the drive shaft would bend. That's exactly what happened. By the time we got a bigger tractor over there to pull it out the drive shaft was bent. We had to have the truck, so I called my friend Paul Johnson at the Fargo International truck dealership for a new drive shaft. He said they could get one in about four days.

"We can't wait four days," I said. I tried the wrecking shop and they said they could probably get one in three days. So I finally went to see my friend Harold Lee who was the father of the legislator Gary Lee. He was a very clever blacksmith. "Harold," I said, "is there any way that I could straighten out that drive shaft?"

"No way could you straighten a hollow drive shaft," he said.

So I called Larson and Thurlow, a welding shop and manufacturing shop in Fargo. "No, it can't be done," they too said.

I was desperate. I began to look at it. Finally I said, "Pull it home to the shop."

They pushed it into our farm shop and I got a couple of hydraulic jacks. I put one big jack under one set of tandems so that I could turn the wheel and make the bent drive shaft turn. I got underneath and I marked the high spot with a piece of chalk. I then took a piece of oak two-by-four, laid it up underneath the drive shaft, and put the other hydraulic jack underneath it. I started slowly jacking with the jack and in twenty minutes I had the drive shaft absolutely straight. It was still in the truck when it was sold many years later. I eventually also did the same process with another truck that had the same thing happen—it too sank and settled onto the drive shaft. I told a longtime truck dealer that story and he had never heard of anyone successfully straightening a drive shaft. Fortunately it wasn't kinked, the whole thing just curved. That probably wouldn't have worked had there been a kink in it.

I had started running all the equipment on the farm early. I operated the bucker—a great big wide thing that you pushed with a tractor and it had a lift on it. The back end ran about ten inches off the ground and the front would drop down when you wanted to pick up a shock of bundles. This was the era between the first major advance of the grain binder—which bundled the grain that was then formed into shocks by hand for hauling to the threshing machine—and just before the advent of the combine, which eventually consolidated the grain cutting and threshing. We'd pile the bundles by hand in shocks that would sit with the kernels up and the straw down so the grain would not lie on the ground. The grain shock was the method used to dry the grain so the thresher could separate the grain from the straw and chaff. When the shocks were dry enough we'd pick them up with the bucker and haul them to the thresher. The bucker had replaced the old hay wagons, the bundle wagons, of the early days. It was a dirty, tough job, but I was good at it. There were two guys—spike pitchers—who shoved those bundles of grain from the bucker into the machine, the thresher. We had to be careful we didn't drive up with the bucker and have them not see us and get pushed into the machine. I never did hit a spike pitcher.

I also ran a boom and shovel that mounted on the back of the tractor. It had foot and hand controls that you had to coordinate. I remember being young and doing that and being good at it. I was well coordinated. It too was a dirty job. I've often marveled that I didn't suffer lung damage from all the dust. When I'd get home at night I'd be as black as the ace of spades because of all the dirt. Then we started getting combines later on and that was dirty work too because there were no good cabs in those days. It's a wonder we don't all have emphysema from the dirt we ate.

Later, I spent thousands of hours on a Bobcat skid-steer loader. As governor, when we dedicated the Melroe building expansion at Gwinner, they let me practice on a Bobcat a little bit at the airport.[21] Bob Spolum, the CEO, likes to tell that story. The plant workers had parked a semi trailer as a stage for the program and they had bleachers set up around a half circle. Bob announced that I would turn the first shovel. I went around the truck and started the Bobcat and wheeled it toward the audience. We had a pretty good crowd. I drove it right at them and then turned away. People were scrambling out of the front seats. I didn't get that close to them, but what a clown I was.

Lessons from Farm Hands

Eric Hanson, one of our longtime employees at the farm, had a mangled left hand. He told me many times how it happened. I'd say, "Eric, I've forgotten, what happened to your hand?"

"Vell, yah know, I vas helpin' Leo, yah know, ve ver driving some stakes, ve ver gonna pour cement," he said, "and I got down there and I lined up the stake and I had my hand on top holding it. Okay, hit it, I sez to him. And he did!" Leo took the sledgehammer and whap, right on top of his hand. Leo was pretty impetuous and was sure Eric would move his hand.

Another time we were pulling up a tree. Ellery and I were there and one of us fastened the chain around the trunk. We had it hooked on a big tractor. There was no cab and most of the time we stood when you drove it, as Eric did in this case. We didn't realize there wasn't enough chain. He started ahead and we both screamed at him: "Stop, Eric!" But Eric didn't stop.

The tree came down and hit him across the head, damn near knocked him off the tractor. He had one hand on the clutch and as he went forward it pushed the clutch ahead. When the tree hit him he flopped back and the clutch came back. We thought it had killed him.

Looking up at us, Eric muttered, "Dangerous yob!"

Sid Gregorson, another employee, could repair just about anything. He had grown up as an auto mechanic and could fix engines. He wasn't the most imaginative when it came to making do—he had to have new parts. In contrast, that's all some of us do is piece stuff together. Sid was good at things like getting lawn mowers to run. He'd take the needle valves out and clean them. He understood how things like the choke should work. Everyone would bring their cars out for Sid to fix. Sid was from Kathryn, North Dakota, south of Valley City. I came from Bismarck for his funeral, which was a rewarding experience. Our whole family was there—although Mother and Dad and Bill were gone by then—and we met Sid's relatives.

Sid and Eric and a lot of the other men would go out and drink beer on weekends and quite frequently get picked up by the police. They'd barely be moving driving down the road. Usually one of us would go in and get them and take them home. More often it was Bill than me because I was much younger.

They worked for us pretty much year round. We had an insulated bunkhouse, not fancy but they thought it was pretty good. Sid used to hate Bill Barney, the highway patrolman from Casselton. Bill picked him up two or three times and Sid was sure he just laid in wait, watching for him. Sid could swear like few people I've ever known and used cuss words I'd never heard before or since when he talked about Bill Barney.

We laughed a lot about those days. The weekend of fellowship enhanced by three or four beers was wonderful for them. Too bad they always overdid it. They always had trouble driving but they wouldn't steal if it was the last place on earth to get income. They were certainly not organized-religion people. In many ways they had an acceptance and a trust that was amazing. They just never complained about life.

We were concerned about one employee, Martin Peterson. I don't know what happened to him. He used to go to Fargo for a couple months in the winter and he once had tried to hang himself in a hotel room. We didn't know what drove him to that despair. He was happy on the farm but it worried us because sometimes he would disappear and we would look for him with terrible apprehension around the hay mow. He eventually died in the old soldiers' home at Lisbon, as did Eric. We grew up with Martin—he was always wonderful to us kids. He'd bring candy home. He was not the fall-down, staggering-drunk type either. He loved his beer, the main effect of which was that he got talkative when we helped him into his house.

Martin Schmeltzer, who came along after Martin Peterson, was a World War I veteran, a short man of German ancestry who had fought in horrible actions. He was in both the Battle of the Argonne and the Battle of Bellow Wood. When drunk he would get into terrible crying jags remembering the war and the experiences that were so ghastly to him. Two of the stories he told me many, many times when I would sit with him, after he had gotten back from town, until he quieted down. Tears streamed down his face. Always these two things came back to him. They both just made him sob. His best buddy stepped on a mine that literally blew out his stomach. He was conscious and just horribly torn up, pleading with Martin to kill him. And Martin did. He shot him to put him out of misery. Martin just sobbed in sorrow over that. The other one that I will never forget him telling happened during the Battle of the Argonne. Martin told about it being bitter hand-to-hand fighting. "I came around a tree and ran into this beautiful little German boy and I shot his face off," he said. "I just sobbed—he was such a beautiful young kid."

Martin was a kind man, but oh, how he suffered with those awful memories of World War I. Those stories made me hate war. I came to love Martin too, and appreciate the humanity of all these people whom I knew and saw as fellow workmen. Mother and Dad, too, were always kind to these people. Even though Dad could be pretty tough with us kids, I don't remember him ever being hard on the employees.

I had another episode with an employee who came from north of Detroit Lakes. His last name was Ness and I want to say Arvid, but I'm not sure of his first name. He was a good man who had lived in abject poverty all his life. He was running a beet harvester and somehow or other he left the machine running when he got off to lubricate something. He got his hand between the big chain and the sprocket it turned on. His hand went around the sprocket, which mutilated his hand. Fortunately, the chain had a little bit of slack in it and it gave some, but he was pretty badly torn up.

When I got there I saw it and I ran to get the pickup to take him to the doctor. But instead he said, "Yah, I'll fix it." He goes behind the harvester and takes out his penis and he pees all over his hand. That disinfected the wounds and his hand eventually healed without further treatment.

I've told a couple doctors about it and they said, "Listen, uric acid is stronger than hell and will in fact help sanitize things." Ness didn't even wrap up his hand.

Something I did one time was a little bit similar. We used to have a great big drag affair that you'd pull across a stubble field after you combined. We used it particularly to burn flax straw because flax straw was difficult to plow down. So, you'd pull this thing with the teeth pointing forward. The teeth were a few inches off the ground and they'd catch the flax straw and once you got a bunch in there you'd light it. Then you'd drag it, go forth and back across the field. The dryness of the air and the dryness of the flax straw controlled how fast you could go.

I went too fast one day and rolled up a big mass of hot burned flax straw. The machine toppled over, got all tangled up and one of the back sections toppled forward. I was impatient and despite my pretty heavy leather gloves the damn thing was hotter than a two-bit pistol. I grabbed the back and thought I had the back rung. A weight, fastened behind the rungs to hold them straight, toppled over and fell across my arm, which sizzled loudly. I was a long way from home and frantic because I was really burned. I got thinking, you know, they always put Vaseline over a burn. So, grabbing my grease gun, I coated my arm with that black gun grease. My arm never blistered. At home they said, my God, what did you do? Everyone was pretty mystified but it worked, as had the uric acid.

Learning to Learn

Ellery Bresnahan was a prankster with our seventh grade art teacher, Miss Syma TaBelle. A class rule dictated that not more than one person could go to the bathroom at the same time, and we had to sign out on the board. The rule was that, only one set of initials could be on the board. This prank involved another friend, Jack English. Jack would get up and put his initials JE on the board. Ellery would then get up when she was looking the other way and add his B on the bottom of the JE. Miss TaBelle had noticed this before and one day when they both came back she asked these two, why is it you always have to go to the bathroom in art class? "I guess we just formed a habit," Ellery said. We all laughed and Ellery always had a devilish grin on his face anyway so the teacher had to laugh too.

A lot of teachers at Casselton had an influence on me—four or five were outstanding. Esther Lebus, first grade, was the kindest, most encouraging woman of the teachers I ever had, although many others were similar. I don't think this woman ever said a critical word to me, and rarely did to anybody. She got people off to a good start as a first grade teacher. Laura Port, third grade, was good also. She was a little sterner, but an extremely good teacher.

I was always a fan of a teacher who was then named Ella Sailer. She was twenty-two or twenty-three, right out of Valley City State College. I was sort of in love with her. She was a special teacher. When I was in fifth grade she got married in mid-year to a man named Buck, so her name became Ella Buck. Then she went on to graduate school or something. Her husband was in the State Department. She traveled all over the world and is a very knowledgeable woman. Miss Sailer—who became Mrs. Buck—was a fascinating lady. I remember her kindness. She was firm but with gentle discipline. All the teachers who were special managed to maintain discipline without high decibel or high energy. They kept things in control.

Our eighth grade teacher probably more than anybody else encouraged me and engendered my love for mathematics. I have always been good at math. Agna Presthus taught math to freshmen and sophomores at Casselton. She was one of the foremost teachers I had. She just made it so clear. She often asked me to help the people having trouble in class get their homework done, help them understand it. So I did a lot of that as a sophomore, even as a freshman. Both years I coached four or five senior girls who had put off taking math courses.

I eventually considered getting a minor in math at St. John's, but I was already taking twenty-two and twenty-three credit hours at the time. It was my senior year and I was carrying a major in philosophy, almost a minor in education, and a minor in language, and trying to get a minor in math. I had a B at the quarter but I saw myself getting so far behind in calculus. So I dropped it and didn't complete my minor.

Many of my college teachers were memorable. Father Polycarp, OSB, a Benedictine monk, who was also a math genius, was classically known for his practice of holding an eraser in his left hand and when he'd write a formula on the board with his right hand his left hand came behind erasing it.

Without question, Father Ernest Kilzer, my ethics professor, influenced me the most. He spent a lot of time on government. I remember him mostly because I had a memorable experience with him. I broke my hand in a softball game. I tried to bare-hand a line drive, so I had to take an oral exam from him because I couldn't write the test. It didn't take him long to find out what I *didn't* know. He was just that kind of mind.

One of the areas I studied a great deal was natural law. I wrote a good paper on that for Father Kilzer that he duplicated and handed out for years. My paper was three or four pages, listing the major statements about natural law throughout history. I remember so many things he taught me about medical ethics. I later became active in the legislature with pharmaceutical legislation principally because of what he taught: that you can't let a profession like that become economically involved in what they're prescribing when what they're doing is so tied to human well-being.

Father Kilzer also taught us that the great thing about American government was honoring individual freedom and individual rights. I learned from him that government should not limit the rights of people unless it must do so to protect the rights of others. If an individual in exercising his rights damages other people's rights, then government has to step in. Father Kilzer was an expert on the works of American government and I absorbed an awful lot about it from him. He was fascinated by the US Constitution and the American scene. He was also big on freedom. He wasn't an arch liberal, nor was he an anarchist. He believed in government but he knew its limitations.

I learned to love Shakespeare from a brilliant course taught by Conrad Diekman. He was the brother to one of the foremost theologians in the United States, Godfrey Diekman, another good friend. The two brothers were both priests.

A wonderful man named Farley taught me educational methods. It was one of the requirements in education, kind of a joke course. I never bought a textbook, never took notes, and studied other subjects in his class. I reviewed a friend's notes from the previous year for about two hours before the final exam and pulled a B. The professor seemed to understand that much in the methods course was changing rapidly and it was mostly common sense anyway.

CHAPTER FIVE: from seminary to father of ten

A Tale of Two Sinners

I was an altar boy, not particularly pious, but not causing a lot of trouble either. I followed my older brother Dick to St. John's Preparatory School my junior year of high school and did fairly well in all my studies. I can't remember anybody persuading me to attend St. John's. It was just something I thought I wanted to do.

Those years were tremendously interesting and informative. I was probably a B-plus student. It was a little difficult down there at St. John's because I had a bunch of "brains" around me—they were pretty tough competition. But I did all right despite being a slow reader, a weakness that lingered all through college. That made for difficulties, particularly in history and even in philosophy, although I did pretty well overall. I would never trade that philosophy education because it taught me so much about humanity and learning and life in general.

My time at St. John's also gave me an intense commitment to public service, to working for and with other people to improve society and the life of people. I grew interested in the inequality of racial minorities in this country and developed a strong desire to make society and our communities better places for people to live.

I was in the seminary for six years and actually wore a Roman collar and cassock for two years. You didn't get to be a sub-deacon or a deacon, which are the only names I can remember, until your second-to-last year, when your sub-deaconate came.[22] In 1950 I had gotten my bachelor of arts degree and went home for the summer before starting my graduate work. But the approach of this even more major commitment spurred me to take a serious look at the growing doubts that I'd been having about going on to the priesthood. Through the years I wondered whether I could deal with celibacy, but I had just put it out of my mind and kept on going.

Following a liturgical conference in Missouri, I stopped to visit relatives in Illinois. While there I met a young woman, Rosie Fuesting, whose mother was a sister to my uncle. We became pretty good friends in four or five days. She attended Webster College, a Catholic college for women in St. Louis, where my future wife Janie was a student. After I met Rosie I knew I didn't want to go on into the priesthood, but I was having a hard time finalizing the decision. So I went to a Trappist monastery called New Melleray, outside Dubuque. I was there for a week, praying and thinking and being counseled by an old priest whose family name was Smith. At the end of the week I remember sitting in his office with my packed bags beside me. He said, "Go home and forget about the priesthood. God will give you other signals if you should be a priest."

And then he said, "I don't want you to try to remember everything I've told you, I just want you to try to remember that whatever happens to you in your life, even things you choose sinfully, God will make work for your good. Because," he said, "that's who God is and that's what salvation is. God is all love and will make it all work out. He doesn't control our lives."

That hit me like a ton of bricks because in all the studies I'd done no one had ever described salvation that way. What he taught convinced me that there is no such thing as God *running* our lives. That's not what it's about. The world is free and we are free. The significance of salvation in Christian terms—I'm not sure of the other religions—is that somehow as we go through, God makes it work out. That's a strange mix of providential dabbling and of freedom, but that was one of the huge lessons I learned that day from that old monk.

Not long afterward I was visiting at St. John's with a couple of theologians who were old friends and I told them what this priest said. Father Godfrey Diekman, who was probably among the major theologians in the United States certainly and maybe even worldwide, said that was the best description of salvation he'd ever heard.

Father Godfrey said Father Smith had given me two valuable pieces of advice. "He told you that God doesn't run the world. He created the world free and he created us free. But when he gives the gift of salvation what he does is make things work out okay. He doesn't cause the storms. He doesn't condone the errors we make. But he makes it somehow then become a source of good things."

He said, "You hang on to that."

And I always have. That has been a huge lesson to me.

In the seminary I loved the studies even though I wasn't an astonishingly good student. I wasn't upset with the church because back then, unlike now, church leadership was going in the direction of humanity and service to people, not away from it. But I knew myself that celibacy wasn't going to work. I just made the decision to not pursue the priesthood with the help of that old monk in the Trappist Monastery. All my classmates were shocked to hear I wasn't coming back.

I liked Rosie Fuesting a lot but it didn't take long to find out that she was already almost engaged to Fred Crowe, an ex-seminarian from Notre Dame, who became one of the foremost CPAs in the nation. Rosie decided she wanted to stay with him so she told Janie that I was hers. Or something to that effect. Janie and I had a couple dates and started exchanging letters. It wasn't too long and we decided to get married. Janie and Rosie were good friends and continue to be good friends. Janie communicates regularly with Rosie and we always look forward to seeing her and Fred when we have that opportunity.

Janie's memories about all of that are clearer than mine. Here's what she has written:[23]

A handsome young man named Bud Sinner had graduated from St. John's and was visiting his relatives in Mattoon (Ill.) and had a few dates with Rosie Fuesting. He was rather "taken" with Rosie and in the fall when we were back at school in St. Louis he decided to make a trip down to see her. Rosie was not at all "taken" with Bud, as she was really going with another guy named Fred. So she fixed me up on a blind date with him. This blind date in September of 1950 was an instant connection between Bud and me. We spent the entire evening talking and discovering the many ideas we had in common. I came back to my room that night and told Rosie, "This is the man I'm going to marry."

She was shocked. I had a lot of skeptical roommates who would constantly chide me. After that weekend, Bud and I wrote letters to each other once a week from that September until April. This was long before e-mail had ever been invented. In April of 1951, when Bud and his cousin Tom Sinner, both now in the North Dakota Air National Guard, were activated and sent to Moody Field in Valdosta, Georgia, they stopped in St. Louis for a brief weekend. This is when Tom and Lois first met (Cousin Tom Sinner and his wife Lois AuBuchon of Elmhurst, Ill.)

We were married in Valdosta on August 10, 1951. We had not intended to be married until later in September, and actually the invitations were printed for the later date. But Bud's National Guard unit was advised to be ready to move to California after the 15th of August and all leaves were cancelled after that date. So we quickly changed our plans and moved the date up. It was a small wedding with few guests.

We were in California only a year when Bud's unit was deactivated and we were on our way to North Dakota. Bob was only two months old and we traveled in the car with some buddies from North Dakota. NOT the most pleasant five-day trip, if I remember. Except for a brief two or three days when Bud's brother Father Dick was ordained, this would be my first real visit to North Dakota, or even that far north.

North Dakota was a stark change after growing up in the hills of Kentucky. If the Mojave Desert was depressing, Casselton was even more so. The streets were just dirt, no paving. That didn't happen for another nine years. This 'backwoods' country was a far cry from the green and lush areas of Kentucky with its large stately homes. I missed my home in the rolling green hills. It gave me pause many times, wondering just what I had gotten myself into. I told Bud one evening when I was pretty despondent, "Well, I'll only promise to stay for twenty years!"

But I had a very kind and considerate husband and we were very much in love. In addition, Bud's family and especially Jeanne and Ellery who came home a month later, were very good to me. His dad never quite accepted this "southerner" and once told me he didn't like me wearing shorts. I told him I wouldn't change because Bud liked seeing my legs. I know he didn't like me, but he did try to be gracious, and we were invited to their home many Sundays for dinner. However, many conversations were very tense as Al was a right-wing conservative and Bud was quite liberal. And Al did not like anyone to disagree with him. Katherine was wonderful, however. She treated me just like a daughter even though I knew they always considered me an outsider. Which I was.

Force Be With Me

After finishing my philosophy degree and deciding against pursuing the priesthood I was eligible for the Korean War draft. On September 20, 1950, I enlisted in Air National Guard 178th Fighter Interceptor Squadron at Hector Airport. I joined along with a large contingent of people from the Casselton area, including my cousin Tom Sinner and Ellery Bresnahan. I was called to active-duty status in April of 1951 for the Korean War and assigned to the Strategic Air Command at Moody Air Force Base, Georgia. Our unit was later transferred to George Air Force Base, California.

I ended up with the rank of airman first class and was supposed to go to officers training camp but I had no interest in it. I was in the motor pool when we were activated, then went into headquarters squadron, did secretarial-type duties, then was in medics for a while. Finally I was asked to take over the Information and Education section, which was officially headed by an officer, usually a clueless second lieutenant.

I got my boss in trouble. This unit in Victorville was made up of Air National Guard personnel from Idaho, Montana, California, and North Dakota. My role was to prepare the weekly information and education lesson. There were several squadrons within the framework of the base—all motor pool people, for example, were in one transportation squadron. Each of these squadrons had an information and education officer who would give a lecture on the week's lesson, mostly drivel that had come out in printed form from the Pentagon.

I would give lectures to these officers on Thursday afternoon and they would go back and spread the word on the various issues to their people. The pablum from the Pentagon was really very milk toast and boring. For the Fourth of July in 1952, I had the Pentagon information and it was particularly awful. So, I decided to do my own version. I wrote a lecture on the Declaration of Independence and emphasized the section where Jefferson said, at the beginning: "We hold these truths to be self evident: that all men are created equal; that they are endowed by their Creator with certain unalienable rights; that among these are life, liberty, and the pursuit of happiness." Nobody ever notices the next line, which is interesting because Jefferson said, "And to secure these rights, governments are instituted among men." That was a key phrase in Jefferson's Declaration of Independence that no one wants to remember because people like to abuse and damn government.

I became so enamored with the Declaration of Independence and the way it was worded—the concept that it is not about power, it's not about party. That was on my mind all the time because we studied it so much in ethics at St. John's. I quoted current news reports about issues on life, liberty, and the pursuit of happiness to demonstrate the importance of this basic American policy statement. In talking about the equal rights of all people, I cited a *Time* magazine article on the Cicero, Illinois, race riots and how it pretty well illustrated that we were far from meeting the goals of their demonstrations. I also talked about the Watts riots in Los Angeles. I quoted exactly from all the articles and handed out printed sheets with the lectures. The officers went back and repeated it at their squadron lectures on the following day, Friday.

My boss, the officer in charge of my office, was a wonderful man named Bill Flood, a second lieutenant from Wisconsin. He was new there and didn't even know what I was doing. On Monday, I'm sitting about four feet from the lieutenant and all of a sudden I heard him say on the phone, "Yes sir, no sir, yes sir." His face turned beet red and after several minutes of this I realized he was obviously getting chewed out.

He hung up and said, "George, what the hell did you do?"

I told him.

He said the commanding officer wanted me to know that "we do *not ever* have race issues on this base."

Lieutenant Flood knew how terrible the Pentagon material was so he wasn't a bit upset with me. He was pleased, I suspected.

In that Air Force experience, my rank and my position were not important and it didn't take me long to learn that one has to think his own thoughts wherever possible. And even though the information and education lectures I occasionally wrote offended certain superiors, they were the times in my work that I felt satisfied and reassured about doing something worthwhile.

I played shortstop for the base fast-pitch softball team. A big red-haired captain from Montana was determined we were going to have softball fields come hell or high water. So he performed a midnight requisition and the next morning announced, "Boys, we've got our posts and fence, let's go do it." We then had all kinds of equipment, enough for about four softball fields.

More than anything the Air Force gave me an independence that seems to accompany an awful lot of veterans. They go away as young kids and suddenly discover there's a mystique of respect and maturity that is accepted and expected. You can see it in some of the politicians. You can see it in John McCain and you can see it in John Kerry. Lots of people have it and get it from different sources. I felt that maturity, the confidence to say "I disagree" and not be uncomfortable doing it.

It did that for me, even though I had an awful experience with a crude and tough major. He interviewed us for job assignments when we were first in California because it looked like we'd be heading to Korea. He looked at my file and literally scorned my bachelor's degree in philosophy. "Philosophy? What the hell are you going to do with that?" he said. "That is the most ridiculous major anybody's ever taken."

I wasn't rebellious enough at that time to tell him to stick it in his ear, but I probably should have. In later years I would have. That experience didn't dampen my independence at all, or my self-esteem.

Of course, the highlight of my military time was when I got married to Janie and we had our first child, Bob, while I was on active duty. He was born May 10, 1952.

All In the Family

Our children came fast, and life was pretty crazy busy. Lots of things were taking place at the farm and changes were happening regularly. As I mentioned, between my two partners and me, there were thirty kids. Many summers there were eight or ten boys home who needed to work and wanted to work. We did all kinds of things with them.

There was too much going on and I wasn't always a father when I should have been. Janie filled in a lot of the blanks for me. She was extremely attentive to birthdays and all the things that were highlights in their lives. People used to say she was the most organized mother they had ever seen. I don't know to this day how she did it.

I talked to the kids a lot about how to live, emphasizing that *truth* is fundamental. The teaching of forgiveness came along later. I had never articulated that until I heard it from my friend Dr. Ralph Dunnigan. It's impossible to be good parents without being mindful of the need to always forgive and forget, which I think I practiced but may not have taught other than verbally. Janie could be mighty tough, but half an hour later it was forgotten. She did it all the time. She combined the toughness and the astuteness with almost instant forgiveness.

All through the raising of the children I was the soft touch. Janie was often angry when I wouldn't back her up. I thought we shouldn't gang up on the kids—somebody's got to be there to catch them. I remember one or two instances of being pretty tough. But I've always told the kids: "I don't care where you are or what you've done, if you need help call me right away. No questions asked." That was the standing rule and I never had trouble with them, they always called except for one incident and I don't know what happened with that one—one truck accident I never found out about until years later.

I laughed so much with our kids on the farm. There was always humor. One of the classic tricks that always got everyone giggling was when the boys would stand on the back of the trailer and pee over the end of the wagon as we were driving to and from the field. Of course it was damn near impossible to urinate straight with all the bumps and the ditches so they would pee all over themselves.

One time in the fairly early summer we were up at the International Music Camp, held at the International Peace Garden near Dunseith. The Ford LTD quit running—it would just cough and choke and chug along. I thought sure as the world the fuel line was loose so I crawled under the car, tightened up the fuel line. By golly the car started, went a little ways, sputtered and then started in again. I said that sure sounds like dirt in the fuel line because fuel gets to it for a while then it gets plugged. Finally I limped into a filling station. The service attendant came out and took the air cleaner off. It was absolutely plugged with fluffy white cottonwood seeds.

"How often do you clean that?" he said.

"Oh I don't know, whenever somebody changes the oil," I said. I remember everyone was getting pretty nervous—this had gone on for quite a while because I was determined to fix it, to show my skills to my kids, before I finally broke down and went to that filling station. That was the trip where we left our son Jim behind when we drove off and we didn't discover it until we were ten miles down the road. I don't know that there was any particular lesson learned there or specific point to make about it now, but family episodes like that are memorable for me.

My time with the kids in the summer was probably the most enjoyable part of my life. Always smart remarks, always laughter, on occasion one of the older kids hungover. We poured cement in feedlots, we threw bales, and it was a fun time for all of us. Plus, there was a little teaching along the way. But there wasn't a lot of time. I couldn't get to all of these kids' athletic events. I went to basketball games but I remember missing football games because I couldn't get away. Our oldest boy, Bob, got hurt, broke a collarbone. It happened out of town, and I was not there. I always felt badly about that. We were not rich but had enough income to live a happy life, however busy.

We use to put up about 25,000 bales of straw. So we'd be out loading bales, sometimes two trailers in tandem behind the tractor. One of the boys had been out partying the night before and he'd been half asleep all morning. We had a double load and he was asleep on top of the bales on the back trailer. I was driving the tractor and probably going too fast and the back section of the load fell off. I didn't see it until I turned the corner and looked behind me and here comes my nephew and behind him is a big pile of bales. It was riotously funny and of course the rest of the guys just gave him the what-for for shaking the load loose. There were lots of episodes like that.

One time son George backed a combine out of a Quonset and rammed into a utility pole, bending the back of the combine pretty severely. My brother Bill, who was under a lot of pressure and a bit short tempered, came running out: "What the hell are ya doing... look what ya did!"

As Bill continued to express his frustration, George said to him, "I did it on purpose, of course." Later on it became kind of a standard line—*I did it on purpose, of course*—whenever some accident happened. It became the source of a lot of laughter, and also some learning.

The farm also taught me an ability to turn around and say *Oh-oh I've made a mistake*, and stop it. That was part of a philosophical background, my belief that somehow things would work out. I believe that even mistakes will turn out all right if you are confident enough to make the judgment in the first place and then not be afraid to change it.

They Were Positive Influences

Adlai Stevenson, who ran for president against Dwight Eisenhower in 1952 and 1956, was one of my early heroes. There wasn't any dark side to Eisenhower, but a cartoon by Herblock (Herbert Block) at the time said better than anything else I ever read or saw who Ike was. It showed Eisenhower sitting in a helicopter with his golf cap on, holding his golf bag, and down below the people are wrangling over problems, economic crisis, racial problems. The caption reads: "He's above all this."

People who knew Eisenhower say they saw him as a great man. I personally admired him for something he said in a farewell speech he gave just before John Kennedy's inauguration. This former five-star general, who had led the nation through World War II, surprised everyone with this warning:

> In the councils of government, we must guard against the acquisition of unwarranted influence, whether sought or unsought, by the military-industrial complex. The potential for the disastrous rise of misplaced power exists and will persist.

> We must never let the weight of this combination endanger our liberties or democratic process. he continued. We should take nothing for granted. Only an alert and knowledgeable citizenry can compel the proper meshing of the huge industrial and military machinery of defense with our peaceful methods and goals so that security and liberty may prosper together.

Eisenhower's speechwriter Malcolm Moos, who later became the University of Minnesota's president, inserted that language into Eisenhower's speech, and Ike didn't see it until he gave the talk.[24] But once Ike said it, he defended it and argued for it. Clearly he must have understood that in advance even though he probably wouldn't have said it were it not for his speechwriter. That was a significant bit of history because it was a fundamental important warning to the nation.

I quoted Eisenhower in some of my speeches, but was more impressed by Stevenson with his understanding of the complex issues and his need to bring a fresh approach. Even though I had terrible misgivings about his decision to drop the atomic bomb on Japan, Harry Truman was also kind of a hero because of his common-man characteristics and because he wasn't afraid to "tell it like it is."

Of course, Abraham Lincoln is one of my heroes. Along with the Declaration of Independence, I love to quote the Gettysburg Address.

Believe it or not, I really became a big fan of Allen Olson, the man I defeated to become governor. Though he sometimes made mistakes as governor, and we all do, his strength was that he listens well and has more intellectual honesty than an awful lot of people. I've always felt badly about the way he was treated by his party after he lost the election. He didn't deserve that.

I've worked with Olson a lot in the last few years. But as governor he wasn't able to tell people how to do things. He was a college good-old-boy with Dale Moug, his Office of Management and Budget director and Al Lick, Director of Institutions. The only negative position I raised in the 1984 campaign involved a sale of state land. It appeared afterward that Olson didn't even know about it. Lick departed at the end of Olson's term. Moug had gone earlier, after embarrassing his boss. After three years, Dick Rayl brought Lick back to be the director of juvenile services within the Department of Corrections.

Obviously I have really strong feelings about the work that Bill Guy did as governor. He really set a new tone in government. Bill was probably my idol. And then Art Link came with a different but equally sincere understanding of the people's needs. Art did amazing work in the environmental area of land reclamation. I think he understood the budget, and things were pretty sane when he was there.

When I ran for Congress in 1964, I'd been in Bismarck and was flying with Senator Quentin Burdick. He had an event in Minot, and I gave a greeting even though I wasn't a candidate in the west district. It was a hot, hot August day and Burdick had been carrying his raincoat all day long. As we got to the event in Minot, I said, "Senator, let me carry your raincoat. It's hotter than blazes and I'm not going to be meeting many people here anyway."

He said, "I would, George, but my zipper's broken." I was on the platform with him and two or three other people and I noticed that the cuffs of his trousers were all frayed. I thought, my God, you'd think he'd buy new clothes. We rushed to get to the airport because we were flying over to an event in Grand Forks. At the Minot airport, as we walked in the door, the senator handed me his briefcase and that raincoat. He said, "George, you catch up with the pilot, I'm going to slip into the men's room and put on my *old* suit."

Jocie Burdick, his wife, hated these stories. But they were just so funny and Quentin was such a dear man. He understood the issues and he was brighter than a new penny. He had a kind of a wink in his eye about half the time and he was as unselfish as the day is long.

I felt much the same way about Art Link. Art was a great guy and was always considerate and never uttered a negative comment that I know of, unless it was kind of tongue in cheek. Along with Buckshot Hoffner and Walt Hjelle, Art and I were running for the party's gubernatorial nomination in 1984. Having four of us trying to get the nomination was a good thing. While we rarely traveled together, we all appeared at the same political meetings and district conventions. That drew larger crowds in every case and made those into significant events for the Democratic Party. Art was just a great campaigner, there's just no question. I remember kidding him once when we were on the podium about every night. I noticed that in the West he always wore his cowboy boots and his western suit. And then we'd be in Grand Forks and he'd have a different suit and regular oxfords. I said to him one night, "Well Art, I see you've got your eastern clothes on." He laughed. He knew exactly what I was talking about.

When I won the party's nomination at the party's state convention in Minot, we brought our family up on the stage. Art said he didn't know we had that many kids working for us.

Itinerarium Mentis in Deum

Pardon my French, I mean Latin. To introduce this section, "The Mind's Road to God," the title of a famous work many centuries ago by a profound Christian thinker named Bonaventura.

Two life-changing learning experiences have so deepened my religious faith that it is impossible to ever forget them. The first occurred in the summer of 1950, when after meeting Rosie

Fuesting I visited Father Smith at the Trappist Monastery. His wise counsel has always reassured me and given me the courage to make difficult decisions and to go on without worrying needlessly about the consequences, which no amount of worrying is going to change anyway.

The second great teaching came to me fifty years later from a dying friend, Dr. Ralph Dunnigan, my beloved doctor in Bismarck. It was March of 2002 and Ralph was coming to the end of a long fight with prostate cancer. I had driven to Bismarck just to see him. He knew he was dying and he knew that I knew that he was dying. After visiting for a while, I said to him, "Ralph, are you all right with death coming on?"

He looked at me quietly for several minutes and said nothing. There was peace in his face and in his voice. "Yes," he finally said, "I've been fine ever since I learned that God's love is all about forgiveness. I've been praying a lot and studying scripture a lot, and I've discovered that every reference in scripture to salvation is about forgiveness." He went on, "When we pray the *Our Father*, we pray to be taught to forgive. When Christ gave us the Eucharist he said it was for the forgiveness of sins. And, Bud," he said, "human love is all about forgiveness too. I know that love is all the things St. Paul said it is, and I've come to understand that all of the things that he wrote about—patience, kindness, and all of the rest—they all come together and come into fullness in forgiveness."

And then he said, looking intensely at me, "If you and Jane can't forgive each other right away when something comes between you..." He poked his weak and tired forefinger into my chest and continued, "You've got to work on that."

I've never forgotten what Ralph told me. I see the truth in his words, every day—not just in personal matters, but in all kinds of social and political issues. Harshness and violence and vengefulness just never really work. Ralph Dunnigan was the greatest teacher I have ever had—well maybe Janie has been even greater, because she has taught me by her actions and by her forgiveness all through these years. But Ralph articulated a huge lesson. Especially on top of the earlier lesson from the Trappist monk, the two together became the most profound teaching of my life.

So Christianity remains important to me. I believe strongly in the fundamental Christian teachings of love and forgiveness and in the sacramental core of Eucharist. From those core beliefs flow most of my other more particular beliefs, among them the understanding that in all human beings there is a basic kinship and equality that demands total respect for every person and total respect for the rights of every person. This belief demands acceptance of the social nature of human and divine relationships. It demands an understanding that in serving our fellow humans we are serving God. Christianity involves a cubic relationship with God—a relationship that reaches out as well as up. Christianity is not a linear, individualistic relationship between individual and God. We serve God by serving our fellow human beings: by respecting them and by feeding them and by protecting their rights. When we understand that, it becomes offensive and almost impossible to damage another human, or to deny his or her rights. It becomes almost impossible to ignore another individual's needs. From these basic beliefs flow most of the motivation for my work.

My seminary courses at St. John's—particularly the courses taught by a Bismarck native named Ernest Kilzer—were heavily involved in the discussion of the role of the state, the role of the church, the communal role of individuals in the state, and the communal role of the individual in the church. These beliefs may explain why my own church was in the forefront of the fight for religious freedom in American history. It is true that in the early years of the United States, Catholic leadership rightly promoted separation between church and state. Catholics were a distinct minority in some (not all) of the early colonies and early colonial states. In the end, the fear of religious intolerance (from which many of the colonists had fled) resulted in wide-spread pressure for constitutional expression of separation.

Some of us have short memories. Some actually argue against separation and try to enforce generally religious opinions in public policy. Their righteousness frequently reaches the point of claiming that God is on their side. And yet, if history is clear about anything it is that tyranny emerges when sectarian religious views dominate a government. At the same time internal church bureaucracy has become an overburdening encumbrance on many Christian churches. It is part and parcel of the goal of power in the world. Christianity has suffered with this syndrome since Constantine. It has led to abuses in many areas of human life, at times even drowning out the voices of those living and preaching the teachings of Christ. Pomposity and pretense are not infrequent components of it, and they lead to intolerance of even other Christians.

I most heartily applaud the fact that Christian churches do honor the teachings of Christ through their extensive charitable works of feeding the hungry, clothing the naked, housing the homeless, and harboring the harborless. But church bureaucracy frequently ignores the changing lives of people. That tendency in church bureaucracies is even more frustrating than it is in public bureaucracies, but the same tendency exists in all bureaucracies. Bureaucrats seem to have difficulty understanding that the practices of a certain era need to be regularly reviewed. World relationships change, people change, and good and evil exist in new forms. Because each new era challenges not only people, but bureaucracies as well, many church leaders struggle to maintain the status quo, believing that what happened fifty years ago was clearly God's way. The fact is that Christianity has also never really gotten over the terrible prostitution of it by the alignment with government powers and the establishment of the spirit of royalty among the hierarchy. Even some regular clergy are caught up in it. I can't find anything in the gospels that leads me to believe that such a mentality is part of the teachings of Christ.

Bernard Häring, the leading moral theologian at the Second Vatican Council and one of the greater theologians of this era, wrote extensively about the church's need to be relevant to the society and the era in which it lives. His last work, written about 1998, is called *My Hope for the Church: Critical Encouragement for the Twenty-first Century.* In it he talks of the need for the church to take a new look at things like divorce, birth control, and capital punishment. In my mind, Häring's final work was truly great because he said again that the church has to open the windows and let the sun and the daylight in, which was the message of Vatican II. Many of us are hanging on to the hope that Christianity will win out and that all the Christian churches will work together and in that way make progress in interpreting and living the gospel. We are hopeful they will then escape the unfortunate influence of the age of Constantine, which brought church officials into the realm of princes and lords and sterile bureaucracies.

I initially saw some signs of hope that the new pope, Benedict XVI, may yet bring a fresh outlook to the church. One or two of his recent writings have been somewhat encouraging and we're starting to hear some new discussions on some human issues that churchmen have been absolutely silent on. I read a piece by the European theologian Hans Küng, a long time friend of the pope when the pope was still Cardinal Ratzinger. Küng spent four hours talking with him after his selection as pope. He wrote some hopeful things about where he thought Ratzinger would move the church to become more Gospel centered and away from its bureaucratic tendency toward rigidity in rules and laws. That gave us some hope, but those hopes were dashed by later pronouncements from Rome.

Some pretty significant groups within the church, particularly the Opus Dei element and those who are friendly to it, constantly struggle for bureaucratic power and monetary power. They're reading a different Bible than I read. Unfortunately, I think much of the attitude portrayed in Dan Brown's novel, *The Da Vinci Code* is true in spirit, if not in fact. I know that the bishop of Fargo attended one of the really far-right world meetings in Lima a few years ago. The fact that Ratzinger may not be captive to this right-wing power group is good news. Christianity is based on the principles of faith, hope, and *love for God and for our fellow humans*—not faith, hope, and *law*. Christianity is not about power and crime and punishment. It is about love and forgiveness.

CHAPTER SIX: legislation and leadership

Updating the Constitution

Subsequent to my time in the State Senate I was elected a delegate to the North Dakota Constitutional Convention in 1972.[25] That was a great learning experience because there were so many things I saw from a constitutional point of view that constantly took me back to my experience in ethics class at St. John's. All the topics we talked about so frequently in terms of governmental ethics—the separation of church and state—kept coming up.

One episode at the Constitutional Convention became highly public. A problem that existed in the constitution then and still does now was the provision that exempts property owned by the churches as well as non-profits and fraternal organizations from taxation. Abuse was pretty widespread. Restaurants and other operations escaped taxation because they traveled under the guise of non-profits. In an attempt to provide for some discipline, the tax committee, which I was not on, voted to change the constitution so that it read that the *Legislature may grant* tax exempt status to certain kinds of organizations, instead of the constitution mandating that. The committee brought the measure into the convention and by the time the delegates—including several who were Catholic—got home that weekend many of them were chastised from the pulpit because they were threatening to take away the tax exemption for church property. Buckshot Hoffner was one who got blasted by the clergy.

I was angry about what happened. Back in Bismarck on Monday, on a point of personal privilege, I got up and read a statement that I had handed to the press in which I said I was embarrassed to be a Catholic, that the convention had talked about a whole host of social concerns including legal aid to the poor, capital punishment, corrections versus imprisonment, and punishment, and we'd heard not one word from the churches. I said the convention takes one turn into their tax-exempt status and they descend on us like wolves.

Here's my entire statement that was recorded in the *Journal of the Constitutional Convention* following a newspaper story about the defeat of the proposed change to the Constitution:

The story in the press on Saturday about tax exemptions and the role of the Catholic Church in this issue here forces me to make a response.

I rise to express my regret and embarrassment that the Catholic Conference has brought pressure upon this convention to place the language of specific exemptions in the new constitution.

Nearly every delegate here believes that the details of tax exemptions have no business in the Constitution. They know that people generally are sick and tired of the tax loopholes that develop from such constitutional language.

But I accept the collective wisdom of the convention on the matter, in the face of the thinly veiled threats to defeat the Constitution if we did otherwise.

What hurts is the fact that the Catholic Conference forced us into the compromising decision. What hurts even more is the fact that tax exemptions of all things should be the only issue that the Catholic Conference found to exert its pressure upon, when the issues of legal help for the poor, the death sentence, and so many others with moral and ethical implications have been before us. It is with some reluctance that I make this statement, but the whole thing seems so out of joint that I could not help but make some public response to the unfortunate public statement made last week.

I apologize in whatever way I can for the Catholic Church. I'm embarrassed about the Catholic Church.

Joe Lamb, who was also a delegate, got up on the floor and proclaimed that he wanted to be on record supporting everything I had just said. Joe also expressed amazement that the lobbyist for the North Dakota Catholic Conference, former legislator Ed Becker, would claim that keeping the tax exemption in the Constitution was vital to the concept of separation of church and state. Joe said, "I am sure that future legislators and the people of North Dakota are happy that this lobbyist and the group he represents have such an interest in the separation of church and state, particularly in regard to funds for a certain form of education."[26] Of course, he was referring to the interest of church schools in receiving state money.

Boy it rocked in every paper that published our statements. I didn't get any direct confrontation, though, except about a week later Joe and I both received a letter from Bishop Hilary Hacker of Bismarck in which he said some pretty strong things—he thought we were betrayers of the church. I didn't answer mine but Joe took his and wrote across the bottom: "Dear Bishop, some idiot's been sending stupid letters and signing your name to them," and he forwarded it back to the bishop. Everyone saw Joe's letter before it left and laughed joyfully. We never did hear back.

Making Laws

I was involved with huge issues in the 1963 and 1965 legislative sessions. Few legislators were eager to speak on the floor, so the chairman, Senator Gail Hernett, asked me to carry half the Industry Business and Labor Committee bills, even as a minority member. Those weren't partisan bills at all. They were just concerns that people tried to address. Hernett was a wonderful senator, a banker from Ashley whom I liked. The huge advantage of bipartisan effort became apparent early, how much you could get done if you just didn't play partisan games and tried instead for a workable solution.

Some unusual things happened that first year. An effort developed on the House side to amend the anti-corporate farming law. I knew enough about it to realize the existing anti-corporate farming law had some bad effects so I went over to the House and testified on behalf of an amendment that would have allowed small farmers to use the advantages of incorporating for their own operation. I can't remember details of the amendment but it caused consternation among some of the traditional supporters of the anti-corporate farming.

In addition to doing quite a bit on Hernett's committee in the Senate, I was also on the Education Committee.

Lee Brooks sponsored the repeal of the food-liquor divorcement law and I testified for it. The antiquated law prohibited the sale of food where liquor was sold. Frank Knox of Fargo, an attorney who represented the hospitality industry, lined up a Lutheran bishop and a minister, among several others, to testify in favor of changing the law. The hearing was set for one o'clock in the Capitol's Large Hearing Room, now called the Brynhild Haugland Room. When this bishop and minister got there they saw hundreds of people, a packed house, so they told Frank they were backing out. He came and asked me to answer the opponents who quoted the Bible. I'd promised myself I wouldn't do that but he said it was an exceptional case because they would be reciting scripture *ad nauseam* in there. After finally agreeing, I worked over the noon hour to put together three quotes from the Old Testament and three from the New Testament.

I was the last proponent of the bill to speak. "Everything can be abused, alcohol can be abused too," I said. "But it's not a bad thing and if it's used properly it's a good thing. People abuse clothing, they abuse cars, and they abuse food. All these things can be abused, but the proper use is a good thing."

Then I offered some scriptural quotes that speak admiringly about the use of alcoholic beverages. One of them was Psalms in which David praised God for giving us wine to cheer the heart of man, and also, of course, was the wedding feast of Canaan. Those are the two I remember. The silence that fell over the room after my quoting scripture was deafening because a lot of people had their Bibles. Lee Brooks asked if there were any questions.

Judge P. O. Sathre was the spokesperson for the Women's Christian Temperance Union.[27] "Senator Sinner," he said. "Everyone here knows that the wine that was spoken of in scripture was really grape juice." He said, "It's very serious for you to be quoting these passages and telling us all that these were really alcoholic beverages when all know they weren't, they were really grape juice." He made a sermonette out of his statement, but never asked a question. The ladies all clapped.

When it got quiet I said, "Your honor, with all due respect, I defy you to quote a single scripture scholar to support that position." He got red in the face and said not one more word. This was all being broadcast statewide.

And yet later, Lee Brooks was forced to withdraw his own bill. He was a Fargo attorney and a good legislator. He came in for a night session, just before crossover. We were up against a deadline so we were meeting after dinner. He'd had a few drinks and he stopped by my desk. "Those God-damn Republicans made me withdraw my own bill," he said. "A lot of those Bible carriers will vote dry as long as they can stagger to the polls." That's an old line—I've heard it used about the Mormons too. So the bill was withdrawn, but later on a Fargo merchant named Omer Mathison started an initiated measure to repeal the food-liquor separation law and the voters approved it by a good margin in the November 1964 general election. Lee Brooks was involved in that campaign. The new law allowed food and alcoholic beverages in the same room as long as gross sales of food during the calendar year at least equaled the gross sale of alcoholic beverages. It also permitted individuals under twenty-one years old to be in those places if accompanied by a parent or guardian.

Another bill that comes to mind from 1963 got my attention as I was sitting at my desk on the Senate floor and heard Al Doerr, who represented the pharmacies as their lobbyist, talking to the president of the pharmacists, whom I knew from having a couple uncles in that profession. They were discussing whom they might get to sponsor their legislation because nobody would take it. I knew a little about it, had studied medical ethics in college, and didn't like what was going on with physicians taking over the pharmaceutical business. So I got up and went back. "What is your bill and would you consider my taking it?"

Al looked at me. "You're kind of young," he said. "You're pretty new."

"I know. I'd work hard on it. I haven't got any other bills."

He said the bill would simply require that the ownership of any pharmacy in North Dakota must be 51 percent pharmacists. They wanted to think about me as sponsor. "We'll come and see you in the morning and we'll tell you if we want to let you take it."

"Who are the senators most likely to oppose this?" I inquired. They named off about a dozen. "I think I know what to do," I said, and then went to each of those twelve senators and asked them if they would co-sign it and help me. To a man each of them said, "George, we can't sponsor it but we won't oppose it."

I introduced the bill and told the pharmacists: "I want you to call the hometown pharmacists of every one of the committee members and tell them to call their senator and ask for their help with the bill. If it pans out in committee you better do the same things with the other senators on the floor."

Finally we passed it in committee and then on the floor with few dissenting votes. The House did exactly the same thing, passed it with about ten dissenting votes.[28] One of the witnesses in the first hearing was Ed Leibe, who was a pharmacist from Ellendale. He came in and said that at one time the doctor in Ellendale owned all three pharmacies and the funeral home. That sounded like a strange combination for a doctor, but that's what he owned. Gratefully the testimony was recorded because that summer, US Senator Phillip Hart was holding antitrust hearings in Washington on medical involvement with the pharmaceutical business. The North Dakota bill became the battle cry for pharmacists all over the country.

The pharmacists' national journal published a big article, a front-page headline story in the organization's national paper. I got a call from Hart's committee inviting me to Washington to testify, which I did in mid-summer. I repeated the story that Ed

Leibe had told the North Dakota Senate Committee. It wasn't a long presentation, ten or fifteen minutes at the most. I was doing some other things in Washington and didn't think a lot about it. In Bismarck for the 1965 session, the organizational session the first of the year, I ran into Senator Earl Redlin of Ellendale. "Hi George, did you know you were being sued?" he said, explaining that the doctor in Ellendale read the story in *The Wall Street Journal* about my testimony to Senator Hart's committee and claimed it was absolutely not true.

"Really, did *The Wall Street Journal* print it?"

"Every word of your speech."

"Holy buckets," I said. "That could be serious."

I went to my desk and called John Kelly, my attorney. "Bud," John said, "don't worry about it, you have legislative immunity. If your testimony and your repeating of the story were anywhere near true then it's especially clear that he can't touch you."

We checked the legislative hearing records and I had it exactly right, didn't go an inch beyond the mark.

Nothing happened until after the legislative session when letters came from this Ellendale doctor containing copies of checks. He was trying to prove he sold one pharmacy the same day or day after he bought the second one, so he didn't own all three of them. I didn't bother to send it to John, as it didn't really matter to me. I didn't really have a dog in that hunt.

Then one day came a phone call from California. It was the Ellendale doctor, who had moved to California. He was coming back through and wanted to know if I'd meet with him. So we had lunch together out by the interstate. "I wanted to tell you that you were right, this is not a good thing," he said. "I didn't see it until I got to California and found out that there the doctors also own the hospital." He said, "You think there might be graft in what's going on here. Hah, you ought to see what's going on out there."

So, in the end, he came back to say I was right, there are some dangers. For instance, perhaps the doctor owns the pharmacy that's got an oversupply of a drug. Who is to say that the whole clinic can't be asked to prescribe that drug even though there's a newer, better one on the market. That was part of the testimony. I was careful not to say that was going on, but who is to say it couldn't happen.

Sometime in the middle 1970s the law was appealed all the way to the US Supreme Court. John Kelly defended the pharmacists. The law was upheld by the US Supreme Court and is still in place. That was a fabulously interesting episode. The clinics that owned pharmacies before the bill was passed were grandfathered in but this law has made it difficult for other hospitals and clinics to dispense medications, and they can't operate pharmacies at different locations. It's also difficult for some patients, such as those treated in emergency rooms, to get prescriptions filled during hours when community pharmacies are closed. So, in retrospect, improvements in that pharmacy-ownership law are now called for.

In 1963, Bill Guy asked me if I would fight a bill that the sign companies had gotten introduced. The measure, which was heard in my committee, intended to waive the agreement between the state highway department and the Federal Bureau of Roads controlling billboard advertising along the interstates. He said the Republicans are going to pass this no matter what you do but we need to go through the motions of fighting it.

I didn't sponsor a lot of legislation that first year so I studied the bill, which was sponsored by veteran legislator Ken Fitch of Fargo, who was a former House Speaker. I knew the language in the bill like the back of my hand. When it came up for final vote, late in the legislative session, I got to my chair after dinner and looked across and there were sign company representatives all seated up in the gallery on the opposite side of the Senate so they could stare at me when I spoke and try to intimidate me. It was a crazy experience. Lee Brooks chaired the committee that year and he was handling the bill for the committee. Lee got up and explained the bill, saying it was an attempt to take away some of the restrictiveness of the federal highway beautification act that had been passed through the influence of President Lyndon Johnson.

I had filed a divided report in opposition. Explaining my disagreement with the bill, I cited road beautification, highway safety, inconvenience to farmers—all the traditional arguments about billboards along the interstate. "I think everybody understands what the implications are, that the people who drive highways can see the beauty of the countryside, and we can all understand the effects on highway safety when you have distracting billboards,"

I said. "The farmers have to farm all around these darn things again if we change this."

And another argument: "We should kill this bill if for no other reason than that this is a very bad draft to put on our law books. If you look on page 32 of this massive bill you'll see a sentence there that's two-thirds of a page long. It has two double negatives and I contend it's gibberish."

Senator Roland Meidinger of Jamestown was ardently supporting the measure for the Newman sign company, which is located in Jamestown. He got up and spoke. "Senator Sinner is a very young man, he doesn't understand these complex, legal bits of language," he said. "Senator Brooks is an expert on that sort of thing—he's been in the committee all the weeks we've had this bill. If Senator Sinner had only asked Senator Brooks, I know that Senator Brooks would have helped him understand it."

Well, he talked just long enough for me to get my wits about me. When he was finished I got up. "Mr. President, if Senator Brooks will explain that sentence I'm all ears." And I sat down. It got deathly quiet in the chamber.

We had the old huge bill books—they weighed about fifteen pounds. Brooks put on his half glasses and got up. He picked up his bill book and started to read. He got down about two lines and he stopped. Ceremoniously he laid his bill book down on his desk and after removing his glasses he looked at the lieutenant governor and said, "Mr. President, I give up."

A thunderous silence permeated the chamber. It was just too much. I got up again and said, "I think you can see that this is indeed a bad draft and it shouldn't pass."

Of course they passed it anyway. Unknown to me Bill Guy was in the gallery and he came down just beaming. "You darn near ruined a perfectly good veto," he said to me. And that's what happened, he vetoed the bill.[29] It was fascinating and you can imagine what that experience did for my self-confidence.

One of the other bills Bill Guy asked me to fight was also in 1963. The measure was introduced to reinsure the state fire and tornado fund, a self-sufficient pool of money that insured all the state and county buildings. The bill included a pretty high deductible clause. Lee Brooks was handling that one too. I was raising questions and finally said: "Members of the Senate, the major thing that troubles me about this is the deductible that was written into this bill. It's larger than any one year's total losses for the state's fund. This doesn't make sense to me."

Jud (Aloys) Wartner, a senator from Harvey, asked me to repeat that. "I've got the book," I replied. "I've got the figures on all the losses."

"Let me see that."

I handed it to him, he was about four seats away. He looked at it for about fifteen seconds. "Mr. President," he said. "Senator Sinner is right. This is crazy—we can't do this."

"You got me this time," said Brooks, who carried the bill. That bill was passed by the Senate but eventually died a big-time death. A rewritten version passed two years later and Bill Guy signed it. The tornado that hit Fargo in 1957 had triggered that effort. Despite still having second thoughts, I ended up voting for it the second time. Instead of defining all the details, the companies had to bid and provide alternative packages in their bids. Ultimately the program was never implemented because they couldn't get a decent bid. I never did know who was right, but if we had a catastrophe you would look pretty stupid if you voted against reinsurance.

I came to the Senate during a period where many people didn't care which party you were with. They just wanted to solve problems. Activity during those years was much more nonpartisan. Jud Wartner was one of those people to whom political party was not a big deal. He wasn't intent on embarrassing Democrats. I loved learning so much and found there was continuous opportunity to provide some input that was meaningful. I loved carrying bills on the floor and saying what to me seemed right, not what would serve the party.

The following session I co-sponsored more than two dozen bills with George Longmire, a Republican from Grand Forks who was a pretty darned progressive senator. One of the pieces of legislation that we handled was the bill to set up the legal provisions for regional mental health clinics, now known as regional human service centers.[30]

Another memory from my term in the Senate was a vitriolic debate over the amount of higher education spending. "My God, all our kids are leaving the state anyway," argued one of my conservative colleagues.

Senator Evan Lips, to his credit got up with a great response: "What do you want us to do, send them out dumb?"

After court challenges delayed reapportionment earlier in that decade, legislative districts were reapportioned prior to the 1966 election and gerrymandered me out of my strong areas in Fargo and West Fargo. The new district was carefully redesigned to be hard-line Republican. I liked campaigning, but we knew it would be a tough re-election race. Nationally it was a Republican landslide in an off-presidential-year election. Republican candidates also ran strong across North Dakota that year and ended up owning 82 of 98 House seats and 44 of 49 in the Senate. Ernie Pyle beat me 2,091 to 2,006. A friend told me afterward that if he'd had known it would be that close he would have gone out and voted. I was so busy the loss didn't leave a big void in my activity. Being happy with my life and whatever came along, I didn't view that defeat with any great alarm.

Guiding Campuses

In January of 1967, Bill Guy asked me to serve on the Board of Higher Education, for a term to run from July 1, 1967, to July 1, 1974. My appointment was subject to confirmation by the State Senate. The other board members when I was appointed were Henry Sullivan of Mohall, John Conrad of Bismarck, Elvira Jestrab of Williston, Albert Haas of New Rockford, Fred Orth of Grand Forks, and Allen Hausauer of Wahpeton.[31]

I drove from Casselton the morning of a board meeting at the Prince Hotel in Bismarck. I arrived at the meeting about a half-hour late. When I walked in they were in the midst of a discussion about a demand from a state senator and a house member that we fire the faculty advisor of the student newspaper at University of North Dakota and expel the student editor. I didn't get the full story and didn't know really what had happened; only that something in *The Dakota Student* had upset some people.[32] I asked to table it until after lunch so I would have a chance to get caught up. Elvira Jestrab was chairing and she granted my request.

Over lunch I went out to the lobby and called a friend of mine at UND to find out what happened. He said a jazz festival failed miserably, and the kid who chaired the event spelled S-H-I-T on the carpet with the leftover tickets. They took a picture of him sitting staring at the tickets and ran the photo on the front page of *The Dakota Student*. That's what people were upset about. Well, I wasn't particularly enamored with the board members who raised the question—they weren't exactly paragons of virtue. While I had been on the phone, all the dignitaries were sitting around the little lounge there telling dirty stories. Isn't this a fine kettle of fish, I thought. They're going to complain because kids spell out *shit* in the paper, as if that were really so terrible, but then it doesn't bother them at all to sit around and tell dirty stories. (Neither bothered me.)

"Listen, it will be over my dead body that anything is done on this," I said. "The university can take care of it. They can acknowledge to the young man that it wasn't a very good idea and that's as far as it's going to go as far as I'm concerned."

I became a hero at UND. President George Starcher thanked me over and over. Because I became the target of criticism from a few phony politicians, I deflected the pressure from him and the university.

At the same meeting, two popular people in the university system—one from North Dakota State University and one from University of North Dakota—had reached mandatory retirement age. They both were in for exemptions. "Why do we have a rule?" I said. "If the rule's bad, let's change it." And they were both denied exemptions. One of them—Ben Gustafson—was head of university extension at UND. So I again became the target big time. Some who supported them being granted the extensions lobbied legislators against my confirmation as a member of the board. The legislative session came around after I'd been defeated for re-election to the Senate by Ernie Pyle and they were going to reject my nomination for the board.

"Aren't you going out to testify, to make a statement?" everyone asked.

"No, it wouldn't make any difference," I said. "They didn't ask me to come out."

Some supporters of the extensions we disapproved lobbied against my confirmation. Finally I was approved by a 27-26 vote. Landslide Sinner!

I chaired the board when a man was chosen for a high position on one of the campuses. I wasn't that sure about him because another candidate had a wonderful resume. But this man was selected. The three people who were really supporting him, hard core, were Fred Orth from Grand Forks, Albert Haas from New Rockford, and Al Hausauer from Wahpeton. If I remember correctly he was appointed in March or February and he took office in time to be in place when school started in the fall. It was harvest and I was on the combine when I went home to take a phone call that two of these guys who had strongly supported this man were demanding we fire him immediately. Apparently he'd had a "lost weekend" with the wife of a prominent person in that city. His car sat in her driveway all weekend.

The call came from Al Hausauer. He told me Albert Haas and one of the other members were fighting mad. I handed off my combine to somebody and I drove to Bismarck where I sat down with Ken Raschke, the higher education commissioner. "I think we should risk it," I said. "We ought to tell these guys to shut up and go home and we're going to fight them. We're going to give this man one chance."

"You got the votes?"

"I will get the votes."

So I called Peter Hinrichs, a board member from Dickinson. I told Peter what had happened and what I thought we should do. He said he absolutely agreed with me. That gave me lots of confidence because he was such a sound guy. I called Fred Orth and he agreed too. I called Elvira Jestrab and got her vote. Harold Refling was the other one. I then called the other three and said, "If you guys bring this up I'm going to hang you with it in the end. I've got the votes. I understand how you feel but we need to give him one chance."

I then called the campus official. "I don't even want to know what happened," I said. "Just don't ever let it happen again."

"I won't," he said.

He never had another drink, and I bet he's thanked me countless times for saving his career. I think they were all grateful that we toughed it through. I had no idea who the woman was. I didn't want to know.

Years later, Minnesota Governor Jesse Ventura was here for a meeting on the flood problems. I was sitting with him and the meeting was actually kind of boring. In Minnesota a big story had just broken about his chief of staff getting picked up for indecent exposure. I was familiar enough with the guy to know he was probably the one person who was keeping some sanity in Jesse's administration. Jesse and I were whispering. I said, "You know what, you ought to give that guy a chance, because if you abandon him his life is over. You might be able to save him. Give him a chance."

Then I told him this story about the campus official who had his lost weekend. "Jesse," I said, "that guy you've got is pretty good, I think."

"Yeah he is."

"Gamble," I said.

"You know what, I'm going to do that." And he did.

It was an incredible lesson to me that so many people could find themselves in the same predicament. I did try whenever I had a chance to practice that. Highway Commissioner Walt Hjelle's drinking incident in late 1988 was really the only time a similar situation came up. He hit a couple cars driving home. It was pretty bad. Walt was so upset with himself he wouldn't even talk to me. He wasn't going to listen to me or discuss me not accepting his resignation. I think maybe he was ready to hang it up anyway. But I would have kept him. I would have tried.

Walt had been the highway commissioner under two former governors, Bill Guy and Art Link. He was a superb public servant.[33] Early on I was concerned about the need for jobs in the state. I asked Walt Hjelle whether in highway projects they could go back to using jackhammers and other smaller equipment that required more manpower than did the large machines that tore up and recycled road material. He found out from his engineers that the cost and the outcome would be about the same so the department started doing that. It created a lot of jobs that summer, particularly for college kids.

I've always felt badly that Walt didn't let me give him another chance and help him deal with that drinking problem he had.

A fire at the Ellendale college in January 1970 sparked a hot controversy. That winter blaze destroyed Carnegie Hall, the college's main facility, which contained classrooms and an auditorium. It also leveled the home economics building. Ellendale's enrollment had been declining. When I moved that we not rebuild the college I got three other votes. Peter Hinrichs' was the only one I remember for sure. "There's a time to live and a time to die," he said to me. Then we had to go to the legislature because we didn't have authority to close the college. We would have lost it if it hadn't been for two tough legislators, two Republican Appropriations Committee leaders, Bob Reimers and Clark Jenkins.

Following our board's decision to not rebuild, the legislature was petitioned by everyone from the Ellendale region to fund reconstruction. Had the legislature done that we would have been bound by the state constitution to maintain the school. To their undying credit, Reimers and Jenkins stood strong beside me and the other members of the board who had made the decision to not fund it. Reimers was from Melville, a little town near Carrington. He chaired Appropriations. Jenkins was a state representative from Fargo. They were both moderately good friends of mine, but we were not political allies by any stretch of the imagination. They were able to garner enough votes to stop the appropriation. They cut the college off and the board was then able to sell the property.[34] Voters in the 1972 election approved a measure that removed the college from the state constitution.[35]

The Ellendale closure was a challenging situation for the State Board of Higher Education. Colleges in a town are like cornerstones. They mean so much to the community that losing one becomes a huge civic concern. One of the arguments used by the Ellendale people for keeping the college open was that so many of the children would not be able to go to college if they had to pay room and board. They said that was why they needed this nearby school. That seemed questionable and one night I mentioned it while visiting with a man who was a highly educated person and an educator. He said that was exactly the wrong attitude. He told me the most important thing about going to college is getting away from home. For many of the children, it is not until they leave home and have to make do in other circumstances that they really begin to mature and face the reality of an independent life. He said to act for themselves really is better for their intellect as well as their will to learn to think for themselves.

One side effect of closing Ellendale was political when in the summer of 1972 I lost the party's nomination for governor on the seventh ballot to Art Link. No votes or few votes came my way out of the six counties around Ellendale. I didn't blame them. That fallout was probably predictable and in some ways a badge of honor because I had done what I really believed needed to be done even though it was not popular.

Reimers sought the nomination for governor from the Republican Party that same year and experienced the same thing I did. There weren't any votes for him either out of that area.

That episode turned out for everyone's betterment, I think, because Trinity Bible College bought the property for the price of one dollar, moved from Jamestown, and started classes in the fall of 1972. The town has had a better and more stable facility as a result. The college recently completed a major building project. The space didn't go empty and the community maintained an institution of higher learning, albeit a private one.

Not long after we ended up having to close Ellendale, we helped start community colleges on the reservations. The timing was ironic. That also happened in 1970, the summer before the legislative session.

The other big matter that year was UND's proposed expansion to a four-year medical school. Supporters had politicked with the doctors around the state. I just didn't believe it would work because a lot of people I knew said there's no way we even have enough patients so we can train doctors well enough about some of the sophisticated rare diseases they might run across. Dr. John Gillam, a physician who was head of the Fargo Clinic, thought it was a big mistake and we wouldn't do well. The case for the four-year program was sold on the basis of federal capitation grants. That meant the federal money was based on a per-student grant. I knew and everyone else knew those funds weren't going to continue long and then suddenly the state would be left with a hell of a budget item.

The board voted 4-3 to approve the four-year program, but as chair I went before the legislature to oppose it. It was approved and funded. Needless to say I wasn't elected board chair the following year. That was fine because I kind of asked for it. I was pretty sure then about being right, though.

In retrospect, the medical school has served the state pretty well. I wasn't wrong about the high cost. It is expensive, but I was wrong about the quality of the doctors. University of North Dakota has produced a lot of good physicians.

Our Prairie Oxford

In early June 1968, I was asked to give the summer commencement address at North Dakota State University. The ceremony was set up in the old football stadium, Dacotah Field, before the Astroturf was installed. Because of a fifty-mile-per-hour wind blowing they talked about canceling it. But I said I didn't care. I could get by. There was no way I could read my notes and deliver a prepared address. So I just wrote down about five things I wanted to talk about.

A friend of mine named Seth Russell, who was a history professor at NDSU, had talked years earlier about a common market for education. He had advocated that the three schools in Fargo-Moorhead should be doing more together. It always struck me as an idea that clearly needed to be fulfilled and activated. So in my remarks I said something I had written in my prepared text, that we had the opportunity to develop an "Oxford on the Prairie." Of course, Oxford was a combination of small schools that became a world-class university. I said we had that potential because we had universities with different specialties—one was principally in physical sciences, one was in education, and one was liberal arts. I said several things about that and how I thought it was time we developed some sort of understanding.

I've always remembered the headline in the next day's *Fargo Forum* saying: "Oxford on the Prairie Proposed." However, we dug up the actual article to find that the headline read: "Sinner Proposes a Single School from the 3 in Fargo-Moorhead." Close enough.[36] The story didn't make the front page and the Oxford on the Prairie concept in the story didn't make it into the headline. But the idea rang around both towns. Of course, why don't we do more to work together? I had been appointed by Governor Bill Guy to the Board of Higher Education a year earlier. In that role I one day called Herb Albrecht, who was the president of NDSU, John Neumaier, president of Moorhead State, and president Joe Knutson at Concordia. I asked them if they would consider having lunch with me.

So we had lunch. I asked them how often they met. It turned out they had never met to talk about common problems. So I said, "There's a lot here and I'd like to help. Why don't we meet the first Wednesday of every month?" And so we did. Slowly but surely things began to look like there was a willingness to go ahead. They then agreed to hire Albert Anderson, head of the Concordia philosophy department, to do some brainstorming and grant writing. It was the genius of Al Anderson that really put Tri-College University together.

Before we knew it they had a library agreement that still functions today by which you can check a book out of any of their libraries. The libraries can buy esoteric volumes in singles so each library doesn't have to spend huge amounts of money. The card catalogues were matched and listed the inventories of the other libraries. The three agreed to a credit exchange and allowed students to take classes on any of the three campuses even if they were enrolled at one of the others.

In the meantime the presidents changed. Laurel Loftsgard took over at NDSU and Roland Dille at Moorhead State. They were both very supportive of Tri-College, as was Joe Knutson at Concordia. The board included the three presidents. Doug Sillers, the State Senator from Clay County, was also interested. He became part of the effort and started meeting with us almost from the beginning. There was no question that in the early years Dille was the most aggressive mover among the three presidents on the joint board in getting things approved, along with Doug Sillers and me. Doug had been forceful in getting the tuition reciprocity passed in Minnesota about the same time it got passed in North Dakota. I think they may even have initiated it before North Dakota.[37] From the beginning he saw what I saw was the potential of much greater enhancement of student offerings. I don't suppose either of us has realized our wildest dreams. But there's been an awful lot of good accomplished through the years.

The surprising thing was that in the first years Concordia was the least convinced about the three schools working together. A registrar there named Jim Rendahl thought Concordia offered superior programs and other students would take advantage of the Tri-College to get into their courses. That was only true in part. While Concordia had some good courses and some good areas, to some extent it was the classic case of believing that others aren't as good as we are. Somehow the love for Concordia that Rendahl had warped his attitude toward the other two institutions. Knutson saw the merit in trying to do some things together and was supportive of Anderson, who was subsequently appointed the first Tri-College provost. Al put together the library program with the help of Jan Janasek from NDSU, who was in many ways the main architect of it. That was immediately perceived as a really good idea. What facilitated it at the beginning from the point of view of the students was the Tri-College bus route, which was already in place. I think it was making a round every half-hour and you could get on the bus at any school and get back home after your class.

It was always difficult to get a balanced exchange that everyone was comfortable with. Sometimes there were more Minnesota students coming over and sometimes it was the other way. I can't remember the history of the equity formula but it was pretty satisfactory. We had a lot of students moving back and forth. The fact that a student enrolled in any institution could take courses at the other was a huge bonus. And then eventually after a library agreement, there came the development of an education administration master's program, which was badly needed in the region. It has produced many, many graduates. As I remember, rather than any kind of Tri-College diploma, those students received their graduate degree from the school at which they had matriculated as an undergraduate, which kept students loyal to their own institutions. Concordia was unable to participate in the education administration program then because Concordia didn't grant graduate degrees.

Tri-College has produced several such joint efforts. Early on an environmental studies group provided a research base in environmental issues where all three institutions and faculty could participate.

After Nathan Davis became Tri-College provost in 2000, he soon found himself somewhat frustrated with his inability to get new programs started. We together hit upon the idea of broadening the reach of Tri-College in a regional effort for bringing public issues to public discussion. Obviously there were many people on the campuses who were expert in the various fields.

During my years in Bismarck I called and sent letters telling them many times that I needed to get off the Tri-College board. I thought I should resign. I couldn't contribute. But they wanted me to stay on. So when I finally retired from the board in 2004, Nathan asked me how I would feel about a banquet. The presidents wanted to hold an event to wish me well. But I attended a lot of banquets and had my fill of them. So I said, "If you want to do something, let's try to do something in the public policy area." That's when Nathan got together with Dick Gross to write the grant application to the Otto Bremer Foundation. The Governor George Sinner Public Policy Symposium resulted.[38] The first year we received $30,000 from Bremer with no strings attached. We had to raise a $10,000 match the second year and $20,000 the third year. We have completed the three annual forums.

The first symposium explored the impact of the use and abuse of addictive drugs—especially methamphetamine—on the criminal justice, corrections, and healthcare systems and the appropriate public policy response for this region. We had the three attorneys general from Minnesota, South Dakota, and North Dakota along with the justice minister from Manitoba. That event was a key part in awakening the public to the difficult challenges involved in methamphetamine. Wayne Stenehjem, North Dakota's attorney general, did a terrific job as one of the keynoters at that inaugural symposium. So also did the representatives from the other jurisdictions.

Dr. Lisa Faust of MeritCare did a masterful job of explaining the problems addictions cause for everyone involved, as did Karen Larson, a former State Department of Human Services employee and deputy director of the Community HealthCare Association of the Dakotas (CHAD). Prairie Public Television aired the event. The production was played over and over across the region. I'm even told that parts of it were shown to the west-

ern province premiers. Later on the western governors and western premiers both passed resolutions in support of most of the
findings of that symposium.

The second symposium focused on a similar problem—alcoholism. It resulted from two or three serious drinking episodes
on the campuses and turned out to be a powerful *exposé* of the
problem of alcoholism in the region. It was reported at the symposium that we rank number one in student alcoholism and we
rank number one in *adult* alcoholism. The problem extends beyond North Dakota and into Minnesota and Wisconsin, too. No
one seems to be able to put a finger on the cause of that except
that it was pointed out the northern countries of Europe have a
similar problem.

The discussion was extremely worthwhile. Addiction was
recognized as a problem for not just individual lives but for businesses and for primary and secondary schools. So we decided to
take it up again the third year and see if we could find experts
on what is working to help reduce this problem on the campuses
and within businesses and anywhere else. Everyone knew there
weren't going to be any short-term fixes, but it was obviously a
major cultural problem. We also wanted to find people who help
leaders cope with the problem in their own organizations.

So the final symposium brought together experts with proven
solutions to the problems of substance abuse in schools and college campuses, the workplace, and in the community. Initiatives
that followed addressed the problem in three ways. The broadest
of those was expansion of the successful Healthy Communities
program in Moorhead to Fargo and West Fargo. In addition, we
sponsored presentations and distributed information through the
Chamber of Commerce to employers on developing and using
drug policies. We also lobbied to generate support for drug courts,
which have been effective in helping people kick their substance-
abuse addictions.

That work all flowed out of the fact that I didn't want to have
a retirement banquet. Nathan Davis and Dick Gross did a great
piece of work. The Otto Bremer Foundation has been wonderful
and the Consensus Council was a huge help.

After we passed enabling legislation when I was in the Senate, the committee that had been established to begin the Southeast Region Mental Health and Retardation Clinic came to me and asked if I would chair the board of directors. Paul Beithon, a physician from Wahpeton, became board vice president and a close friend. He and I hired the staff. That was a difficult, whole new experience for me in hiring professionals and helping manage a sometimes difficult entity. It was a great board. Our efforts turned out pretty well.

The clinic needed space so it moved downtown to the second floor of St. Mark's Lutheran Church just west of the Powers Hotel. Eventually it was melded into the state human services division.

This was a non-political form of public service. After losing the Senate seat I then took kind of a hiatus from political activity. I didn't even go to the political conventions a lot of times, concentrating instead on what I was doing at the farm.

Sugar beets were a major part of our farming operation. When the sugar beet growers were buying the company, American Crystal Sugar, and turning it into a grower-owned cooperative, I offered a motion at the growers association annual meeting to dissolve the separate growers organization.[39] I thought there was a danger if we kept both, we would end up being a two-headed monster. A good friend, Hank Schroeder, got up and moved that the proposal be referred to a committee that would report back at the next annual convention. I ended up on the committee and became convinced in the discussion that maybe eliminating the growers association was the wrong idea. I realized there were certain areas of grower activity—such as migrant labor and farm agronomic research—that didn't lend themselves well to corporate handling. Grower production research, for example, was also probably better handled and understood by a growers association that concentrated on it.

I was selected president of the Sugar Beet Growers Association at the next meeting. The language outlining the structure was part of the motion to adopt the new format and elect the new officers. Basically the old officers became the corporate officers. I was president for four years, nominated and elected by secret ballot of sixty-five growers. It was my first episode of designing a structure where nominations and voting for all officers and board members were by secret ballot. It was extremely reassuring to be elected that way. You knew darn well you better do your job because people trusted you. That system is still in place.

One of the first things that happened, a grower named Alvin Hanson proposed a significant change. He advocated setting up a growers research plan, checking off grower money, and having a grower research board to define what needed to be researched. It became an almost classic research effort. That research, generally speaking, has been given credit for reducing cost of production in the Red River Valley and for getting the growers to go to payments based on extractable sugar content (actual sugar produced), not tonnage. There were more facets to it but it was an almost unparalleled example of research sponsored and paid for by farmers that produces huge advances.

Later, during the years in Bismarck, I insisted on starting a lignite research council and I modeled it after the sugar beet growers. It involved professional researchers and members of labor organizations, but it was dominated by people who paid for it. I cited the sugar beet growers example to the lignite industry. I tried without any success to get other organizations to do the same thing. It was a new idea that still has not really caught on. It's a powerful tool and one of the great developments of that period.

As president of the beet growers I wanted to bring together leaders of the various commodity associations so they would talk to each other and understand the importance of research. In doing so we realized the need for a new greenhouse complex at NDSU and were able to obtain the necessary federal and state funding. NDSU President Laurel Loftsgard wasn't aware of the project until it came to the 1979 legislature, which changed higher education's building priorities to include the greenhouses.

That led to establishment of the Northern Crops Institute (NCI), which was approved by the 1981 legislature with the groundbreaking in December of that year. NCI is a collaboration among the Dakotas, Minnesota, and Montana to support the promotion and market development of crops grown in the region. It focuses on learning rather than selling and provides an international meeting and learning center on the NDSU campus that brings together customers, commodity traders, technical experts, and processors for discussion, education, and technical services. I was the first chairman of the Northern Crops Council, NCI's governing board, and served on it for several years.

Then came my election to the State House of Representatives in 1982. The House was evenly divided among Republicans and Democrats in the 1983 session and I was chosen to chair the Finance and Tax Committee. It was the year that the chair of the Senate committee, Chuck Goodman, was very sick with diabetes. His committee wasn't functioning well. So we carried a heavy load on the House side.

Only one person on the committee played politics. He was a bright, young man who seemed to think it was all a big game. I think his colleagues, in the end, told him to either shape up and get to work or get off the committee. That great committee rewrote practically everything in the tax code. We got Governor Olson's budget out of trouble and the following year *U. S. News & World Report* ran a feature story on state tax structures and called North Dakota's the most fair, most even-handed tax structure in the United States. We were all proud. The great people on the committee were: Ron Anderson, Clare Aubol, Bill Goetz, Steve Hughes, Roger Koski, Bruce Larson, Bruce Laughlin, Clarence Martin, Marshall Moore, Glenn Pomeroy, Allen Richard, Emil Riehl, Alice Olson, Gene Nicholas, John Schneider, and Mike Timm. It was a class act. They were good people and all worked hard.

Late that summer I announced I would be running for governor.

CHAPTER SEVEN: becoming the governor

Winning Campaign

As coach Durenburger said to me, if you can do it better, you better do it. Looking around it seemed to me there weren't a lot of people who knew all the facets of government like I did. Even my knowledge amounted to little when you get down to it because there was such a huge volume of things to know. But I thought I understood education and the economic factors and the different things in the business community that were going on. That prompted my decision to run for governor. I didn't agonize over it and announced my candidacy early.

There's no way that I would ever have won had it not been for Chuck Fleming. He thinks well, he has a mind like a vacuum cleaner, and he has the perseverance and drive to get things done. And he doesn't do it deviously. It's all honest and above board stuff. No dirt. Sometimes with a chuckle or two, his sense of humor carried him. But when he had something to say you listened. Who could ever equal Chuck Fleming when it came to organizing at that 1984 state convention? He was the most tenacious, energetic campaigner that I have ever seen anywhere.

Chuck was my campaign's chief of staff and manager, as well as a friend and confidant. Chuck had been in the legislature and had a vision that was hard to copy. He and Jim Fuglie, who was the Democratic-NPL Party's executive director, were just tremendous helpers during the campaign. My kids, along with my wife, were also tremendously helpful. My press secretary worked for us, as did a woman named Carol Siegert. Rita Moore, who later married Fuglie, was employed by the State Democratic Party then. Rita was with us all eight years in the Governor's Office and continued for a while as my transition secretary after we left there.

After winning the party nomination, I didn't try to influence the convention on selecting my running mate. A substantial movement supported Ruth Meiers. Dick Backes was also a candidate.[40] Either would have been acceptable to me. Ruth became North Dakota's first woman lieutenant governor and was absolutely wonderful.

Chuck still has his handwritten lists on four separate sheets of yellow legal pad paper of what he identified as my assets and liabilities. Here are some of what he saw as my strong points: my ability to attract Republican and independent votes, my character, a woman on the ticket as my running mate, my broad background and large family, my enthusiasm, appearance, lack of baggage, strength of organization, gubernatorial demeanor, support from constituent groups and our Congressional delegation, intellect, political party organization, strength of the party ticket, and good relations with the news media.

Among my liabilities were lack of money and name recognition and that I wasn't an incumbent. He also listed my speaking ability and my lack of fire and brimstone or killer instinct. My nickname among some was "Mr. Doom and Gloom" because I talked about the problems of our economy. Chuck saw negatives in the perception of me as a rich farmer coming from "Imperial Cass" County, my early liberalism and later involvement with controversial issues, and my lack of support for a four-year medical school. A woman on the ticket could also be a liability with some voters, and Chuck thought my candor could be a problem.

A statewide Bureau of Governmental Affairs poll conducted in September, 1984, less than two months before the November 6, election, showed Olson leading by 52.5 percent to 33.1 percent.

Then, about two weeks before the election, Fuglie proposed that we put together a tabloid type paper with pictures of my youth, my work on the farm, my sports activities, children, Janie, all positive stuff about my life. Party Chairman George Gaukler encouraged us to produce the campaign piece, but I had made up my mind that I wasn't going to spend any money I didn't have. "No we can't do this," I said.

My wife, on the other hand, decided we *were* going to do it. She wrote the check for $40,000 while I was out of town campaigning.

On the weekend, Fuglie and my daughter Mary Jo and our press secretary worked through the night to put together this simple, straightforward, positive tabloid. It was two-colored, as I remember it was red and black on four pages on inexpensive newsprint. In addition to photos and information about us, it contained personal letters from both Ruth and me thanking friends and people around the state for listening to us and treating us well during the campaign. Janie wrote the letter that had my signature. Chuck organized an effort to hand-carry that tabloid to every North Dakota community.

Our son Jim was also a tremendous help on the campaign. He took the car and an overloaded trailer and delivered those tabloids, which were inserted in newspapers throughout the state the weekend before the election. That piece hit the homes at the same time the news broke that Governor Olson had not filed an income tax return.[41] I've always thought if there was a secret weapon in the campaign that tabloid was it.

I knew from my own personal meetings that people were listening and understood what I was trying to tell them: that the state was in financial trouble and we had to start being realistic about what we really could pay and what we really could spend. But the arrival of this tabloid helped people decide. One of the pictures was of Janie and me feeding the kids at a picnic table and it was a great picture. There was another one of me playing baseball. Oh, maybe I've mentioned that I was a pretty fair baseball player.

No one ever wrote any stories about that tabloid. But it was an incredible coup. That entire campaign cost $400,000 and we were able to raise $360,000, all but that final $40,000 for the tabloid. I didn't look at the lists to see who donated to my election campaign. Janie wrote more than a thousand personal thank-you notes. Lucy Calautti, who is now married to North Dakota Senator Kent Conrad (1986 – present), organized a fundraiser in Washington, DC, to wipe out the remaining balance.

My re-election effort in 1988 produced a bigger debt. Chuck Fleming and Dan Ulmer, who managed that campaign, organized fundraisers after the election to pay it off. Included in the re-election campaign material was another tabloid, a newspaper pull-out section that featured a photo of Lloyd Omdahl and me on the front. It was printed in black and white to save money. The contents primarily featured photographs of my first term in office. Pictures of Janie and me and of Lloyd and his wife, Ruth, graced the back page, along with personal messages thanking the people of North Dakota for the honor of serving them. [42]

Janie recalls that we made a lot of connections around the state to the college friends of two of our sons who were then students at the University of North Dakota and North Dakota State University. During that first campaign we weren't aware of anything negative coming out on the sitting governor not properly handling his income taxes. I knew we were in the race but when the election came it was much to everyone else's amazement that I ended up victorious, with 55 percent of the vote. I suppose it was nine-thirty or ten o'clock when I was declared the winner.

Before the night was over I received a call from Dick Rayl saying he wanted to help me. Dick was the CEO of Mayrath Industries, a farm equipment manufacturing company headquartered in Illinois. He later became the vice president of administration and finance at NDSU after we left our office. "Man, come on home as fast as you can," I said. "We want you."

So, almost within days he was back and working on the budget trying to sort out what we could really afford as a state. He remained throughout the years there as one of my top advisors. Dick Rayl was always there with me. No one will adequately recount the work he did. He put together a team of budget analysts that has two or three times been recognized in the United States as the best in the country. They were all women. I later wrote a letter to support the nomination of the leader of the analysts, Sheila Peterson, for the most outstanding budget analyst award. The whole team was wonderful. Dick knew how to get good people, encourage them to be professionals, and empower them.

The second person I called on immediately was Joe Lamb. He was a lifelong friend and totally unselfish when it came to what he wanted out of anything. I asked him if he would come and help me with the transition into the office. Joe led the team that analyzed the qualifications of the sitting agency heads Governor Olson had in place. Joe's committee also included Ruth Meiers, Dick Backes, Ted Hardmeyer, Dave Kemnitz, Darlene Leinen, Lois Schneider, and Mart Vogel. I also had two other committees, headed by Art Link and Bill Guy, to help us prepare for the legislative session and develop plans and policies for the Governor's Office.

After Joe's transition team professionally analyzed the sitting department heads of Governor Olson we kept almost half of them. Joe and Dick provided the leadership. Governor Olson's appointees proved to be professional people who didn't have a political ax to grind so much as they saw themselves as having a job to do. For the most part the people I kept were wonderful administrators and became great friends. I wanted them because they were professional staff, not necessarily because they were party loyalists or because they were even supportive of me with their dollars. In the end I think most of them—at least from what I heard—were grateful for the way we ran the government and we let them run the agencies. We didn't try to do it either by intimidation or too many suggestions.

Chuck and I had some arguments because I wouldn't let him ask the people who worked for me for a political contribution. It seemed to me that can be the source of an awful lot of ridiculous intimidation that disrupts the relationship between a sitting administrator and staff. I didn't want to compromise their independence and I suffered for it because I was always short of money for campaigns, but I was willing to live with that because I was so pleased with the honest, aggressive involvement of the agency heads.

I divided up the major responsibilities. I did that in the interim for staff in the office too, as much as I could. I remember telling Chuck one day there were two areas where I would probably want to keep a leadership role. One was agriculture and the other was energy. In energy I had a lot to learn but nobody else in the office was an expert in that area either.

Joe Lamb was a banker and advised me on myriad things. I soon discovered that I had to have someone that I completely trusted as president at the Bank of North Dakota, so I asked Joe to take that position. He worked to straighten out the bank by identifying some of the inaccuracies and the truth of where we were with loans that were bad. As a result we were able to get the state moved from a B grading with Moody's and Standard and Poors grading agencies up to an A-. The state was then able to borrow at less cost to our citizens.

We eventually set up a bonding agency for the state to help the smaller communities handle the technicalities of their bonding authority. The concept was developed by Joe and Dick, both of whom were constantly a source of good ideas.

We Had a Two-Headed State

North Dakota made headlines when we had two governors at the same time—or at least two of us who claimed to be the governor at the same time. And two heads of a state aren't always better than one.

Of concern to Olson supporters were appointments to fill two seats on the Supreme Court. Justice Paul Sand died on December 8, 1984, and Justice Vernon Pederson had announced his retirement effective January 7, 1985. Names of the nominees from the recommendation committee were about to come in and the governor in office at that time would make the appointments.

Newly elected state officials had long taken office when the legislature convenes on the first Tuesday after the first Monday in January during a ceremony established by legislative action. In this case, that would have been January 8, 1985. But in early December, Governor Olson's chief of staff, Bill Wright, acknowledged in news media reports that I could take office as soon as January 1 if I chose to. He also told Chuck Fleming that over lunch, as I recall. That indicated to me there was something serious going on that they knew was wrong. I didn't figure out what it was until months later but I accepted their judgment.

Then, as the end of December approached, Chuck reported to me, "I don't know what's going on, but they said they can't give up the office."

I believe Bill and Allen Olson initially wanted me to take office early, but that they changed due to heavy outside pressure. "I know what I'm going to do," I said to Chuck. "But I don't think I'm even going to tell you, because you don't need to know." I called Secretary of State Ben Meier. "Ben, will you swear me in Monday morning?"

"Sure, Jorch," Meier said in his famous German-Russian accent. "It's my chob."

I went ahead and played out my hand on Monday, December 31st when I was administered the oath of office by Meier. The news was out and Governor Olson announced that they would not surrender the office because he was still the governor.

For details of the actions that followed, I will essentially rely on the mind and memory of Dick Gross, who would become my legal counsel in the Governor's Office. Dick worked night and day on the legal research and processes to assert my position. While I returned to Casselton to be with my family, Dick spent all of that Monday night, New Year's Eve, in the law library of the North Dakota Supreme Court trying to figure out a legal solution. Dick flew to Fargo on New Year's Day to meet with me and we consulted with the newly elected attorney general, Nick Spaeth. I also talked with other leaders of the Democratic-NPL Party who had legal backgrounds. We decided that day to ask for an attorney general's opinion, and had a Bismarck legislator, Serenus Hoffner, sign the request. The following morning we received Spaeth's opinion that I was governor.

But Olson claimed he wasn't bound by that opinion or one he himself had issued four years earlier as attorney general. "I don't know how you should do it, but you've got to go right to the Supreme Court," I said to our attorneys. "Figure out a way and see if the court will hear it." And they did. We asked the North Dakota Supreme Court to take original jurisdiction over the case and the court required legal briefs be submitted by five o'clock Thursday night the following day. Both sides met the deadline.

As this was unfolding, Janie and I and our son Eric had moved into the Governor's Residence, which was available because Governor Olson and his family had chosen to not live there. So, as it turned out, we had one governor in the Governor's Office and one governor in the Governor's Residence for a few days.

Dick told me that after the legal briefs were filed by both sides he asked Spaeth to read them. The new attorney general did so and concluded that Olson's case was "dog meat."

I'll not try to summarize the legal arguments and other details except to say it was Governor Olson as attorney general who first pointed out that elected officials are qualified to take office, according to the state constitution, on January 1. In his attorney general's opinion, dated December 24, 1980, Olson stated that "the powers of the offices of Governor...devolve upon the persons elected at the November, 1980, general election, at the earliest moment of January 1, 1981, or at the moment the oath of office has been taken, subscribed, and filed, whichever moment is later."

However, one of Olson's arguments to the Supreme Court a little over four years later was that since he filed his oath of office on January 6, 1981, he was entitled to serve through January 5, 1985, to complete four full years in office.

The court heard arguments in the case on Friday morning, January 4th, and delivered its unanimous decision that same afternoon. I was represented in court by attorneys Malcolm Brown and Dick Gross. Dick was prepared to give the rebuttal to Olson's case, but that didn't become necessary. By the end of the day, the unanimous opinion of the Supreme Court, written by Chief Justice Ralph Erickstad, concluded: "The term of office for which Olson was elected in 1980 commenced on January 1, 1981, and terminated on December 31, 1984. Based upon the foregoing reasoning, we hold that George A. Sinner is currently, and has been since the first moment of January 1, 1985, the Governor of the State of North Dakota. We therefore grant an original writ enjoining Olson from exercising the powers and duties of the Office of Governor of the State of North Dakota."

It's interesting to note that three Supreme Court justices disqualified themselves from the case because they had either worked for Olson or had been appointed to the court by him. So, the chief justice was joined by four district court presiding judges: Benny Graff, Norman Backes, A. C. Bakken, and Maurice Hunke.

I went into Governor Olson's office and did my best to console him. I didn't know what had gone on, but it appeared there was some hellish pressure on him from someplace.

Meanwhile, among the names submitted that same day by the state Judicial Nominating Committee were Herb Meschke, a brilliant lawyer from Minot and a solid Democrat, and Beryl Levine, who some Democrats didn't want because she wasn't an active Democrat. Later, on January 17th, I appointed Herb and also Beryl, who became the first woman to serve on the Supreme Court.

After the Supreme Court decision on Friday, January 4th, I was sworn in again on Tuesday, January 8th, during a ceremony held when the legislature convened.

With other commitments at hand we were busy. Though frequently a point of discussion, the mystery of why Olson changed his mind about giving up the office on January 1st remained unsolved. I should have realized that it was a serious matter because I was told law firms blackballed Olson after he left office. At one point I actually called and offered to help him find a spot in a good law firm. He said I shouldn't intervene, because his wife, Barb, wanted to leave North Dakota anyway.

It was only months later that I figured out what was going on. I was returning from Washington, DC one night. In the back of the Northwest plane, too tired to work, I sat thinking about all that had transpired. Suddenly it was clear to me. I realized somebody had tried to control those appointments to the Supreme Court and Governor Olson wasn't buying it. I concluded and continue to believe that Governor Olson and Bill Wright set up the whole process that would lead to me taking office early and making the Supreme Court appointments.

I could hardly wait for morning to come. When it did and I reached the office the first thing I did was call Olson.

"You will always be one of my heroes for what you did, Al," I said. "I have finally figured out what was going on here last December—somebody was trying to fix the court, weren't they? You showed terrific courage, because I have a hunch the pressure was huge, and withstanding it took great heroism. I'm proud to know you!"

"Whatever," was Olson's immediate response.

In our subsequent work together we became close friends and Al eventually told me I had it right. It *was* a tough time.

In the Governor's Office

Everyone on the Governor's Office staff had an important role.

Chuck managed the discussion of economic development with the Committee of 100. Nobody who witnessed that doubted his brightness, his tenacity, and his success at molding and guiding a very independent group toward developing a good program.

Janis Cheney superbly handled constituent services and all kinds of other areas.

No way can I ever adequately describe Dick Gross's brilliance. I don't remember ever asking Dick a legal question that he didn't either have a ready answer or quickly developed an answer. He also handled planning. His good sense and acumen when it came to the legality of things was unbelievable.

As I said a few years ago in her eulogy, Rita Moore Fuglie, my scheduler, was wise way beyond what we realized. I don't know how many times Rita would smile and say are you sure you really want to do that. It always made me stop and think and revisit the idea and invariably she was right—I didn't want to do that.

Kathy Dwyer did a fabulous job managing the support staff downstairs.

Carol Siegert was great with the appointments. Sometimes she got a little too politically partisan, but she knew I wanted professionalism.

The role of the press secretary is spotlighted elsewhere.

Several people who joined us on a more temporary basis also did outstanding work and were key players on the staff when they were there. Everyone had a special niche that they filled and made the office both happy and self-confident.

I think so highly of everyone who worked there but I'm particularly close to several members of my Governor's Office staff who remain such close friends with me as well as with each other. They still get together regularly for brunch and they share fun events and the sadness of family funerals. Rather than Bud, they prefer to call me "The Gov." I think it's a term of endearment as well as respect for the time and wonderful experiences we had together.

I was extremely impressed by state employees in general. It's just astonishing that new governors come in to office, time after time after time, knowing little about the state, and yet everything runs normally and efficiently well into the first year or two.

We saw so little evidence of any graft in state government. I do know of one case that I ran across. To his credit the guy who was involved—an Olson appointee—told me that the governor had no knowledge of it and had nothing to do with it. He openly admitted his mistake and expressed his regret for what he had done. Other than that, there were probably only small incidents.

I got aggressive about leadership. Somebody used to ask, why are you always leading with your chin? I had watched one of my predecessors take forever to make appointments and it was dragging a lot of people through a murky course of campaigning and soliciting support from others, so I determined right from the beginning that I was going to study the candidates in the best way I could...and then move!

For example, I interviewed candidates for judicial appointments and discussed the interviews in the evening with Dick Gross, who sat in on them. I usually made the decision that night, and before I went to bed I called those who were not going to be appointed, I thanked them, and I told them the announcement would be made the next morning. I suppose there's the possibility you make a mistake, but I don't think you make any more mistakes than if you wait, and wait, and hear from a zillion people and from campaign teams that are built up for the candidates. I've always thought that waiting was unfair to the candidates, unfair to the public, and unfair to the organization.

I believed ardently in candor and transparency, and hated trying to hide things from people or doing them in a sneaky way. We wanted everything in the open as much as we possibly could, sometimes to people's aggravation I guess. That came from working on the farm, where I was with all the employees every day. It's easier to change an honest opinion than to say oh, I was really waffling.

As I talked about earlier, I was once lectured at a think-tank meeting in Colorado by a man who was upset with me for a speech I gave and the discussion that followed about all the major concerns of the country but didn't mention what's happened to the poor along the way. Those kinds of reminders were pretty shocking and upsetting to me. I think that's at the root of all the things going wrong in the country now. People tend to worship a certain economic model that's in their mind, such as trickle-down benefits from huge profits.

I've always known that government's main purpose is to secure the rights of the people. There aren't a whole lot of other things that we serve. The economy is important to people, and the environment is also important, but it's how they affect people in the short term and the long term that's important. It's not how they affect the economy per se; it's how the economy's *effects* impact people.

The other main principle that I tried to follow when choosing among candidates was to make sure women and applicants of all sexual preferences were given equal consideration as we searched for qualified people. There were some situations where I had to follow certain prescriptions of the code. But there's just no replacement for professionalism and that's why my staff and agency heads were so superb. They were pros. It would have been stupid of me to try to give them advice on how to do their jobs because they all knew their jobs far better than I.

I'm the Governor

As governor, I never professed to know how to deal with the legislature. For the most part I stayed out of the way. I made one stupid mistake at the beginning and sent a letter to the party and said by God I wanted a certain thus and so. That went over like a crude noise in church. It was not well received, it was not well done. I learned early on that it was stupid of me to write a letter to all the legislators telling them what I wanted done. They resented it.

In that regard, when the telephone service deregulation issue began to surface, Nebraska had already deregulated and as nearly as I could tell hadn't done a perfect job because there were some details in the Nebraska plan that weren't working out so well. I relied on Bruce Hagen for advice on what to do. He thought the bill under consideration was pretty good and an improvement on some of the mistakes made in Nebraska. He advised me to support it.

Meanwhile, a partisan battle was developing in the legislature. By this time I'd learned to be careful how I spoke to legislators.

Two or three Democrats were supporting the bill when it got to the Senate. One of them was Joe Satrom. But on the Republican side it wasn't clear at all that they had enough votes. I knew quite a bit about public utilities and cooperatives. I read through and studied it and discovered a terrible flaw in the compensation for rural telephone companies when they had to give up an urban franchise because a town grew to be bigger than the 2,500 population limit for cooperative franchises. Because I had dealt with that in the legislature years earlier in a territorial integrity bill, I understood it was grossly unfair to the cooperatives.

So I wrote a letter to Satrom and told him I couldn't support the bill unless they cleaned up the problematic section. Then I called Joe. I told him I'd written the letter and I wanted him to quietly pass it around to the Democrats. Fixing that section became the battle cry in the Senate.

Theresa Wahlert, head of Northwestern Bell in the state, asked for an appointment and came in. "Governor, you were right about that section," she said. "It was poorly drafted and we thank you for getting it corrected. You know what, it's going to help to get that bill passed because otherwise it probably wouldn't pass." I think the bill got the reputation as being one of the better deregulation bills. Bruce Hagen's advice on things like that was always valuable because he was so sane and so aware of the real-world consequences.

The same process came into play a couple other times where rather than send a letter to a whole chamber I simply wrote to one member and said pass it around. It came off as a lot less offensive and yet got the job done. At the beginning of the 2007 session, Senator Tim Mathern asked me for a letter describing the pain that property taxes are causing fixed-income people. So I wrote a pretty straightforward comment on several facets and Tim handed it all over the place. I had told Tim that that's how I approached the legislature.

I'm not sure how broadly my letter to Tim was distributed, but I think it was influential. It indicated a lot of city people are unhappy that the same value property in rural Cass County pays less than half the property taxes we do in Fargo. In addition, city people pay for county government, where the money is spent in the rural areas. My letter also emphasized that the locus of suffering has switched from the farmer going broke to the city homeowners struggling to remain in their homes. Observing developments in the legislature, I did see more and more expression of concern for the elderly poor particularly and the damages caused by property taxes.

CHAPTER EIGHT: taking firm action

Big Decisions

I have always felt comfortable with making decisions. Maybe some of that came from my military experience, but it was the farm more than anything. There's so much to do on the farm. We had a lot of people, during the summer particularly. There were often seven or eight boys wanting to work so I was moving fast and making decisions. Sometimes they were wrong but we'd go right back and correct them whenever we made mistakes and not get too shook up about errors and mistakes. That experience taught me you have to move. You can't sit and ponder it, you've just got to do it. I learned to trust my own mind. You had to decide to work a field for planting. You would send a tractor and cultivator out. If it was too wet you had to make an instant decision to stop, don't perpetuate the mistake.

Just out of the sheer burden of my obligations, I started praying quite regularly to the Holy Spirit for help when there were major decisions to make. That was not an infrequent occasion. There was a lot of heavy stuff. It isn't that there will be some sort of divine guidance that helps us make decisions. More likely, as I've explained, it was divine intervention to help make the thing work out.

My one bad decision as governor was to veto the first coal severance tax bill in 1985.[43] That bill would have frozen the tax in the future at its rate in effect on July 1, 1987. It was the one time that I let staff and the party people shout me down. They didn't want to limit the tax and I reluctantly went along with them The coal severance tax is imposed instead of sales or property taxes on coal mined in the state for sale or industrial purposes. Two years later we supported a larger cut in the tax. We also initiated and included a provision that allocated two cents per ton for a lignite research fund. I knew quite a bit about that coal issue because research had been a similar discussion with sugar. Growers wanted to buy North Dakota coal but they couldn't afford it. That bill became the cause *célèbre* of the Republican majority.

I remember Montana Governor Ted Schwinden called me one of the first days we were in the Governor's Office. He introduced himself and asked if Democrats owned the legislature. "No," I said, "we have one house."

"You should thank God you don't own both. It is the bane of governors to own the legislature because they always insist that you do things their way. You lose your ability to be an intervener and sort through the issues and do what's right, rather than what the party wants."

I never forgot that as I watched North Dakota's Governor John Hoeven struggle with a Republican-controlled legislature.

A leader must be willing to do the tough stuff. A leader has to get over the attitude that they're not supposed to do the dirty work. If they do it people understand there's nothing wrong with it. It's got to be done. So on the farm I often took the dirty jobs myself and I sort of learned to love doing it. I suppose it was a matter of pride and I was teaching a little bit, but it was also kind of the way I grew up. I told one of my sons once he should take the job cleaning out the bathrooms because people tended to think they were being mistreated if they got that assignment. That's the way to fairly quickly alleviate that. I don't know if he ever did, but that was my attitude.

One day in the dead of winter, early February in 1989, I was on the phone and it was bitter cold out. Chuck Fleming stuck his head in the doorway and beckoned me to get off the phone and I did. "What's up?" I said.

"They are forecasting eighty-below windchills," he said. "What do you think about the schools?"

"Close them," I said.

He left. I went back to my phone conversation and within the hour, Dick Gross brought in the emergency declaration shutting down all elementary and high schools for two days. We invoked a 1973 section of state law that authorizes school closings based on "acts of God" and we announced it immediately.[44] Dick obviously knew instantly we could do it and Chuck knew too. The only question I can remember asking was is it somebody else's jurisdiction. They said maybe, but clearly it ends with you.

It was front-page news in *The Forum* and a day later *USA Today* ran a feature story about this agonizing decision a poor rural governor had to make that no one had ever done before. We didn't know it hadn't been done and we didn't really care. There was nothing to agonize about. When it is eighty-below windchill you close the schools. Any idiot knows that. *USA Today* thought it was sort of a unique decision to do it when really it was clearly needed.

There were people who were upset by it, of course. Parents had to find babysitters or could not go to work, so there was that repercussion. And some school superintendents thought school closures should be decided locally. But we knew that when we got around to looking at what might happen, I don't think we ever questioned the wisdom of the decision. We were told that a child outside for about four or five minutes would be frozen.

I tried as hard as I know how to be candid and open. We gave interviews to virtually everyone who asked and we tried to tell them as much as we could tell them. I also didn't want my office door closed. For the most part that was honored, but one day a man who thought differently came in. I went over and sat with him at the small table in the corner of the office. He began to say something and then he got up and started to close the door. I said, "Frank, I don't ever close my door—claustrophobia."

I didn't have claustrophobia but I hated the aura of secret meetings so I got up and opened the door again. He really had nothing whatever of importance to say. Maybe he would have if the door were closed. I have no idea what he had in mind and I don't remember what his subject matter was. My open door was almost an ironclad rule even though at times it got to be a bit of a free for all.

Working It Out

I'd begun getting mail and telephone calls from people I respected up in the Lewis and Clark State Park area near Williston. It was kind of a lowland that fell within the Garrison Diversion entrapment area. But it was at the top end of the valley and people were upset because the Game and Fish Department had ordered them to stop farming it so it could be managed as a fish and wildlife area. I didn't know the history at all, but in the subsequent correspondence I received copies of old letters from Senator Milton Young and press statements by Governor Guy about how the farmers would always be able to farm this land as long as they could. If it wasn't flooded they could farm it. That was proclaimed over and over in public statements and documents. I called Lloyd Jones who was then Game and Fish commissioner. "Lloyd, what's the deal here?"

"The Corps of Engineers came to us with a contract and pretty generous reimbursement to manage that area the way the law prescribes, which is to be used for fish and wildlife habitat," Lloyd said. "So we notified the farmers that we were going to do that."

"Whoa, I don't think so," I said. "You just can't do that to people. It's clear in history and in the documents they were told they could farm it and they would be able to do it as long as possible. You better come over and talk about this."

It turned out Lloyd was right. That's exactly what was in the law under the Pick Sloan Plan, a component of the federal Flood Control Act of 1944. Despite what the farmers had been told, the details of the law specified that the area be used for fish and wildlife habitat. I'm sure Governor Link didn't know and I know Governor Guy didn't realize it because I talked to him about it.

"Lloyd, we can't do this," I said. "You'll have to tell the Corps that the governor has ordered you to work out an arrangement to get some of it done and move into it gradually. Lisa Novacek will know how to negotiate this. You two go up there and meet with the farmers."

Lisa, who handled natural resources matters on my staff, accompanied Lloyd to three meetings with the Lewis and Clark working group in the spring and summer of 1991. In the end they worked out an agreement acceptable to both sides and at the last meeting they had a big party to celebrate. Everyone understood and respected the position of the other side and it was the classic example that someone else could do the job better than I could have.

Someone told me that when anyone at those meetings would propose something extreme, Lisa would shake her head and say in a kindly way, "I don't know if the governor will like that." She was using the Governor's Office authority in a nicer, gentler way than anyone else could have done. Lloyd told me he had never seen anyone handle a difficult discussion and intense feelings as well as she did. That's the way the whole staff was. My press secretary, too. If we had media people asking unreasonable questions he dismissed them with an ease that I couldn't have gotten away with.

In September of 1985, I was in Japan with five other governors for an international governors' conference. During that trip I had the opportunity to meet Japanese emperor Hirohito, and while we were there I became quite good friends with Hawaii's Governor, George Ariyoshi. He was informally the leader of our delegation. I was startled as I began to know him and his wife, Jean, and to find that they were close personal friends of the notorious dictator in the Philippines, Ferdinand Marcos, and his wife, Imelda. We discovered in visiting with the Ariyoshis that they babysat for each other's children and they shopped together. I knew that Ariyoshi was a good governor and had heard good things about him. But as the days wore on, I began to see more and more evidence of power politics and how if you were big in politics there was always a party, booze, and whatever you wanted. It was scary at times to be around Ariyoshi. In fact, one night we walked out on him because he had taken us to a party, just the governors, and there were geisha girls and pictures were being taken. Cameras were going off and all of us just left. I think it was fairly innocent, but we couldn't be sure.

I began to understand this was a carryover from old Asia, so I just kind of dismissed it. Then in February of 1986 we were having our Annual National Governors Association meeting at the Hyatt Regency in Washington, DC. On Sunday night, I was getting ready for bed and had the TV news on. Elections had been held in the Philippines that week and I was quite interested in them because when I was in Japan we had some exposure to the Philippine political situation. Mrs. Corazon Aquino was running in place of her husband who had been assassinated and she was leading in the election campaign. On the news I learned that Marcos had declared the election invalid and declared martial law. Rioting had broken out in Manila Square and quite a few people had been killed. I said to Janie, "If they don't get that so and so out of there they are going to have a bloodbath because the people are fed up with him from what I have heard."

The next morning I got up early for a 6:30 AM governors-only breakfast and I was dressing in the bathroom to not wake Janie up. I had a little TV on in there and learned that there had been many more people killed and I was worried about it.

I hurried down to breakfast and was one of the first ones there. I saw my nameplate and next to my place sat Governor Ariyoshi eating all alone. As I walked up to Ariyoshi, a thought struck me, and I told him, "George, you know what you ought to do, you ought to go out and call Secretary of State Shultz and offer to let Marcos come to Hawaii. George, you are the only one who can do it. None of the rest of us can make that work. Think about it. You are leaving office and he is your friend and your people will probably accept him. If they don't get him out of there they are going to kill everybody over there."

As I spoke to Ariyoshi, a mutual friend of ours, Governor Tony Earl of Wisconsin, walked up and heard me. When I realized he was there I turned to him because he was a bright man. I said, "Tony, what do you think of that idea?"

He looked at Ariyoshi. "George," he said, "that's the best idea I have heard in twenty years, you ought to do it."

Ariyoshi, who is Japanese by heritage, said nothing. He got up, left his breakfast half finished, and was gone. The next time we saw him was on national television, welcoming Ferdinand and Imelda to Hawaii. There were so many things that were almost mystical about that experience because I was not a student of Asian politics at all. I just knew that Marcos had been really desperate.[45]

Ariyoshi did it in the face of what was going to be obviously some real criticism in Hawaii. I know it did get to be a bit of a problem because the Hawaii governor who succeeded him in office wouldn't talk about it either. They didn't want anyone to know they had anything to do with it. But in many ways you see those kinds of things happen and you wonder how much divine intervention there is in an experience like that. I don't think I did it myself. I was just a vehicle. There were other incidents, other events that were not quite that dramatic, but that one was almost mind blowing in how it happened.

Carpe Diem

I made a practice of moving quickly to deal with a crisis. One example happened in late summer of 1985. Brian Berg, head of the highway patrol, came into my office one afternoon and told me that there was a problem brewing on the Fort Berthold Reservation. A federal court ruling in 1972 had enlarged the reservation and in so doing took onto the reservation several farms that were owned by white settlers and white landholders.[46] The tribe had begun requiring license plates and hunting licenses from the tribe, and several other things that they had just gotten jurisdiction to do. They were beginning to impose those requirements on those white people as well as Native Americans. This was producing some real tense feelings on the reservation between the whites and the tribal members.

Brian told me the sheriff was reporting that people were carrying guns and bandying some pretty violent threats back and forth. He said frankly, he didn't know how to deal with it. "I don't really know either," I said. "But an acquaintance of mine, Governor Janklow of South Dakota, has a history of working with some difficult things on the reservation and with some offenses by both sides. Let's call and see what he says."

I had met Janklow only once before that and we had an almost instant friendship. We ended up on the same side of a fairly significant matter and he had told me how pleased he was I was in agreement. Anyway, I called him and I told him what I had and asked him what he thought we ought to do.

He answered without hesitation. "Number one, George," he said, "you can't fix that problem because you didn't create it, and it is not going to go away. But what you can do is go up there with a show of force and let everybody know that the first side that steps across the line is going to get it. If I were you," he said, "I would take your adjutant general, I would take the attorney general, I would take the head of the highway patrol, and I would take the sheriff. I would go up there and I would get as many people as you can get into a room and tell them you are sorry about the problem but you can't fix it and that only time was going to take care of it."

I had a meeting arranged and went up a couple of days later. We went to a big restaurant near there and got everyone in the room and told them what Janklow said to me, that I couldn't fix the problem but I wanted them to understand that if anybody on either side violated the rights or property of someone else, we were not going to ask a lot of questions. We were going to come in with every ounce of energy we had and every force we had and there was going to be justice, so help us God.

My staff was just aghast as to how tough I was. Everyone was who knew me. I was surprised, too. Janklow and I became good friends. I respected his judgment, which was sound, mature, and sophisticated. And it worked. I hadn't overstated the facts because we were going to make sure that people's rights weren't abused and the situation was resolved peacefully.

Janklow told me that day the principle of action in a crisis is that you always overcorrect. Always go further than conservative people will tell you to go. Do whatever you must do to make sure the problem is solved.

It was good advice and I put it to work one time several years after that incident. It was a Friday night and I was flying back from Washington, DC on board a Northwest flight out of Minneapolis. We had just gotten up to altitude when all of a sudden the pilot came back out of the cockpit and asked one of the cabin crew where I was sitting. He came to me and said that he had just had an emergency call from the state that three murderers had escaped from the penitentiary. They wanted me to release an Army National Guard helicopter to help in the search for them. Choppers had big lights and they could cover more area.

"Tell them to take *two* choppers," I said. As soon as I got on the ground, I found the officer in charge because the adjutant general was gone and I told him I wanted twenty-five military police just as quickly as he could get them out to the pen.

"Get them out there immediately," I said. "Get them out there as fast as you can."

So I went to the penitentiary and into the office with the warden. The Burleigh County sheriff was there too. I told them that I had these people coming and that they were going to be in charge of them and to use them in whatever way they could in their search. I told them I was going to leave, as it wasn't my job to direct traffic.

They thought the prisoners had escaped just before they discovered they were gone, so they might be close by, perhaps in a high, weedy field of probably about twenty-five acres just south of the penitentiary. They decided to walk that area hoping maybe they could find these people out there. All these military police were walking about eight to ten feet apart. They didn't find them there but one was captured about three hours later near a business in southeast Bismarck, and another was nabbed that Sunday in Linton, North Dakota. The third prisoner was on the lam until July of 1993.[47]

The prisoner they caught first told them he had nearly been stepped on by one of the walkers and that they were all in that field. They just didn't find them. I overcorrected, but I didn't overcorrect enough. If they would have had fifty walkers they would have found them. It is an interesting story and a good principle for governors to remember.

Too Much Regulation

The call came from the Long family in LaMoure County. Wonderful folks. John Long and his wife, Christina, are on the advisory board of Manor St. Joseph, a basic care nursing home in Edgeley. Christina is also a volunteer ombudsman there.

Nursing home regulation had previously been under Human Services and then the legislature moved that responsibility to the State Health Department. An employee of the fire marshal's office was sent to this nursing home by the Health Department to conduct an inspection and see if it was fire safe for the residents. His report included a long list of things that needed to be corrected. Some of them conflicted with what previous inspectors had said. Problem areas included the fire alarm system, door latches and handles, a requirement for automatic door closers on resident rooms even though those doors were too close to the bathroom doors to have automatic closers, and a need to replace room dividers because they weren't fire retardant even though they were previously told that they were. Lots of other things.

These people were just distraught. They had changed most of the condemned doors just two years before to comply with the fire inspector's requirements when it was under the Department of Human Services. Now they were being told to change them by the Health Department. It had cost them a lot of money in the first place and they were concerned about having to do more. An order of nuns, the Sister Servants of Christ the King, had owned and operated the nursing home since 1940. They didn't want to run the place any longer because of all the state rules and regulations and changing requirements. I was infuriated by how outrageous this must seem to them so I called the state fire marshal, Bob Allan. I said, "You and I are going to Edgeley and we're going to meet with this board and you're going to explain why your people don't get their act together and what you're going to do about it." I was furious.

Allan couldn't make it but he sent Barb Skogen, his deputy, along with Fred Gladden from the Health Department. We got there to a meeting at the Transfiguration Catholic Church parish hall with the Manor board and several other area nursing home operators and about 100 community people. Christina had lined up several people to talk to us. When they told me what had happened and the details of it I vented my anger in front of the entire crowd.

"Now listen, we cannot do this to people," I said to the deputy fire marshal.

"I want to tell you all a story," I told the crowd. "Before I was elected, City of Casselton regional airport people came to my partners and me and asked if we'd sell them a diagonal strip of land along the railroad for an airport. I convinced my partners to do it because we'd gotten a lot from the community in the years we lived there. So we sold them the strip, but with the regularly repeated condition that they never come and take more. We didn't want to give up any more and we felt we might get a little benefit from the adjacent land, maybe develop it. The regional airport people always agreed.

"Then right after I took office they announced they were going to condemn another seventy acres and take it. I was livid and so were my partners. I knew that if I got involved it would only make it worse. I told my partners to get the toughest attorney they could hire and make them pay. They hired John Kelly and he just crucified them in court. My partners said they were actually embarrassed for their neighbors because John left the city no room to apologize. No one ever admitted that they lied, but some of them knew all along that they were going to do this. They did lie. They condemned and paid dearly for the land."

And I said to the people gathered at Edgeley, "I want to tell you something. I will never get over it. I will never forget what they did to us. They took advantage of our good will."

To deal with the Manor St. Joseph situation I told the fire marshal I didn't care what the rules say, the damage is done, and I want a written guarantee that for ten years this ruling won't change, again. He first sent me a letter draft saying they would guarantee it for two years. I wrote back and told him that he must do better, that "a nine-year assurance would not be excessive and would allow a facility to get a reasonable return on their corrective investment." I eventually settled for an assurance of about seven years because I knew then that Allan had gone to Nick Spaeth and told him. I wasn't going to start a conflict with Nick. I'm kind of sorry I agreed to the seven years, though, because nine would have been better.

John and Christina Long were the best people on the face of the earth. They never lost their loyalty to me. The nursing home was financed by these people themselves to take care of the elderly in the region. They did a great job. Unfortunately, state government had betrayed them with ridiculous regulations.

Signs of the Times

In early 1990, a letter from Jim Trautman, the mayor of Jamestown, advised me that the town had committed money to a proposed highway paint manufacturing plant. I called Stuart McDonald, the Jamestown-Stutsman County Business and Industrial Development Commission director. He was a former Republican legislator from Grand Forks and a really good guy. McDonald didn't say why but he, like me, was skeptical. "George, I don't believe this thing," he said. "Newman Signs is going to partner with this company and they allege they're going to build this paint plant."

Mayor Trautman said in his letter to me that one of their people had told them not to bother writing to me because I had been bought off by 3M. But he said I just want you to know that we will probably be looking to use some of the state economic development programs. I was just livid because if there's anything we wouldn't do it was be bought off. I had friends at 3M but we didn't have any allegiance there and we certainly weren't bought off.

So I didn't write back. I didn't want to perpetuate the discussion. Eventually, maybe six weeks later, Don Wilhelm, a car dealer in Jamestown, called me and said, "We want you to come over and meet with this Japanese delegation," he said. "They are coming here to promote their project. The city council people will be there and Newman Signs people will be there and the economic development team will be there."

"Don," I said, "if I come, there's going to be words." I told him about the letter, and that I resented it so badly I wouldn't be able to overlook it.

"Well, we want you to come," he insisted.

I said, "I don't think I'd better."

That's where it ended, until he called about a week later and said again that everyone wanted me to come.

So I did and brought Dick Backes, whom I had appointed highway commissioner after Walt Hjelle resigned. One building was already there and they meant to build another one. These five Japanese men from the Tokyo Company, Seibulite International, presented this elaborate plan. But I was pretty sure all they were really going to do was put up a warehouse. That on top of my anger over what this guy had written was boiling inside of me. They gave about a half an hour presentation and finally Jim Trautman said to me, "Governor, do you have any comments?"

"Well, our programs are available to everyone equally," I said. "There are no preferential treatments and they will be available to these people."

"But I want to make something clear. One of your party has written a letter suggesting that he thinks contracts are bought and sold here. I want to tell you something; if that's the way you're used to doing business, don't come here. Our specifications for these highway projects are developed in public, they're open to public critique, and the bidding is public. If that's not good enough for you, don't come here."

"I want you to know how badly I and the people of the state resent the letter you wrote. If that's what you're used to, that's the way you think business is done, we don't want you here." And that's all I said.

The place was absolutely like a tomb. Nobody moved. Finally Jim said, "Well, we better go out and see the site." So we looked at the proposed location for this plant, over on the north side of that long road that comes into Jamestown from the west.

We came back in and Jim said, "Governor, one of these fellows wants to make a statement."

So this Japanese guy got up bowing and uttering a profound apology. I thought, you phony! That was unfair but I was not going to get over it and I never have. I was angry with those Seibulite people from Japan, not anybody local. Jamestown went ahead, put out a bunch of money and the Bank of North Dakota was also involved in financing the project. Guess what happened. They built that one building, kind of a warehouse, and that's all that ever happened. By January of 1992 the Japanese company had withdrawn its plans to locate the manufacturing plant in Jamestown.[48]

This episode had reminded me of a neighbor lady whose husband was dying. She discovered in looking through the farm records that a sign company had not paid them in six years for their right of way where they put billboards up. She was enraged. I was angry about it and I called Walt Hjelle. "They're famous for that," Walt said. "They promise big money to these farm people and unless the farm people remember they don't pay." Walt said unfortunately that's gone on everywhere and he didn't have any means at his disposal to pursue it. I never got over that conduct by a sign company. It left an awful taste in my mouth. I don't know whether I was too judgmental or not, but it created the suspicion when the Japanese joint venture came up that there was something devious going on. The Japanese developers promised they were going to build a manufacturing plant. But that didn't make sense and I was suspicious from the get-go that all they were going to build was a warehouse to store highway painting materials.

CHAPTER NINE: centennial celebration and challenge

We Look Back, then Turn Back

Because of the 1989 referral election, North Dakota's centennial year ended up a *dies irae, dies illa*, which roughly translates as "day of wrath" and "day of mourning."

My state of the state address given January 4, 1989 to the 51st Legislative Assembly was titled "Cherishing Our Past—Shaping Our Future." That was also the theme for celebrating the centennial and remembering North Dakota's heritage.

The first big event of the centennial year was a visit to Bismarck in late April by the president, the first George Bush.[49] With an estimated 10,000 people looking on, he wished North Dakota a happy birthday and planted an elm tree from the White House lawn on our Capitol grounds, along with a bur oak that was placed on the opposite side of the Capitol steps.

"This hardy elm is a descendant of a tree planted on the White House lawn by John Quincy Adams," Bush said with his presidential shovel ready, "and now its seedlings will be a part of North Dakota forever."

As reported in *The Bismarck Tribune*, the president referred to Theodore Roosevelt becoming a man in North Dakota. Bush said: "Let us honor the coming 100th birthday of North Dakota and the memory of the nation's first true environmentalist by dedicating this centennial bur oak along with this White House elm.

Before the year 2000, your state will plant 100 million trees, almost half as many new trees in one state as there are Americans in the Union. May each tree add to the abundance of the good life in North Dakota, cleaner air for North America."

In my brief remarks I used Quaker scholar Eldon Trueblood's famous quote: "A man has at least a start at discovering the real meaning of life when he plants a shade tree under which he will never sit." And I noted that President Bush "had gone a long way down that path today."

Unfortunately, that twelve-foot American elm tree didn't fare so well. It was infested with gypsy moth larvae when it arrived here and a few years later the tree died after it budded out during an unseasonally warm March and then was hurt by a late frost.

My most vivid memory of the state centennial celebration is the coming together of the four former governors: Al Olson, Art Link, Bill Guy, and John Davis. I had known John Davis only a bit. Somewhere along the line I had met him, but he had left office when I was elected to the Senate. Bill Guy was governor then and Charlie Tighe lieutenant governor. It was really good to see all the governors come together and recognize the special gift of leadership that they all had.

I also remember the centennial parades. I didn't mind riding in those. I had learned to catch eyes. You have to be waving but at the same time going from person to person catching eyes. I felt much better about it once I knew that. It's sort of a mechanical, cold affair but as soon as you catch eyes and you see the smiles that quickly emerge it's really refreshing and fun to do. You can only see to one side along the parade route at a time but it really makes a more human connection.

I will never forget the "Party of the Century" celebration on the mall of the Capitol grounds. I remember KFYR Broadcasting's owners, Bill and Marietta Ekberg, stopping by. They were particularly grateful that the event was happening where it was on the mall there. A lot of people who attended didn't often get back to Bismarck. Bill and Marietta told me how special it was for some of their friends who came back to see the elegance of the mall and the way it had been preserved, which I couldn't take any credit for.

The man named Jim Dunn, who took care of the flowers, had a knack and the mall was simply elegant.

I had some concern about Williams and Ree, the entertainers brought in for the evening, because they tended to get a little far afield. I was actually worried enough that I went up there and talked to them. "You guys be careful tonight," I said. "I've heard you and you always go too far." They understood and generally speaking they cleaned up their act.

I also remember that was the first time we heard Chuck Suchy perform. I like him a lot. His albums are plentiful in my car. He's a great human being. I've always wanted him to branch away from his own music. For example, do an album of some of the frontier Christmas music. But he didn't want to do that. He's stood pretty much with his own stuff as far as I know.

There were lots of memories like that. Art Link agreed to be chairman when we reorganized the Centennial Commission and appointed new members back in 1985. I remember the work of Buckshot Hoffner and certainly Dennis Neumann. Karen Aasel was also involved in some of that, with the Parks and Recreation Department.

The state centennial observance's focal event was that July 4th "Party of the Century". In addition, throughout the year some 600 endeavors designated as centennial projects took place and, as President Bush mentioned, the big project was a campaign to plant 100 million trees by the year 2000, the new millennium. We decided to participate by planting a tree in the hometown of everyone who had served as governor since statehood. That would contribute twenty-six trees toward the 100-million goal. We tried to fit these plantings in when I was traveling near a former governor's hometown and when the time of year was right.

In August of 1989 we planted the first Governor's Centennial Tree, a juniper, in Davidson Park at Williston, the adopted hometown of Thomas Moodie, who served the shortest time in office of any North Dakota governor. Moodie was a Democrat and he had defeated Lydia Langer, who ran for the job after her husband Bill Langer was removed from office the previous July. Moodie took office as governor on January 7, 1935, and then left six weeks later when the North Dakota Supreme Court determined that he was ineligible. The state Constitution requires a governor to have been a citizen of the state for five consecutive years prior to the election. Moodie's opponents learned that he had voted in a municipal election in Minneapolis in 1932.[50]

Moodie had grown up in Minneapolis and immediately prior to his election as governor he lived in Williston where he was editor of *The Williston Herald.* Our press release quoted me as saying at the Williston planting that "I certainly hope this tree grows deeper roots in the Williston soil than Tom Moodie did in the Governor's Office."

Trees were planted in honor of the most recent former governors, including Bill Guy who served in office the longest of anyone, but the effort lost steam after the referral election that December.

As that Centennial birthday year of 1989 ended I don't think that there's any question that the most disappointing loss I experienced was the defeat of the taxes in the referendum.

Regrettable Referral Repercussions

As we were taking office in 1985, we went through the Olson budget and asked the legislature to cut out $73 million. That was just the first in a continuing series of actions to deal with the devastating impact of a regional recession and a decline in our state government revenues from the oil, gas, coal, and agricultural industries.[51] The legislature restored $20 million and approved a general fund level that was $107 million higher than the amount of expected income, which left a small projected ending balance. However, revenues subsequently came in far below expectations. I cut 4 percent, a total of $45 million.

In 1986, after we were forced to cut the budget, I called a special session and the legislature bumped the income tax rate from 10.5 percent of taxpayers' federal liability to 14 percent and raised the sales tax and the motor vehicle excise tax. Leon Mallberg ran the petition drive in which the referendum on the income tax hike qualified for the ballot in a matter of days. But the voters sided with the legislature and those tax increases were upheld.[52]

The economy didn't improve. Three years later, legislators knew the problem and by better than a two-thirds majority passed an additional 1 percent sales tax, along with modest increases in the income and gas taxes to fill the gap. Tragically, the taxes were referred by unscrupulous people to a public vote. Eight measures were referred.[53] I remember calling the staff in saying I wanted to go out and fight when the petitions came in and we realized what it was going to do to the state's revenue.

The referral episode was disappointing in lots of ways. I knew if we didn't save the sales tax we were going to be very short of funds for primary and secondary schools, and local property taxes would go up as a result. Of all the things that are important in state government—care of the sick and assistance for all manner of human need—the future depended upon how well we did in education. And everyone who was thinking knew that, but few would stand up and fight and say the tough stuff that you have to say to get new taxes. They liked saying "no new taxes" and it's caused all kinds of trouble. Back then it was more the Republicans who were crying about the folly of deficit spending than were the Democrats. Bill Guy told me it has always taken Democrats who don't run on the principle that they're going to cut taxes to get things straightened out. It seems to be true. This weird obsession with cutting taxes obliterates every other kind of rationality in public policy.

Few of the people in public life came forward to fight and save the sales tax. When the petitions were filed, my memory is that someone in the office, probably my press secretary, told us that the polls showed us down 80-20—only 20 percent of the people supported continuation of the sales tax increase. Two public officials helped. Wayne Sanstead, the state superintendent of public instruction, was consistent but he wasn't able to be out on the road working day after day. The other was Evan Lips, a wonderful longtime Republican State Senator from Bismarck. Evan went out and spoke wherever he could to remind people what I was telling them, that property taxes were going to go goofy if we killed these revenue sources.

I loved that trip around the state on the tax referral fight—not because I convinced everyone, but just because people were honestly interested and listened intently everywhere I went.[54] It was a wonderful experience, contrary to what some people thought. I gave up to five or six presentations a day for six or seven weeks. I was pretty tired but I was never unhappy and I enjoyed the discussions and people were generally good to me. Even when they didn't agree with me they listened and seemed to be appreciative that somebody came out and told them what he thought, with clarity.

I used charts to show North Dakota's taxes were low to moderate. We were running into a situation where we couldn't adequately fund everything we had to support. Because of my belief of what government was supposed to do in taking care of the rights of people, human service programs were a high priority, particularly helping the poor, the sick, and handicapped. Higher education had little place to go other than tuitions, which were raised pretty significantly during that period because we didn't have enough money after the referrals were approved. I warned every audience about the calamity that would result.

In addition to the meetings around the state, I pointed out in a letter to North Dakota newspapers that if a no vote prevailed, there would be cuts in state services and increases in local property taxes to offset the loss in state revenues.

Even with the stakes so serious, I tried to use some humor that was appropriate to the situation. One of the things I quoted during the tax-referral debate was a great line of Winston Churchill. During the war, Churchill had to raise taxes incredibly in England. He had just introduced a substantial tax increase to finance the war effort and was introduced at London Square to about ten thousand people. As he approached the podium, the master of ceremonies said, "Ah sir, Sir Winston indeed, it is a great honor to have ten thousand people turn out to hear you speak."

Churchill arrived at the podium, unfolded an envelope, and finally looked up and said to the emcee, "It is quite flattering, but whenever I feel this way I always remember that if instead of making a political speech I was being hanged, the crowd would be twice as big."

Voters said no down the line, even rejecting a constitutional change that would have allowed a commission to propose a plan to the legislature for streamlining state government by consolidating departments.[55] I think we would have won that election had it not been for an ad the North Dakota Education Association ran that offended people. It showed people slamming the door on education. I don't know that I vigorously objected it when I saw it in advance, but I remember that I didn't like it.

In Lloyd Omdahl's view, the referendum in December of 1989 "snuffed out a lot of the optimism that had been created by the Centennial."

Those who knew how hard I had worked were angry. I remember Dick Rayl being just beside himself with frustration that the people hadn't seen the wisdom of keeping that one-cent sales tax. Dick turned off the holiday lights at the Capitol and I was completely unaware that he'd done it. He was feeling badly for me because he knew I'd worked my butt off. He was angry on my behalf. I was embarrassed. I called up Dick and told him you can't turn the lights off, that's petty. He knew he shouldn't have done it and he turned them back on.

People got the message that there was some anger in the budget office about losing the election and those who didn't support the tax didn't see how disastrous the loss would be. But at the same time we made it clear we didn't really want to get revenge. That incident with the lights was kind of like during the 1984 campaign when we cancelled a wonderful TV ad I had that portrayed a farmer with a pitchfork full of manure. The manure was supposed to portray what the Olson campaign was saying about me, but some people didn't get the connection and were offended. It worked out all right but only because I knew enough to pull the tongue-in-cheek ad when I realized we'd made a mistake.

We had to reduce general fund spending $110 million by using up the projected balance of $12 million and cutting $98 million. I had learned the first time I cut the budget in 1985 or the first part of 1986 that in order to do it right you had to accept the legislative prioritization and do an across-the-board cut like we did that year. There was little complaint because everyone got treated the same. Within the agencies there were some tough decisions to make but for the most part people were pretty understanding and were pretty good about it.

The tragedy of it was after the loss of the sales tax in the 1989 special election the only program that could make up for lost state funding was primary and secondary education. The schools could increase property taxes to get revenues. I had told everyone during that campaign that that was the only alternative because if it happened the state would not be able to honor its 70 percent support of education.

University of North Dakota President Tom Clifford was one of the people who I remember was extremely helpful. The only way we could get adequate funding for higher education was to raise tuitions. I remember him telling me, "Bud, you know it isn't all bad that the kids have to pay more because they then understand how important it is for them to pay attention to what they're doing. As much as I wish you didn't have to do it, I think it's okay." I never forgot that. It was something I needed to hear because having been on the Board of Higher Education I was truly worried about the implications of raising tuition. That was a meaningful discussion.

Somebody said to me not long ago, "You told us our property taxes were going to go crazy. Do you remember?" You're damn right I remember. Despite our efforts to cut, we found ourselves unable to adequately fund schools. It's clearly the cause of so much trauma today. We have cities like Fargo where the percentage of homeowners is just abysmal by any standard. People can't afford to own their homes because they can't afford the property tax. Of course no phenomenon in history is single sourced and there were other reasons. Certainly the lack of diversity in the economy was part of it. But the fact is we were in fair shape after increasing the sales tax 1 percent in 1989, but we fell a long way after we lost it.

The Room Got Quiet

I'm a Democrat. I care about people. Certainly there are many, many Republicans who do too but generally speaking it's been the Democrats who've kept human rights targeted. Neither party has a corner on idiots or good people, and to get the job done you must work with the ones that are serious and are good people, no matter which party they're in. The only people who disappointed me after the 1989 referendum vote were the Democrats. They thought I had painted our party into a corner of being the tax-and-spend

Democrats and they were so sensitive about being called that. About six weeks after the special election, Rita Fuglie stuck her head in the door and said the Democratic-NPL Party Executive Committee was meeting at the Seven Seas and wanted me to come out and visit a bit. I wondered what that was about, but she didn't know. Chuck Fleming didn't know either but Rita said she could move my scheduled appointments.

Chuck and I walked into the meeting at the Seven Seas and everyone was there, from Nick Spaeth to Heidi Heitkamp and Earl Pomeroy, maybe ten to a dozen people in all. I don't remember who their spokesperson was, but I asked, "What's up?"

The response was, "We want you to fire Dick Rayl and Joe Lamb." Dick and Joe were clearly the strongest people in the whole administration at helping guide the state through the various problems that we faced. Dick was responsible for straightening out the state budget and Joe had gotten the Bank of North Dakota into good shape.[56] The three of us just shortly before that had gone into Moody's and Best and gotten the state bond rating up from a B- all the way up, I think, to an A-. That was a huge benefit to every jurisdiction in the state. Dick and Joe were also part and parcel to the development of the PACE program, one of the best economic development initiatives in state history.

It was quiet in the room.

I looked at them and in precise, graphic words told them what they could singularly and collectively go do to themselves. (I'll spare you some of that specific language). And Chuck and I walked out.

They never did like Dick and Joe because they believed those two weren't politically partisan enough. Joe, who lampooned idiots and didn't tolerate fools well, was particularly unpopular with them.

Some of them were disappointed office seekers and angry all the years since I made the first appointments. But we as a group ran the state for the good of the state, not the party. We didn't jump every time the party hollered rabbit.

It never came up again. Somehow or other they kind of understood that discussion wasn't going far.

Chuck told me afterward I was as white as a piece of paper I was so angry. Janie, when she heard about it, called Sarah Vogel and Nick Spaeth and gave them a piece of her mind.

I didn't let the defeat in the referral election get to me. I could be pretty argumentative when people refused to listen to my reasoning but I didn't take their criticism personally. You do what you do. If it's not good enough, if people have differences, that's okay. I still kind of live that way.

We were struggling to maintain that motivation and the reward came about a month later when the North Dakota Newspaper Association ran a poll that showed I had something in the area of 60 percent approval rating. It was a great relief to me because I didn't really know what the people thought. I realized people generally appreciated that I told them what I thought even if they didn't agree. The special election was a terrible disappointment but maybe in the end a reassurance as well.

Looking back, it seems that a few lines near the end of my 1989 state of the state speech were even more appropriate than I realized at the time. In concluding that presentation I said: "If history faults us, let it fault us because we tried too hard—not because we did nothing. Let it fault us because we loved the past but we looked to the future. Let it fault us because we took seriously the commission of the people 'to govern.'"

CHAPTER TEN: government must not play god

Law Would Be Too Strict

A bill I vetoed in April 1991 would have been the strictest anti-abortion law in the nation.[57] Along with the general need for separating church and state, the ambivalence of my own church's position on abortion throughout history meant we should not legislate on the issue. The proposed law would have banned abortions except in cases of rape, incest, or if the mother's life was in danger. Rapes leading to pregnancy would have had to be reported within twenty-one days of the crime or within fifteen days of when the victim was capable of doing so. Those who performed illegal abortions would be prosecuted, with a maximum penalty of a year in jail and a $1,000 fine.

My position on abortion, which I have long made clear, directly flows from my education at St. John's. I was a student of church teachings through the centuries on when life begins and major inconsistencies in the position of the church on abortion.

The bill came down the hall to us in the latter part of the legislative session. I was ready for it and acted quickly. This was an example of standing for what I believed in. I didn't waffle or give in to the pressure of lobbying groups, including churchmen of my own Catholic faith.

I wrote in my veto message: "History is full of accounts of the misuse of governmental power, often for a 'good' cause. Such abuse must be resisted vigorously on both sides. Government must not overstep its bounds. It (government) must not play

God." I explained that I am a Catholic and I agree with the current Catholic judgment that abortion is wrong, but that Catholic writings on when life begins vary throughout history. I included statements from various Catholic and other caring faith communities that indicated heartfelt differences of opinion. In concluding the four-page veto message, I indicated that "there are many other historical writings as well which have led me to conclude that since neither I nor anyone else can prove the presence of a separate human person at the moment of conception, women's consciences must be respected."

The North Dakota House then voted, 63 to 43, eight votes short of the 71 needed to override my veto.

My press secretary's perspective shed some additional light on the scene in and around the Governor's Office, which was barraged with letters, faxes, and phone messages from impassioned people on both sides. He later wrote:

Highway Patrol officers responsible for the governor's security—usually not much of a responsibility in this civilized and minimally populated state—were concerned about the potential for verbal and even physical threats so they increased their vigilance of the Capitol building, the Governor's Office, and the Governor's Residence. Troopers also escorted the Governor or were at least present at some of his public appearances, a practice that was unnecessary at any other time during his eight years in office.

We informed the news media that there would be no comment on the abortion bill until the legislation reached the Governor's desk and he had an opportunity to study it. This bought time. It was clear what the bill said and what it meant. No further study was necessary.

After the bill passed the House and the Senate in its final form and the paperwork arrived at the Governor's Office, we immediately scheduled a news conference. The Governor had been working on his veto message for weeks and already had it carefully written.

When asked later how he remembered public reaction to his veto, Governor Sinner said he was shocked by the silence. The Right-to-Lifers had been mobilizing to rally at the Capitol later in that week. His moving so quickly and decisively negated that. Darrell Dorgan, then news director at a Bismarck radio station, had tipped the Governor off about the planned rally.

But that silence was only temporary. Governor Sinner was condemned by many who preach against passing judgment on others. Talk of a campaign to remove him from office didn't find life. Janie Sinner, also a devout Catholic, made headlines when she publicly proclaimed that she supported her husband's decision. And several months later it was front-page news in *The Bismarck Tribune* when the name of North Dakota Governor George Sinner was included on a list of twenty-seven Roman Catholic politicians and public figures whom abortion foes had asked Pope John Paul II to excommunicate for being "accomplices" of abortion.

Nothing came of that. I elaborated and further defined my views in December of 1991, with a short paper titled "Abortion in Public Policy." Along with the historical perspective of Judeo-Christian thought, I indicated the need for a compromise position from the Supreme Court. "It would be intelligent for the court to declare that there should be no abortions after a certain month of pregnancy and that there is no obligation on the part of the general public to support abortions," I wrote. "Clearly, we must be careful to support the poor generally, however. It is the establishment of a punishable prohibition in those early months that is the most offensive and that honest Christians especially should avoid. Public policy people absolutely must avoid such impositions (See Appendices for full text)."

Here are some additional thoughts excerpted from my 1991 policy paper:

In light of history, even within the religious community, few "absolutes" exist. Certainly even fewer can be legislated and are more helpful if recognized as ideals.

For many of us, morally, abortion is abhorrent. Teaching and preaching against abortion and the conditions and mentalities that cause and promote it is not only appropriate, but obligatory, if our consciences so guide us. The legal question, in the public arena, is a different one—and must be based on historical analysis of what this society can legitimately develop (without absolutes) about the beginning of human life. That is essential in public policy. When do a woman's rights come into conflict with the rights of a new person?

In making personal decisions, we will have to deal honestly with our own convictions and emotions. We also have a responsibility to educate ourselves. It is not a given that our personal conviction will be identical to the posture we take on public policy. It seems appropriate to add here that even an "I don't know" is an acceptable position, or "I cannot prove what I believe," since these may be the most honest for many in the absence of absolute or even apparent scientific conclusions.

Faith and public law bring forth the constitutional question of separation of church and state that is quite clearly at the heart of much of our current controversy. It is not surprising that otherwise disparate religions and dominations have become bedfellows. It is also not surprising that abortion continues to divide otherwise united religious groups. The Christian position changed substantially since the early thinkers tackled the question of when human life begins. It varies widely even today. The difficulty is essentially to determine when the human soul exists. Since our constitution is pledged to protect human beings, we cannot risk setting policies based solely on current religious thoughts of a portion of the people. Clearly a historical perspective is imperative.

The facts of Christian history (to say nothing of the pre-Christian era and to say nothing of other-than-Christian thought) display a wide divergence of thought. St. Augustine talked clearly about the time of quickening (movement) as the time when human life begins. St. Thomas talked about vegetable life, animal life, and human life. Some people think you could probably go to the seventh or eighth month as the time when St. Thomas talked about human life. It is fairly clear that for those leading thinkers in Christian history, the time of presence of human life was not at all clear. Many other writings display similar conclusions.

In addition, for years after St. Thomas wrote, the Christian church actually prohibited baptism to a prematurely born fetus precisely because the fetus was not a human person. Probably more importantly, the church has generally taught that human beings are unique and even like God because of their intellect and will—that makes them human. The question then becomes: when can intellect and will be demonstrated? Many of the advocates of constitutional amendments (that would equate abortion to murder and subsequently to the punishments of capital punishment or life imprisonment) allege they can demonstrate response stimuli of several kinds in the fetus at an early age. I'm sure that's true. You can demonstrate those same kinds of response in the animal fetus, too. The question of humanity, however, is the question of intellect and will and the unique and emotional and social characteristics that flow from them.

No matter what one's present personal position is on abortion, it seems safe to assume that everyone is interested in protecting human life. This is a good place to start. However, agreement about the beginning of life, and therefore when it is protected is unlikely. Compromise will be the only valid approach in public policy.

All of us who truly care about human life have much to do. We must embrace all who are pregnant. We must help and support them. We must not make them social outcasts as several religious groups have done. We must help society care for dependent children, handicapped, ill, and elderly. We must work for the cause of peace and against capital punishment.

I've never believed that abortion was a good thing. But when dealing with public policy you have to scrupulously avoid giving credence to the idea that the state can impose church opinions, even when they are the opinions of the majority. That was a difficult issue but I had studied it extensively in college and had pretty vivid memories of the writings of St. Augustine in the fourth century and later on of St. Thomas Aquinas in the thirteenth century, probably the two most prominent "doctors" of the early church. This title of doctor indicated that the writings and preachings of such a person were useful to Christians in any age of the church. Such men and women were particularly known for the depth of understanding and the orthodoxy of their theological teachings. St. Augustine and St. Thomas Aquinas both wrote about the time during pregnancy when God breathes in the human soul and life begins. Both of these saints concluded that human life began sometime *after* conception. In public policy that really is the issue because it's quite clear if it is a human person the state is obliged to protect the rights of that person.

I had watched the abortion discussion kind of quietly in my early years in government. Then when I decided to run for governor I knew I had to figure it out and make clear decisions so I went back and studied it and discovered much to my amazement that until late in the nineteenth century the Catholic Church had banned the baptism of a fetus precisely because it was not yet a human person. Then I began to find out from people outside the church that there are great differences of opinion about when in fact a human person exists. One learned Lutheran theologian told me that he believed human life was present only after separation from the mother because that was the first he and others saw true intellect and will. That became a point that I had to clarify and did clarify. I wrote a paper on it in my first campaign, even before I was nominated, to explain to people what my conclusion was.

I was frustrated with the local Catholic bishop's position during the 2004 election campaign saying that those who didn't agree with his pushing for criminal punishment for abortions were somehow not worthy and that they were violating some Catholic or Christian principle. It has offended me grievously that church leaders presume that they know more about the constitutional law than the people in public life. They pretend to tell public officials how they're supposed to vote and how they're supposed to decide public policy on the merits of church policy rather than on the merits of the act itself.

In March of 2005 *The Fargo Forum* published an exchange about abortion.[58] A woman named Jan George wrote in critiquing my judgment on the question of abortion as public policy based on natural law. I can't find the copy of it any more but at St. John's I wrote a paper on natural law that for years afterward was reproduced and given to students in ethics and history of philosophy. So I am quite familiar with natural law writings. Natural laws are basic and fundamental to human nature and are discoverable by human reason without reference to specific legislative enactments or judicial decisions. St. Thomas Aquinas perpetuated this idea, asserting that natural law was common to all peoples—Christian and non-Christian alike. Natural law certainly is a consideration. Jan George concluded that Thomas Aquinas and Augustine and all of the serious writers, religious and otherwise, through history and even today have not been aware of natural law or have not considered it on this issue. That was a rather disdainful inference about these great men. Clearly she ignored the fact that they knew all about natural law but they differ with her conclusion that human life begins at the moment of conception.

I disagreed completely with imposing legal sanctions on people who were involved with abortions. All through history the attitudes on when human life is present have changed and there's a wide range of thought among Christians even today on when there's a human person present. So I didn't mention my abhorrence of abortions in my newspaper discussions about the attitudes of the public policy. That was a mistake. I had made it clear in the earlier writings that I disapproved of abortion because I personally believed a human life was involved. I also believed it was wrong for the general public to pay for abortions. It's probably not ethical for a society to use people's money to pay for something the vast majority doesn't agree with. The idea of publicly funded abortions has always been a misjudged and mistaken notion in public policy. Admittedly people who are poor and pregnant deserve help, as they do for their food and medical care. But I think it's a miscarriage of that concept to conclude that because some of them want to have an abortion the public should pay for it.

When I was governor, I called Department of Human Services Director John Graham one day and I said, "I don't want to see us paying abortion clinics—be sure we pay out all the money we're supposed to pay out, but be sure the money goes to the needy recipient, not to the abortion clinic."

I ended up not being particularly beloved by either side of the abortion discussion. It should be pointed out, though, that I received many, many commendations for my work in clarifying public policy in this difficult area. The abortion veto didn't deter one significant Catholic university—St. John's—from awarding me an honorary doctorate, as did two other universities.[59]

CHAPTER ELEVEN: Part of the Job

New Portraits in the Hall

One of the honors I had in office was bestowing the state of North Dakota's highest distinction, induction into the Theodore Roosevelt Rough Rider Hall of Fame.[60] We gave the prestigious award to federal judge Ronald Davies, basketball star and coach Phil Jackson, writer Larry Woiwode, and actress Angie Dickinson.

For me the highlight among those was Judge Davies, who was honored and best known for challenging Arkansas Governor Orval Faubus in 1957, during the Little Rock Nine crisis.[61] The judge from Fargo had been temporarily assigned to deal with that segregation problem. He nullified a local injunction and ordered the school board to proceed with integration of Little Rock Central High School. His was the first of the four Rough Rider Awards we presented during my eight years. I will never ever forget something he said to me that night. We were sitting at a state bar association banquet. I was on the left side of the microphone and Judge Davies was on my left. As I was being introduced to go to the podium, I all of a sudden felt a tugging on my coat. I looked around and here was Judge Davies with tears streaming down his face. "I'm no racial justice hero. I didn't even know what the problems were," he sobbed. "I just did my job."

I put my hand on his hand. "It's okay," I said. "You've done very well." Then I went and introduced him.

I couldn't get his emotional words out of my head because I realized that here's a guy who really understood what it was to be a hero. He had all kinds of threats to his life and probably to everything sacred to him, but he just went down the road doing his job. It was a fabulous experience for me, one of those rare times in my life when I learned something important: damn the torpedoes and just do your job.

I had and still have a deep admiration for Phil Jackson. I had met Phil years and years before when he was a student and basketball star at the University of North Dakota. Eleanor Roosevelt had come to Fargo and I went to visit with her at the reception held at the Episcopal bishop's home. I walked in and Phil Jackson was sitting there. I'm not a big sports nut but I never forgot how impressed I was that this jock in college was interested in a former president's widow who had lots of ideas of her own about the world. She was pretty crippled up by then. He came to Fargo to visit with her. Phil is so widely respected for his class and his discipline, his style, his brilliant coaching. He was a natural choice and I was really honored to give him the award.

It was our goal to induct somebody from the literary arts field into the Hall of Fame. Larry Woiwode was one of a group of writers who should have all been honored. I wanted to name one of them so we consulted with several people including Jerry Lamb. Jerry actually suggested that we select a North Dakota native who wrote for *The New York Times*, Richard Critchfield. But Woiwode was probably more widely known in the state by the non-literary people. That was really why he was chosen. I didn't know him that well but I had read some of his stuff and he certainly deserved the award.

I had not had a particularly high opinion of Angie Dickinson until one day I was told she was going to stop by and wanted to visit with me. She was in my office for about two hours. I was astonished to find out what kind of a person she was. It turned out she was taking care of her sister who was in the early stages of Alzheimer's. Angie had brought her sister back to see her roots in Kulm, where they were born.

Angie told me a little bit about her daughter Nikki who also was the child of Burt Bacharach. I kept hearing things from this woman that were not the classic thoughts of a movie star. To be honest about it, I was pretty impressed.

It was the former governor, Bill Guy, who nominated Angie for the Rough Rider Award. He wrote a long and pretty convincing letter why she should be appointed because she had brought fame to North Dakota. He had heard her interviewed on some nationally broadcast program and she said great things about the state.

It was true she'd made some rather flippant comments about her home state at one time many years earlier.[62] But she told me later how much she regretted having done that and she had said very positive things about North Dakota since then. In visiting with her I discovered that her early life was not happy. Her father had a problem with alcohol. Angie was fifteen when they left Kulm. There was no question that she was widely known and that honoring her with the North Dakota Rough Rider Award was appropriate.

She came back to help me with the campaign in 1988. She did a great job and impressed lots of people when she played a starring role in a series of birthday parties that were fundraisers for me. Janie and I were on the plane over to Grand Forks to meet her for one those rallies. I was sitting in the back of the plane and I realized I had nothing to say. So in about ten minutes I wrote the limerick titled *Angie I,* which was probably one of the better ones I've done. It just spilled out. It was one of those days when the words were just falling.

There was a young lady from Kulm,
Who amazed both her dad and her mum.
She traveled afar
and became a great star,
But now she's back whence she come.
We love her sparkling smile.
It beats all the rest by a mile.
When she catches your eye,
She gives you a high.
She's a lady with marvelous style.
I thank you for coming, my dear
For our fondue, our brunches, and beer.
It's ordinary fair
Done with flair.

The best people on earth are here.
The lady from Kulm is our friend.
She's part of a positive trend.
North Dakota is proud,
We say it out loud,
Angie, our love will last 'til the end.

About three years later she came back to North Dakota and I wrote another for her. I didn't like that poem nearly as well as the first one. I have written quite a few more poems, none that I like much, none that worked as well or flowed as well as did that first one I wrote for Angie.

This Was My Style

I have learned to not doubt my own judgments, not be afraid to express them, and always listen carefully to other people's judgments. I came to the conclusion that the art of politics is the art of finding the truth and making it understandable and acceptable to the people. Anyone who wants to influence people cannot bludgeon them. Lots of folks understand issues and understand the positions, but somehow can't make it acceptable. They want to hurt people with the truth. Politics is often described as the art of compromise. But the real art of politics is making the truth acceptable.

At the same time, I had to be careful myself about speaking strongly about things I did not understand. That often happened at press conferences. Reporters would ask, "Governor, what is your opinion about such and such?" Some politicians say you answer the question and don't have staff answer it. I rejected that out of hand and tried to have experts there so we would have the story straight.

Many times somebody would ask me confidentially about why I was so open and willing to try to answer so many questions. I understood the only way to communicate with the public was through the media. If we didn't tell them everything we could, how were they going to know? And if we didn't make things clear, people weren't going to know. We almost never turned down requests for interviews. In turn, the media were awfully good to me. I think my press secretary's friendship with so many of them was a big factor, too.

The other area with the media that I always found rather humorous was whenever editor Mike Jacobs would do one of his he-knew-better editorials in the *Grand Forks Herald*. I would insist that we not answer them directly. We would just write and say we were glad it had been brought up and tell them what the true facts were as we saw them. Somebody told me that really bugged Mike.

When I took office we tried to curtail proclamations for the first year but I finally figured out it probably wasn't wise. Some organizations were very offended. And although we initially questioned their value, proclamations were more important than I initially thought because they bolster good ideas and good projects that benefit the public. I was probably more interested in substance than in form but the form is important too and proclamations were one way to help some causes. Whoever wrote them usually knew what he or she was doing.

I admit that I'm not a good politician. At least I'm not that competitively partisan. I had learned a long, long time before I became governor that you couldn't be any good if decisions were made based on partisan politics or even if the right decision is made and an effort to skew it for partisan benefit follows. I set out from the beginning with the view that every single issue is sacred and must be dealt with honestly without gain for myself or for the party. People tried to influence us to do things for political benefit. We fought that almost continually.

Time for visiting with people was always too short. It struck me many times in the first year or two that I would so often just be getting to the nub of a problem and understanding it and seeing possible solutions and then someone would come and say my next meeting was waiting. In the early years I made up my mind that I'm not going to do this. I'm almost done and I'm going to finish it. Otherwise I had to go back and learn it all over again.

In order to make that work I began to use a white board in the office to focus people on a part of the problem or a possible solution. It worked. As the years went on I became more and more expert at getting a group of maybe five or six people to concentrate on one thought. Now is this what you mean? Is this a possible solution?

That became an office joke: we've got to get the governor's white board, got to get something for the governor to write on.

One day years later I was watching Dick Gross at the Tri College symposium. I was just astonished, again, at watching him pull and extract conclusions out of this group. I was writing down my conclusions and when we finished I was the last person to be called on. I answered, "Well, these are the things I think I'm hearing." I cited six or seven. Later on Dick showed me his sheet and he had the same six or seven. I also watched him on the International Flood Mitigation Initiative.[63] Man, he was brilliant.

One day I asked how he learned all this. "You don't know?" he replied.

"Not really," I said.

"That's what you did with the white board."

Only he did a much more thorough job than I did. It's interesting to see the perfection that he has brought to the technique because it does help everyone focus on one thought, to get clarified and get things moving.

I don't remember well my first day in the Governor's Office. I do recall one of my first decisions, though. We didn't have nearly enough space for staff and I believed the back office that had been used before as the Governor's Office by my predecessor was way more than I needed. So we made that switch immediately and I moved into the traditional, smaller office up front. For senior positions in the office I chose three people from my campaign—Chuck Fleming, Carol Siegert, and my press secretary Bob Jansen—along with Dick Gross, and they helped find talented people to fill the other positions. Many of them stayed with us the entire eight years.

From the beginning I wanted people to be happy and in good spirits and not be bashful about laughing and singing and doing the things that make life better for everyone. I had a passion for having people happy and comfortable in their work. I hated the quiet offices where people shut doors for fear they will upset someone. We had a wonderful staff. Everyone was usually in great spirits. It meant so much to have happiness around. There are plenty of things that make life difficult so if you don't enjoy every minute you can it's sometimes pretty grim.

I loved having children visit. I enjoyed having them sit in the governor's chair or on my lap. They could fiddle with my desk. I didn't care. Children brought a wonderment that was special to have around. Sometimes they had their picture taken. To this day I bet once a month somebody says they were in the chair and had their picture taken when they were five or eight or twelve years old. Several other groups have told me that somehow I seemed vitally interested in them when they were at the Capitol, with bands and groups that came in. I do love children. I couldn't have ten of my own and not love them.

One day I went to speak to a class at one of the religious grade schools. Dick Gross was with me. I didn't have anything prepared. I don't know what got me going but I said, "You know what your job is, kids? Your job is to study, not to become big athletes. I have a job and I have to do it. I work every hour I can to do my job and take care of the needs of the people. Your job in school is to learn from your lessons, and it's very important."

It was really quiet in the room and the children were listening. These were third or fourth graders. Dick later asked, "Where did that come from?" That was kind of typical of the way I loved children and teaching children.

On another occasion I found myself in the ironic position as the father of ten teaching catechism to teenagers and dealing with the discussion of birth control. It was an interesting time for me. Here I am with ten children of my own, or nine at that time I think. And I'm telling them to do what I had not done, obviously.

Many years before, when I said something stupid about that, Father Godfrey Diekman told me, "Listen, I work with people in the cities every weekend for whom it would be a sin to *not* practice birth control." Wow, that pulled me up short.

That was the beginning of my learning about that. More recently, Father Bernard Häring, in his book *My Hope for the Church*, said it is clear now given the population situation it would be a complete error to teach people they should not practice birth control. That and many other things Häring wrote are considered revolutionary but are logically undeniable. The people who want to take the church back to their childhood or the childhood of their parents don't want to hear any of that. Someday they'll wake up to the reality of the world.

Running for Presidents

As the many candidates for president can attest, getting to the White House can be difficult.

Every year the National Governors Association holds its winter meeting in Washington, DC. It includes an evening reception at the White House with the president and first lady. That's a special honor. A new governor from North Dakota had a few things to learn about such events, including how to find his way there. That was literally true for Janie and me and is now always humorous to look back on.

During the 1985 NGA winter meeting, our first, we were due to head for the White House and Janie asked Chuck Fleming to get our car. Chuck always did more than probably any other chief of staff, but he knew nothing about a car because he thought our son Jim was providing transportation. So Chuck scrambled and borrowed a rental vehicle from Dan Garry, whom we knew from his position with 3M Company. Then Chuck had to ask directions to the White House so he could drive us there.

The next year, son Jim did provide our transportation to the governors' reception with the president. Jim was a graduate student at Cornell University and hauled us to the White House in his ten-year-old Chevy Chevelle. Jim's old jalopy generated huge attention among the limousines that dropped off the other governors and spouses. The Marine Corps sergeants who met us were laughing when they opened our doors at the White House entrance. Actually it was great comic relief.

By 1987 we thought it would be simple to just take a taxi to the White House. But the cab driver was irritated about something and his reckless speeding and careening down Pennsylvania Avenue really frightened Janie. She told him to shape up or stop and let us off. After that we sent Steve Sharkey from the Governor's Residence to Washington ahead of us so he could arrange reliable transportation to the annual receptions at the White House.

George H. W. Bush was elected vice president with President Reagan in 1980. As vice president, the first thing he did at the beginning of 1985 was go to the Middle East to try and convince the OPEC leaders to raise the price of oil because the price of oil had crashed in 1981.

I was troubled by what had happened and had no clue about some of the things I know now. There'd been quite a bit of press about Bush saying it's insane to keep prices this low because it meant that people were just going to gobble up oil and it was going to ruin the industry. I agreed with him as I watched the industry in North Dakota shut down. When Bush got back everyone just beat him up publicly, even the Reagan people. So I picked up the phone and told him I wholeheartedly agreed with what he had done and admired his courage for doing it. What was interesting was I couldn't get him off the phone; he was the loneliest man in Washington. He was delighted to find a friend out in the boonies, even if it was a Democrat.

When the senior Bush was then elected president in 1988, his first trip out of Washington was to North Dakota to plant a tree on the capitol grounds. We had a warm meeting. In my office he visited and had pictures taken with everyone. I thought here's a guy who could do a lot of good. The friendship never really waned. He appointed me to a couple of federal commissions.[64]

Janie has written her memories of the White House receptions:

The White House dinners were fabulous. I wish I could re-member all of my tablemates, but unfortunately it's too late now. However, one I do remember—President Reagan. I was seated at his table in 1991. He really didn't converse with any of us, but instead rambled on about World War II throughout the dinner. He didn't ask any of our names or even pretend to have an interest in us. My impression was that he was in a world all by himself. I also remember another dinner be-ing seated next to Jack Kemp and the new governor from Minnesota, Arne Carlson, and my impression of these two was not favorable. They both were full of themselves.

Following dinner we were all ushered into the East Room for entertainment, and afterward, with the band playing, we danced. On one of those evenings, I danced with Governor Clinton, and remarked that I hoped he would someday be president.

In addition to the White House dinners, it was a custom for the First Lady to host a luncheon for the governors' wives. In the Reagan years this luncheon was in the East Room. I always felt as if Nancy Reagan was just doing what protocol required, and wasn't exactly happy about doing it. When we were introduced, she seemed to be looking through me with no expression in her eyes. She always seemed very aloof. But in the Bush years, Barbara was very warm and gracious, and invited us upstairs to the president's private quarters. I sat at Mrs. Bush's table and was impressed with her down-to-earth friendliness. She was a great conversationalist and seemed genuinely interested in each one of us.

At the invitation of a different president, we returned to the White House after I left the Governor's Office. Here's Janie's account of our visit with the Clintons in June of 1993:

Hillary asked for us to let them know the next time we would be in Washington for they would like to have us stay with them. We arrived in Washington about noon on Tuesday, June 1. We were met at the airport by White House security and taken directly to the White House. At the gate we were announced as the "president's guests." Carolyn Huber, the White House manager, was waiting and took us directly up to the second floor to our quarters, the Lincoln Bedroom. She gave us badges to wear, allowing us to go wherever we wished in the house or out on the grounds and told us to feel free to browse. Then she left us to ourselves.

We stood in awe at our surroundings. The Lincoln Bedroom, where Lincoln actually slept, where he signed the Emancipation Proclamation. On a desk in a far corner was one of five original copies of the Gettysburg Address that Lincoln made by hand. The bed was immense, but its size was diminished by the height of the room—fifteen or sixteen feet. We studied the paintings, the furniture, the books from the early 1800s, and realized how few people in the last hundred years had actually used this room and how much history was here.

It felt so incredible to be there, in the White House, sitting outside on the Truman Balcony, and watching all of the tourists below at the fence taking pictures of us. It's a moment I'll never forget. And then President Clinton arrived in a car caravan below us and we watched from the balcony as he came quickly into the house. It was several minutes before he joined us as he had taken time to change into sport clothes. Now he was just Bill, and I got my familiar hug. He was so grateful that we had come and we all sat down to visit. Hillary had not yet arrived.

I pulled out my granddaughter Courtney's letter to "Mr. President" that she had written to him just a few days before and gave it to him. Courtney was six when she wrote it. He loved it. Then he put it into his shirt pocket and said he would answer it before we left.

Hillary received about 2,500 letters a day and they were just not able to stay on top of it. Volunteers were there every day, reading and sorting the letters into twenty-six categories, from health care to personal criticism. There were many requests for help and for photos and each request expected a response. I worked with the volunteers for six hours and I was quite exhausted. And I was only reading and sorting.

Wednesday evening we attended a small dinner in the White House Green Room. In attendance besides Bill and Hillary were Vice-President Al Gore and his wife, Tipper, Mr. and Mrs. Bob Rubin (head of the economic advisors), the Warren Christophers, the David Gergens, Mike Mansfield, and a famous opera singer Jessica Norman. I sat at Al Gore's table while Bud sat with the Clintons. On Bud's left was Katharine Graham, owner of *The Washington Post*. Most of the conversation centered on the economy and how to get it moving.

After dinner Bud and I slipped upstairs before the Clintons so we could be out of sight when they said goodnight to their guests. We found Chelsea at the top of the stairs dancing away to the sound of the music below. She was having a great time all by herself. Bud offered to show her some card tricks and while he was entertaining her with that and I was watching, Bill and Hillary, David Gergen, and George Stephanopoulos came up and disappeared into Bill's study for a long discussion. Chelsea finished learning the card tricks long before the discussion ended so we slipped quietly to our room and to bed.

Later, in November of 2004, I had been in Asia when Janie wrote her now infamous letter to *The Forum* about why she had to leave the Catholic Church because of hypocrisy and injustices within the Church and our Fargo diocese. She was particularly disturbed by bishops "using their authority to give voting instructions and ultimatums" to church members during the just-ended presidential campaign. Janie had held it for me to read the day I got home before she mailed it. "I don't think I want to sign the letter," I said. "I'm the only one who can stay in the Church and fight. And besides, it's too deeply ingrained in me to abandon ship."

"I know that," she said, "I just wanted to show it to you before I sent it." It was published on Tuesday, two weeks after the election.[65] That afternoon we left for the Clinton Library dedication in Little Rock and on Wednesday at about six o'clock or seven we went to a VIP reception. It was a room with about 200 people, including a lot of movie stars and famous people. We were standing off to one side and I can't remember who we were visiting with but Hillary and Bill arrived about 9:15. They walked in the doorway and of course everyone started to clap. Hillary scanned across the crowd. The first person she saw was Janie. She cut right through the crowd, walked over, and threw her arms around her. She said, "Jane, I loved your letter."

It was the next night after the thing was published. I couldn't figure out how Hillary found out about it so fast. Janie gets a lot of respect from a lot of people because she's got brass. Her letter was significant enough that it was seen in high places and had reached the Clintons so quickly. It turned out that Byron Dorgan had shown her letter to Hillary in the Senate hallway. We talked about a lot of old times and had a great visit with the Clintons that night.

Gone With a Puff of Smoke

One of the really interesting examples of political fall-out as a result of political actions was my decision as governor to prohibit smoking in the state buildings. We had been very aggressive in the state under the leadership of Dr. Stephen McDonough in the Health Department, which was headed up by Dr. Bob Wentz. Under Wentz, McDonough had begun as many programs as we could to get smoking stopped in the state, and in 1989 we were given the first award from the Centers for Disease Control for having the best smoking-secession effort in the Rocky Mountain region.

I smoked until 1978. In fact, the doctors said my artery blockage that required bypass surgery in 1991 was a result of earlier smoking. But when I quit, I just quit. I had tried once before but got started again. I knew smoking was a stupid thing to do but that really didn't have any bearing on it. I watched and listened to the reactions of the people who complained about smoking. I began to read of the implications of second-hand smoke and it became more and more clear to me that innocent people were being hurt quite significantly by smoking.

I remember it being a Friday and I left the office that afternoon thinking about it. Quite by coincidence Janie and I had a dinner engagement with a man named Jack Schuchart and his wife, Joyce. Jack was the CEO of Montana Dakota Utilities and he had prohibited smoking at MDU. As we sat and were eating I asked him, "Jack what all did you do before you discontinued smoking?"

He looked at me and said, "I didn't do anything. I just announced it."

I realized that was what I needed to do because if we began a long discussion on how it was going to be done it would never get done. So, the following Monday I asked Dick Gross to prepare an executive order.[66] If I remember correctly we had a press conference the next day with no warning to anybody that it was going to happen.

Lots of people were upset, I admit. Many called and wrote letters complaining. They were from all over the state and different building facilities, but the most significant challenge came from a group of Capitol employees who asked to see me. I met with them and listened to their stories. It was a lengthy meeting. They wanted me to give them a smoking room. Probably thirty or forty people attended. Finally I said to them, "Look, we are trying and we are doing the best we can but we haven't got enough money to pay you well. If we are to provide special places for you to smoke here we must do it for all state employees. Do you have any idea what that would cost us?"

I announced the smoking ban in the large auditorium at the North Dakota Heritage Center. I think the vast majority of state employees knew it was the right thing to do. Eventually some of the same people who complained came in and thanked me for helping them quit smoking.

However, several legislators were upset that they wouldn't be able to smoke while they were in session. They insisted that the legislative wing was not under my authority. In fact, it was under my authority but there was no point in my engaging in a big battle. I deferred to them and they had a smoking room. Until I left, they were still smoking there. I was told you could hardly see in that room and people were in there inhaling that stuff. Much later, the legislature finally ended smoking in their private room. At any rate, the smoking ban was something I was proud of.

What I didn't know about my smoking ban decision I learned later. After his election, the early part of December in 1992, Bill Clinton called me about becoming his secretary of agriculture. I told him I would be honored to do it. "I haven't actually decided to give it to anybody but I wanted you to think about that," he said. So he called me back about the 15th or 16th and asked whether I still wanted to do it. I told him that I would be happy to and I could do it. But I told him not to worry about it and do what he had to do if something else changed. I wanted it pretty badly. But I knew that there were some clear doubts I had, partly because I had been sick that summer and I wasn't altogether sure that it was something Janie was going to enjoy.

"Plan to come to Little Rock next Tuesday and I'll introduce you and name you," Bill said.

The following week, when I arrived in Little Rock, I was met by North Dakota native Warren Christopher, whom Clinton had chosen to serve as secretary of state.[67] "I think this has changed, George," Christopher said. "I don't know where he's at but I think this has changed." I eventually went in and sat down with Bill, just the two of us, and he didn't even bring the agriculture secretary appointment up. I think he thought Warren had referred me.

Bill and I talked for quite a while. He was struggling over the interior secretary appointment and had picked Bill Richardson. I liked Richardson a lot. I'd read some of his stuff and I thought he was pretty good. But, I had reservations. "You know that's the department that's really a mess," I said. "They've got so many agencies that have conflicting regulations. And they don't meet and talk to each other." I told him about a meeting we had with Interior Secretary Manuel Lujan when we asked him to pull his agencies in and that they had never met. "I think you need somebody in there who's had some administrative experience and I don't know that Richardson does," I said.

"That's right; it is a mess over there. Maybe I better put Babbitt in there," Bill agreed.

"There's some things about Babbitt I don't care for but at least there's a lot of management ability," I suggested.

According to press reports, Bruce Babbitt, an outspoken environmentalist and a former Arizona governor, was considered an early favorite for interior secretary. Environmental organizations had protested when Clinton shifted away from him and toward Richardson, who was supported by Hispanic groups. I gave Clinton bad advice on Babbitt. From my perspective, he turned out to be disastrous. Bruce was too green and did things that hurt. He got Governor Mike Sullivan defeated for the Senate because he went into Wyoming in the heat of the campaign and said he hoped he could tear down all the dams. That cost Mike the election. I don't think Mike handled it right, either. He wasn't a street fighter. I did Bill Richardson a disservice and have always regretted it since then. In fact, I became a big fan of his when he ran for the presidential nomination. And I saw his ability to speak the truth and make it both understandable and acceptable.

And then, because he'd lost his Hispanic appointment (Richardson), Bill tracked down Michigan Governor Jim Blanchard, who was already en route to Little Rock. He told Blanchard there was a change and he wouldn't be named secretary of transportation. Instead, Bill then named Frederico Pena head of transportation and eventually made Blanchard ambassador to Canada. Even though I had bipartisan support from the Dakotas and Minnesota, Bill appointed Mississippi Congressman Mike Espy agriculture secretary.

I hadn't told anybody back home I was going to Little Rock because I knew things could change. But the news got out after my private meeting with the president-elect. While I was en route back home to North Dakota on the day before Christmas, *The Fargo Forum* ran a story about Clinton's decisions on various appointments. The paper spread a five-column headline on the front page indicating I had been passed over for agriculture secretary.

After leaving the Governor's Office I was then hired by American Crystal Sugar Company to do lobbying work. I spent a lot of time in Washington, DC, for the next three years. About a year into my job at Crystal—it must have been winter of 1994—I ate lunch with a friend of mine who had been in and around Washington, including some time with the Reagan administration. As we were dining he said, "Do you know why you didn't get to be secretary of agriculture?"

"No."

"Didn't the president tell you?"

"No." Clinton's senator, Mark Pryor from Arkansas was big in agriculture and it had always been my suspicion that the president would defer to Senator Pryor on this appointment.

"I will tell you why you didn't get it," my friend said. "You were the first governor to ban smoking in all state buildings and facilities. The tobacco lobby found out you were the candidate, the nominee, and raised all kinds of hell and that is why you didn't get it." He told me that the thing that upset them most was many other governors followed my example and banned smoking after I made the move.

I didn't know I was the first one and I didn't know others followed suit. That was just not the kind of thing we kept track of or worried about. But, I was certainly proud of what I did. You have to suffer the consequences sometimes. You don't plan your life and start making adjustments in what you do. You do the best you can wherever you are and if something falls you do the best you can there. So I don't think I would ever change it, but it was an interesting bit of side play.

This portrait of the Albert and Katherine Sinner family by Casselton photographer George Tise is from 1936. Front Row, left to right: Katherine, Jeanne, and Albert. Second row: Dick, Bill, George. Photo courtesy George and Jane Sinner.

The children of Albert and Katherine on the original family farmstead in 1935. From left to right: Jeanne, George, Bill, and Dick. Photo courtesy George and Jane Sinner.

Albert Sinner is ready to go hunting pheasants with sons Dick and George on the Sinner farm near Casselton. Photo courtesy George and Jane Sinner.

George Sinner and his older brother Dick (at right) played baseball for the Casselton town team. Dick had an incredible batting eye and rarely struck out, but wasn't as interested in the game. Photo courtesy Ellery and Jeanne Bresnahan.

George attended school in Casselton, ND before moving on to St. John's preparatory School. Photo courtesy George and Jane Sinner.

An ex-seminarian, Airman George Sinner drove a borrowed convertible roadster to Florida to court his future wife, Jane Baute. Photo courtesy Ellery and Jeanne Bresnahan.

George Sinner and Elizabeth Jane Baute were married August 10, 1951, at St. John's Catholic Church in Valdosta, Ga. Photo courtesy of George and Jane Sinner.

Jane Sinner, wearing a "Sinner is a Winner" campaign pin, was a delegate to the 1964 Democratic-NPL Party State Convention. At that convention, State Senator George Sinner won the party's endorsement to run for the U.S. House of Representatives against incumbent Republican Rep. Mark Andrews.
Photo courtesy of the Bismarck Tribune.

George and Jane Sinner enjoy a family picnic with their nine children in the backyard at their Casselton home. Their youngest, son Eric, was born later. Photo courtesy of George and Jane Sinner.

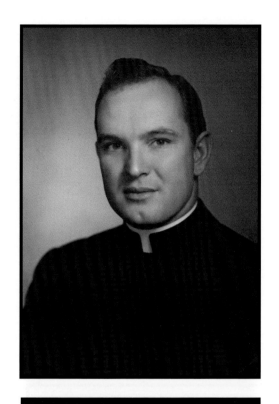

Rev. Richard Sinner was ordained a Catholic priest in May 1952 at St. Mary's Cathedral in Fargo. He is remembered for his compassion and humanitarian work on behalf of people who needed help or sanctuary.
Photo courtesy of George and Jane Sinner.

George Sinner testing a farm product during a trip to France in the early 1970s.
Photo courtesy of George and Jane Sinner.

State Rep. George Sinner chaired the House Finance and Taxation Committee during the 1983 legislative session. Photo courtesy of George and Jane Sinner.

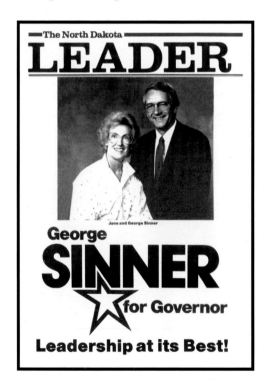

George Sinner viewed the North Dakota Leader tabloid as critical to his winning the 1984 gubernatorial election. The newsprint publication created by Jim Fuglie, Mary Jo Sinner, and Bob Jansen was circulated statewide in the final days leading up to the election.

Ruth Meiers was endorsed by the Democratic-NPL Party and went on to become the state's first woman lieutenant governor. She was diagnosed with lung and brain cancer in 1986 and died in office six months later, in March of 1987.

George Sinner raises his right hand and is formally sworn into office as North Dakota's 29th Governor on January 6, 1985, by Chief Justice Ralph Erickstad at the opening of the 1985 Legislative session. Photo by Garry Redmann.

The Inaugural Ball at the Bismarck Civic Center on January 6, 1985, was a time for expressing congratulations and support, and celebrating the election of the new governor. Jane Sinner was overwhelmed with pride for her husband as they danced in the spotlight to Anne Murray's hit song "Could I Have This Dance." Photo courtesy of the Bismarck Tribune.

Governor George Sinner and First Lady Jane Sinner float on the Boise River during a scheduled activity at the 1985 National Governors Association annual meeting in Idaho. Photo by Bob Jansen.

After eliminating the position of driver of the governor, George Sinner often refueled the Lincoln Town Car provided by the state for his use. He later decided to use his own vehicle, a Chevy Suburban, to save the state money. Photo courtesy of the Bismarck Tribune.

Governor George Sinner demonstrated his skill with the Bobcat loader in 1987 during groundbreaking for expansion of the Melroe plant in Gwinner. Photo by Bob Jansen.

Jane Sinner designed North Dakota's Teddy Roosevelt Bear to highlight the badlands and promote the indomitable spirit and the proud heritage of North Dakota. The stuffed bears, modeled after the U.S. President who ranched in western North Dakota, were presented as gifts by the Sinners and distributed by the Dayton-Hudson Department Store Company.
Photo courtesy of the Bismarck Tribune.

Governor Sinner posed for this formal photograph in the Governor's Office late in his second term.
Photo courtesy of George and Jane Sinner.

*Lloyd Omdahl was appointed lieutenant governor after the death
in March 1987 of Ruth Meiers, the state's first woman to hold
that post. Omdahl, a political science professor at the University
of North Dakota, was a former state tax commissioner and had
worked on Governor Bill Guy's staff.* Photo by Garry Redmann.

On September 6, 1989, Governor George Sinner held a news conference at which he announced he was calling a special election for December 5 to settle legislative measures that had been referred to a statewide vote. Sinner traveled the state that fall to explain the state's budget situation and the need for the revenue enhancements the legislature had approved. Associated Press photo courtesy of the Bismarck Tribune.

Five current and former governors posed for a photo together on July 4, 1989, during the "Party of the Century" held on the Capitol Mall to commemorate and celebrate North Dakota's centennial. From left are Governors John Davis, Bill Guy, Art Link, Allen Olson, and George Sinner. Photo by Garry Redmann.

Whether on formal occasions or more casual and celebratory settings like this one, Governor George Sinner was passionate about issues in many of the speeches he delivered. Photo courtesy of the Bismarck Tribune.

Governor George Sinner commemorated North Dakota's Centennial with a project to plant a tree in the hometowns of former governors. Here he mans the shovel in the park at Alexander in the fall of 1989, as former Governor Art Link and community residents look on. Photo by Bob Jansen.

Governor George Sinner with three men from North Dakota who have served in the U.S. Senate. All Democrats, from left they are: Sinner, Byron Dorgan, Kent Conrad, and Quentin Burdick. Photo by Bob Jansen.

Governor Sinner met with reporters in the lobby of the Rapid City Regional Hospital when he was discharged following heart bypass surgery. Photo courtesy of the Bismarck Tribune.

Lieutenant Governor Lloyd Omdahl and Governor's Office staff members hammed it up for this goofy photo of "running the state" in late July of 1991 while Governor Sinner recovered from heart bypass surgery in Rapid City, S.D. Photo by Garry Redmann.

Governor Sinner and Lieutenant Governor Lloyd Omdahl are shown with the Sinner cabinet during a dinner held in February 1992. Standing (left to right): Helen Tracy, Bruce Larson, John Graham, Bob Wentz, Dick Backes, Jim Sperry, Gary Ness, Glenn Pomeroy, General Alexander Macdonald, Dave Sprynczynatyk, Gary Pressler, Brian Berg, Mike Diesz, Deborah Painte. Seated (left to right): Tim Kingstad, Elaine Little, Lt. Governor Lloyd Omdahl, Governor George Sinner, Doug Eiken, Lloyd Jones, Charlie Mertens. Not shown: Mick Bohn, Joe Lamb. Photo by Garry Redmann.

*Actress and Kulm native
Angie Dickinson was one
of four notable North
Dakotans inducted by
Governor George Sinner
into the Rough Rider Hall
of Fame. He presented
her with a glazed ceramic
bowl by Casselton
native and renowned St.
John's University potter
Richard Bresnahan.*
Photo by Bob Jansen.

*President Bill Clinton
greets former Governor
George Sinner during a
reception in 1995. Sinner
and Clinton worked together
frequently as policy planners
through the National
Governors Association
and became close friends.*
Photo by Lisa Berg.

*George and Jane Sinner
and their next generation
today.* Photo by Haney's
Photography, 2008.

I had another chance to become agriculture secretary about a year and a half later when Espy resigned under some pressure. But the whole debate over the Freedom to Farm bill was going on and I wasn't sure that as a newcomer coming into Washington I could deal with the Republican Congress as well as one of their own could.[68]

When I was in to talk to Clinton about it I told him, "If you can get Dan Glickman, you had better take him. I would love to do it, but I think we have bigger fish to fry than my having a job." So he then appointed Glickman, who was a member of the House Agriculture Committee. He was a good guy from Kansas and a friend of Bob Dole.

I'm not sure I was right, though. Glickman never really used the bully pulpit the way I think he might have. He wasn't a farmer. He's an attorney and his closeness to farming was not as it should have been. I noticed the same thing about several Clinton appointees: they were not vocal or high profile. That may have been part of the Clinton style. He probably didn't want his people out front. All in all, I have no regrets. I think I would have tried pretty hard to have a much higher profile on farm issues than Glickman did, but maybe it was a no-win proposition.

I also had an interesting conversation with Clinton about the question of gays in the military. Our conversation had gone on for a long time and I said, "Bill, I have to get out of here, there are several people out there waiting to see you."

"Wait a minute," he said. "Do you have any last-minute advice for me?"

"Yeah, I do. I have a friend whose son committed suicide because he was gay and so tortured by the society in which he lived. You've got to fix this thing. It's tearing churches apart, tearing the country apart. You know what I know, the Constitution is pretty clear, everyone is the same, is treated the same."

"You know, by God you're right, I'll do that."[69]

The controversy of gays in the military contained a lot of interesting facets. Barry Goldwater put the controversy to rest. A reporter asked him in the heat of that whole discussion what he thought. The conservative Republican senator said he had fought alongside gay people throughout his career in the military and they were among the finest soldiers he'd ever known. That pretty much silenced it. At least it took a lot of people aback. Here we'd had one of the senior Republican statesmen saying it. I watched in agony as the debate played on and I've since learned that this "don't ask-don't tell" policy amplified the hatred that bigots had for Clinton.

I've always felt it fascinating that at the time the policy seemed like kind of a weak compromise. But in retrospect, it was the right approach at the time. It's not anybody's business what private lives are about. At least from the point of view of officialdom it should not be a question that's asked. As revolutionary as that policy was, it didn't turn out to be the perfect answer. After that policy change, Clinton did not have that gays-in-the-military controversy around. At least, not openly. It was not a frontal issue during his re-election campaign, but it was a matter that had to be dealt with.

When you think about the progress that's been made, Clinton did do a pivotal thing. He was without question the quickest study in a political figure I've ever known. Man, he caught on fast. And his perceptions were accurate.

I Was Never Speechless

I had my own homespun way of doing things with speeches. While I greatly appreciated the research and work that went into speeches prepared for me, it was pretty rare that I took a prepared text and used it as it was written. I don't know what that was about. It was just that some expressions seemed too formal for me. However, I rarely doctored up the technical speeches that people prepared unless I couldn't understand what I was saying.

I remember right from the start I never did a prepared speech without having somebody look at what I had written. Admittedly, when others wrote for me I changed pretty much everything in most of them. But there were always two or three hands involved because you can't check it all and you don't think of half of it. I don't present written speeches well. I prefer notes and I like to use quotations because I think they help tell a message.

The best speakers I've heard show some passion about their subject. I displayed that passion frequently in my speeches. The more heartfelt the issue is the more passionate I get. In the sales tax fight in 1989 I was passionate. My son Eric told me I sounded angry.

Another time I found myself pretty passionate during a talk about art to a meeting called the Dakota Centennial Arts Congress in Aberdeen, South Dakota.[70] This time it was passion in a good way. I had been thinking about how to explain the importance of art and what it was and I remember getting pretty strong in my verbal presentation of my thoughts. I remember my comments were applauded because they were heartfelt.

I told that audience of artists and art patrons how throughout history it has often been pointed out that the human spirit has a likeness to God. "And that likeness has for the most part been characterized as existing in the intellect and the will. And serious art, therefore, is a very spiritual experience."

I noted that the individual expanses of the spirit and the will, in each separate artist, determine the purpose and the service of his or her creation. I added that, "It's to the expansion of the human experience and human understanding through these spirited encounters that good art contributes." Also, that, "The artist, in literature and theater and painting and music and in all art forms, broadens our vantage point," and provides an expansion that gives us all new perceptions of truth and goodness. "It's important to understand also that truth, and goodness, and beauty are one."

In concluding my remarks I emphasized that artists have therefore enriched our states, our collective culture, and our collective spirits.

I don't think I had enough passion in my State of the State speeches, though. In the first one, even as confident and self-assured as I was, I remember being nervous. You're looking out at your peers and wondering what do *they* think. Those were the most ceremonial of the speeches. And even though we provided printed copies of the text to the news media, thoughts would come to me and I would pencil in changes right up to the time I spoke the words.

I've seen myself extremely passionate on TV, but usually the passion is more evident in the candid presentations that are less formal.

I remember quoting, in my first inaugural speech, "The Calf Path" poem by Sam Walter Foss, which I loved and still love. I first knew of the piece in January of 1972 when it was placed on the desks of the ninety-eight delegates who assembled in Bismarck for the historic state Constitutional Convention. The poem, which was written in 1895, described how we blindly follow past thinking and resist change. It seemed to me that we were all guilty of being mired in the kind of mindset embodied in the teaching of the "Calf Path" and that we simply have to look outside the box. It's like churchmen who think that church tradition should be just the way it was when they were a child, or just the way it was in a certain era. So we tend to think that political boundaries are sacred and should not be changed. I wanted legislators to do things and not meander along a calf path. The slightly abbreviated version I used of the poem warrants repeating here:

One day thru the primeval wood
A calf walked home, as good calves should,
But made a trail, all bent askew,
A crooked trail, as all calves do.
Since then three hundred years have fled,
And I infer the calf is dead,
But still, he left behind his trail,
And thereby hangs my moral tale.

The trail was taken up next day
By a lone dog that passed that way.
And then, a wise bellwethered sheep
Pursued the trail, o'er vale and steep,
And drew the flock behind him too,
As good bellwethers always do.
And from that day, o'er hill and glade
Thru those old woods, a path was made.

And many men wound in and out,
And dodged, and turned, and bent about,
And uttered words of righteous wrath
Because 'twas such a crooked path,
But still they followed, do not laugh,
The first migrations of that calf.
And thru the winding woods they stalked
Because he wobbled when he walked.

This forest path became a lane
That bent, and turned, and turned again.
This crooked lane became a road
Where many a poor horse with his load
Toiled on beneath the burning sun
And traveled some three miles in one.

And thus a century and a half
They trod the footsteps of that calf.

The years passed on in swiftness fleet,
The road became a village street.
And this, before men were aware,
A city's crooked thoroughfare.
And soon the central street was this
Of a renowned metropolis.
And men, two centuries and a half
Trod in the footsteps of that calf.

Each day a hundred thousand route
Followed the zig-zag calf about,
And o'er his crooked journey went
The traffic of a continent.
A hundred thousand men were led
By one calf, near three centuries dead.
They followed still his crooked way
And lost one hundred years per day.
For this such reverence is lent
To well establish precedent.

A moral lesson this might teach
Were I ordained, and called to preach.
For men are prone to go it blind
Along the calf paths of the mind,
And work away from sun to sun
To do what other men have done.
They follow in the beaten track,
And out, and in, and forth and back,
And still their devious course pursue
To keep the path that others do.

They keep the path a sacred groove
Along with all their lives they move.
But how the wise old wood gods laugh
Who saw the first primeval calf.
Ah, many things this tale might teach,
But I am not ordained to preach.

I also often quoted Sir Alex Fraser Tytler, a Scottish jurist and historian who wrote a piece around 1800 about the folly of democracy, emphasizing that democracies don't last because people want everything they can get from the government while they don't want to pay for it. As Tytler said:

> A democracy cannot exist as a permanent form of government. It can only exist until the voters discover that they can vote themselves largess from the public treasury. From that time on the majority always votes for the candidates promising the most benefits from the public treasury, with the results that a democracy always collapses over loose fiscal policy, always followed by a dictatorship. The average age of the world's great civilizations has been 200 years. These nations have progressed through this sequence: from bondage to spiritual faith; from spiritual faith to great courage; from great courage to liberty; from liberty to abundance; from abundance to selfishness; from selfishness to complacency; from complacency to apathy; from apathy to dependency; from dependency back again to bondage.

Particularly early on with my speeches, partly to offset my serious comments about problems and challenges our state faced, I referred to North Dakota as having "a singular elegance." I called it "a diamond in the rough, a jewel in the crown of states and provinces that is North America." I also used what we called "the litany."[71] That was a list of products and accomplishments where North Dakota ranked first, such as in production of various agricultural crops, and where we ranked high, such as in petroleum and coal and energy. I also talked about our clean air and our clean water and our ranking lowest in both violent crime and incarceration rates. When we left office we also had the lowest rate of repeat criminals. There's been a dramatic change in that whole prison incarceration picture, much of which was driven by two phenomena: mandatory sentencing and methamphetamines. It isn't quite fair to blame subsequent administrations for the incarcerations resulting from the meth syndrome, but it took a long time for people to really push for treatment.

In my speaking occasions, I tried hard to concentrate on substance. Part of it is my nature. As I've said, I'm very issues oriented. Substance suffers when we too often give way to high-sounding, appealing speeches. I concentrate on making the truth as I see it acceptable to people so they can understand what it is about and not be offended by my presentation.

Some people are absolutely expert at making things sound good but don't concentrate on substance. In this regard I was critical of Ronald Reagan as a leader. He had incredible communication skills, but I knew firsthand how distant he was from the day-to-day challenges that affect us. To me, every public servant must avoid doing what Ronald Reagan did so well in convincing people of things that he really didn't know much about.

Keep 'Em Laughing

I don't know why humor is so important in giving speeches but it's always helped me, maybe because it relaxed me and the audience, as well. I wanted people to understand I knew about the real world and that I was just an ordinary guy. A lot of my speeches were heavy and issue-oriented, so it was a way of putting a little ice under the hot stuff.

At major speeches and major undertakings I almost always pray for guidance. I still try to reduce the formality of situations by humor.

There are a lot of people, including my press secretary among the best, who have a way of creating humor. I was never good at that. My one-liners were darn few. But many people remember a line I used to introduce Billy Graham when he brought his crusade to the North Dakota State University football field in 1987. I had been reluctant as governor to participate in public religious endorsements. Howard Binford called me four times so I finally contacted Father Emeric Lawrence for advice. "Billy Graham is about twenty cuts above those other preachers," he said, so I agreed to participate. While meeting privately with Reverend Graham for about an hour beforehand, I was surprised to learn he was self-taught and had never attended a seminary.

Then it came time for his introduction to the huge crowd of maybe 25,000. "It's all together appropriate that a Sinner introduce this man of God," I said at the podium. People still mention remembering that line.

Then I turned to Reverend Graham and pointed out that the crowd was probably predominantly Lutheran and of Scandinavian heritage, including maybe 20 percent Catholics along with several other faiths. That set up my story about the ongoing debate between a Lutheran minister and the Catholic priest over which was the *true* religion. The two of them had agreed whichever of them died first would ask God and let the other know.

The Lutheran pastor happened to go first and when he went to heaven he told God about this disagreement. "You've run the race and finished the course," God said. "I'll take care of it."

Shortly thereafter, the priest got a letter postmarked Heaven. He opened it.

"Dear Father," the letter said, "all religions are the same."

It was signed: "God, ELCA."

Everyone at all familiar with religious denominations like the Evangelical Lutheran Church in America understood that punch line.

Reverend Graham did a fine job, although I wasn't comfortable when he asked all who were making a spiritual commitment to come forward for the altar call.

If I heard a story I liked I would make a couple notes. Then I would try to abbreviate it as much as I could. Too many stories take too long and I tried pretty hard to keep them brief. Some of them defied that. Janie to this day gets upset with me because she thinks my reputation as a storyteller takes precedence over substance. But that's okay; I think it makes me feel more comfortable with people when I laugh with them.

One of my stories at a pretty serious event was memorable for a lot of people. I gave the commencement address at St. John's University in 1992 and they were also awarding me an honorary doctorate.[72] I began by saying that governors generally aren't held in high esteem. As an example I told of my visit one day in Cavalier to Chuck Fleming's uncle Franklin Page who was the oldest living former legislator. Franklin was in a nursing home and he was dying, so I didn't spend much time with him. Leaving through the community room I felt someone tugging on my coat. Here was this old man in a wheelchair. "Say," he said, "are you the governor?"

"Yes sir, I'm the governor."

He looked at me and said: "By golly, you look a lot better on TV than you do in real life." I laughed so hard that night I could barely give the talk at my next meeting.

The other governor joke I dearly love was told by Al Simpson, the former senator from Wyoming, at Governor Mike Sullivan's retirement dinner. It was about the day a highway patrolman stopped a cattle rancher for driving too fast with his eighteen-wheeler, having just unloaded a load of feeder cattle. The trooper walked up to the driver's window and said, "Say cowboy, you're going way too fast."

And the old rancher looked down and said, "Why do you say that, son?"

"Look, I've got you clocked at twenty-five miles an hour over the speed limit. Haven't you got a *governor* in that thing?"

"Nah," the driver said, "that smell's coming from the trailer."

Al Simpson told another one on Sullivan that night, about how the governor had gone to a nursing home to visit a former state employee whose health had deteriorated, but he couldn't find his room. So the governor stopped a nurse, "Ma'am, can you help me find—"

She said, "Sir, I'm on the way to a patient. Look, I've got to go."

"You don't know who I am, do you?"

"No, but if you go up to the front desk maybe they can help you," she quipped.

Humor like that is priceless. If you can remember to tell a joke on yourself it's never that offensive.

The vice president of academic affairs at St. John's was a nun named Sister Eva Hooker. She was an extremely bright lady and introduced me as I sat next to her near the podium, which was on the high altar of the church at St. John's. After being introduced, I was standing with my back to her speaking to the couple thousand people in the audience. I talked to them about not getting any respect. Although I'm not Rodney Dangerfield, self-deprecating humor often works well for me.[73]

And I said to the commencement crowd, "I come to St. John's, my alma mater, which is actually honoring me, and what do I do:

I'm actually seated next to a hooker." The place just burst out laughing. It was one of those fortuitous bits of humor that was a good thing because it took the heaviness off the whole event. It was my best speech ever, by far, and it is one I reuse parts of it often (see Appendix pages 317–327).

Humor in even that serious a setting was really important. Most of that St. John's speech was serious, though. I talked about problems of society but also emphasized that there is cause for optimism. "There is hope that we can learn from our failings," I said. "Democracy, at least American democracy, was born of the belief that the cacophony and chaos of conflicting causes and concepts can be converted into a kaleidoscope of calm compatibility." Obviously I love alliteration. Maybe a bit too much at times.

"That's what we believe," I continued. "That's what we are committed to. We believe that the commonality of human needs is discoverable and governable by a government of the people, by the people, and for the people." It's pretty edifying to see this theme running through a lot of my stuff.

I heard Mario Cuomo[74] give the commencement address at Stanford one year when we had a son graduating there. It's pretty bizarre because the Stanford kids bring in champagne bottles under their robes and when the speaker starts talking they pop the corks to see if they can hit him. They shot corks all over the place and Cuomo was really cool about it. He said, "You know something, you guys, I'd have been hit twenty times in New York. Don't they teach you to aim champagne bottles out here at Stanford?" It broke everyone up.

CHAPTER THIRTEEN: embracing hard choices

Tough Duty

I loved the issues and embraced them with a certain amount of relish. I wasn't frightened at all by the challenge or controversy. Even though I'm not at all an in-depth, scholarly person, I was comfortable with my thought process. I pick up on most things pretty rapidly in conversations. But there were things I worried about until I got at them. Clearly personnel problems were the most difficult and I think that's true for just about everyone.

One particularly difficult instance was when I had to ask Fred Haeffner to resign as Economic Development Commission director.[75] It was hard to find a good person for that position. Fred followed Bob Whitney, who was good but kind of bored with the job. Two of Fred's mutual friends had suggested his name. I was close to and am good friends with both of them. Fred was born in Fargo. He had retired as a major general and he'd had some pretty significant management roles in the Air Force and in the corporate world after the Air Force. Darrell Schroeder had suggested Fred to me and was his main proponent. Adjutant General Alex Macdonald knew him too, and spoke highly of him as a person.

I loved Fred but I had made a mistake in appointing him. Even though he had a passion for North Dakota, he didn't seem to like the complexity of economic development. The programs were so important and unless Fred understood them he just wasn't going to get the job done. Fred had a tendency to give long speeches about his love for North Dakota. That was wonderful but reports were getting pretty consistent that it just was not working.

I agonized over it and I knew I had to do it. Eventually, one morning I walked over there and said, "Fred, it isn't working." It was March of 1991 and he had been on the job only about eight months.

To my great relief, Fred said he already knew. "Don't feel bad that I must leave," he said. "It's okay."

I told his widow this story after Fred died suddenly not long afterward. They had moved to Fargo. He was a spiritual man. I revealed to her the agony I went through but that I knew I had to do it and went ahead and did it. And how he accepted it and made it easier for me. She told me Fred had had a small stroke and was in the hospital and doing rather well by all reports. But then one night she was there until nine o'clock or so and had gone home. The next morning the phone rang early and Fred said "Dear, can you come over right away?"

"It'll be a while before I can get ready," she said.

"No," he said, "I want you to come as soon as you can, I don't think I'm going to be here long."

"Fred, what are you talking about?" she said. "The doctor told me you were doing great."

"Come on over and I'll tell you," he said.

She went over. He said to her, "Honey, when I awakened this morning there were angels all around my bed singing to me and telling me how wonderful life was going to be. It was the most wonderful experience and I think I'm going to be leaving."

"Fred, you must have been hallucinating," she said. "I checked again and the doctor said you were doing fine."

I don't know what time of the morning that was but he died not too long afterward. She never doubted that the angels were actually there with him. She said she'd had two or three friends who had similar experiences and she believes they happen. "So do I," I told her, and I most certainly did and do.

I remember how she appreciated hearing that, but I was sad about losing Fred because he was a dear man.

I should have been better at it, but I did try to go and talk personally with people who were being released; even with the Olson appointees we didn't keep. The only exception I can recall was the

Game and Fish commissioner Dale Henegar, who had lied to me. He had embarrassed me and I was so angry I knew it would be a mistake if I went to see him.

Manitoba Premier Gary Filmon called me and said we were growing a European fish called zander down here. I picked up the phone to Henegar and he said we absolutely do not have zander. So I told Filmon. Several months later the premier called again and told me his fisheries people were still insisting that we had zander down here some place. I called Henegar again; he denied it again.

Finally somebody who worked for federal Fish and Wildlife Service—I can't remember who—came in and told me that we do in fact have zander, in Spiritwood Lake, a closed pool. The Game and Fish Department's experiment with the imported species had begun in 1987.[76] Zander was considered an exotic species in the United States but the fish could thrive in the kinds of turbid water found in many North Dakota lakes.

The zander initiative hit rough water when Manitoba and the three states surrounding us worried about the potential impact of stocking it here. The first batch of zander eggs, which had been imported from Holland, was destroyed over fears of disease but tests later showed the eggs to be disease free. Our Game and Fish Department then got zander eggs from Finland and a large number were eventually stocked into Spiritwood Lake. The department later scrapped the project but some zander still inhabit that lake today.

I was enraged when I learned that we did have a zander population and that Manitoba had it right. Henegar's term ended shortly after that and there was no way I could put him back in. A few people were pretty angry. John Lohman wrote a long article in *The Forum* railing about the evil things I'd done. Afterward I saw Lohman one day at a meeting and he said I never agreed with you but I guess you did okay. I don't recall commenting about the appointment to anybody and I don't know that I was ever personally confronted. But I remember the Canadians were particularly upset about the zander. And with cause.

I do remember going to see Highway Commissioner Duane Liffrig, an Olson appointee. I just had to say I didn't think it would work out for him to remain in that position. That was hard because he badly wanted to stay. But I did it and in a timely fashion. We parted friends, although I did not know him real well.

Dismissing the securities commissioner was also difficult. I'd actually helped him get that job from Governor Olson. I began to learn that however brilliant he was in securities he was a terrible manager and didn't know how to delegate. The work in that office was way behind.[77]

One appointment I didn't make but wanted to would have been Chuck Stroup to head the Economic Development Commission after the PACE program was adopted. I would have appointed him if I hadn't been shouted down literally by some of the staff and others around me. I always thought that Chuck Stroup was the right kind of big-thinking person rather than a detail person. After he was later appointed by Ed Schafer, Chuck in many ways ran that place the way it should be run even though he was criticized by some because he didn't get around to the regions a lot. But it's not a heavily staffed organization. You can't have everyone running around the state giving speeches. Chuck Stroup was wonderful on the Committee of 100.[78] He was not only instrumental in developing the Growing North Dakota Program, he also helped sell it.

Getting It Done

The power in a Governor's Office is incredible. When you think about our executive orders, we did them because they were needed and because they were right. To name just two of the many: the smoking ban and creating the Lignite Research Council were both done by executive order.[79]

A governor can do a lot of things. When we settled the Lewis and Clark area dispute I literally told Lisa Novacek and Lloyd Jones I didn't care what federal law said. People had been told that they could farm that land for as long as it was farmable. We were going to honor that because it was the decent thing to do. It seemed to me there was an incredible amount of power there, properly used and used when needed.

I had no quarrel with the power of the governor in regard to the Bank of North Dakota and its oversight by the Industrial

Commission, which is made up of the governor, attorney general, and agriculture commissioner. That structure is healthy. It demands a competent and ethical administrator running the bank. You must have officers at the bank and at the Housing Finance Agency and other agencies that are honest and open and who tell you the facts. That joint decision making by the Industrial Commission over some of those things is fine. It certainly worked out well for us when we were there.

What Warren Emmer of the Parole and Probation Division did for us was also symptomatic of the importance of competent state agency heads. Warren taught me and everyone else how to deal with prisoners. Even with prisoners for whom the outlook is grim, you absolutely have to apply the corrections philosophy and role rather than just administer punishment. A high percentage of incarcerated people eventually get out of prison. Warren Allen, the parole board member from Minot, was really good. I didn't know him before but I knew his father, who had been a hardcore right-wing Republican. Warren was the longest serving member on the parole board and he saw this whole thing clearly.

When we left the Governor's Office, we had the lowest percentage of our people incarcerated of the fifty states and probably most importantly we had the lowest rate of repeat criminals. It was due to the fact that Warren Emmer and his staff monitored the prisoners and parolees regularly. They tracked people who were going to get out in the next three or four years, made sure they had release time for work, and that they had special training as well as counseling. He would often recommend they be let out a little early so they got out with a good attitude, because attitude was huge.

The probation people helped them get jobs and helped them get back into civilian life. It was working like you'd never believe it could. Warren and the others on that staff were classic examples of how important is it to have professionals and to listen to them.

When I think of all the stuff we did, it's impossible for me to remember whose input was most significant. There are so many good departments and agencies and dedicated people working in them. A few years ago I went out to the Country Kitchen to meet some people who were coming through town. I walked in and there were three highway patrolmen sitting there. So I went over, sat down, and asked them how they all were doing. They said it's going really well. Then one of the troopers asked me whether I remembered the day I told them they were servants, not tyrants. He said that helped the patrolmen finally understand that people treat them well so they must treat people well.

I was really flattered by the whole thing.

The story goes back to 1985 and one of my first agency visits, which was to the Highway Patrol. Superintendent Brian Berg asked me to come over and speak. The troopers were all there. I told them that we're here to serve. That we've got to take crap from people and not dish it out. We've got to treat people right even when they're mad at us. Then I told them a story: "Years ago my dad, who had had two heart attacks, came home after attending a cattle auction. Along the way he'd had a confrontation with a patrol trooper. Dad was as white as a sheet when he walked into the house. The family thought he was having another attack." My audience got really quiet. "My dad was irascible but the patrolman shouldn't have picked up on it," I said. "They came to blows. The patrolman shouldn't have let it happen, even though I knew it was my dad's fault."

When we walked out Brian asked me if I knew who it was. "Of course I do," I said. I told Brian the name of the patrolman who had fought with my father.

"He was sitting right in front of you," Brian said.

And so it was pretty edifying to learn many years later that they had understood what I had told them…and remembered.

Give Me Issues

I hated it when we'd go through an issue and then be expected to turn around and re-discuss it in terms of its political implications. You can't in good conscience make a decision on its merit and then turn around and re-decide it on a political basis and end up with what is right. It was important to help people understand—that's what I loved. I suppose that desire to teach was what made me write papers on some topics and be willing to discuss them with lots of people. I just loved the learning periods. One of the things I cherished about chairing the House tax committee was how much useful stuff I learned.

During an interview when we were about to leave office, Lloyd Omdahl looked back on the 1989 referrals and observed that people were negative about government when our state was struggling economically.[80] He said:

I think the most serious trend that we had to face was the antagonism of the citizenry against the public sector and the refusal to trust state government with the kinds of funds to actually provide the programs that ought to be provided in this state. The people have refused. While demanding increased quality in service and increased services, they have been unwilling to pay for them. Without the tax revenue to do that you're just not going to be able to continue the quality of life in North Dakota. Governor Sinner has done a masterful job, in my opinion, over the eight years he's been in office, and has not had any extra money available for new initiatives and new programs at the same time he was seeing the many needs that were growing in North Dakota. We've really been borrowing time in this state in areas of economic development, in education, in transportation, in infrastructure, and in all of our areas we've just been borrowing time until people realize that we cannot have the quality of life we talk about as long as we're unwilling to pay for it.

North Dakota was founded by pioneers who looked to the future, their lives were pretty miserable but they looked to the future for what their investment would result in a generation or two. And that's how we built this state, but now we seem to have a generation that isn't willing to make those investments in the future, they want to have immediate consumption. And because they want to use all of their resources for immediate consumption, they aren't willing to defer some items for the future like paying taxes now so we can have a better road system for the next thirty years, pay taxes now so we can have a better education system and kids can have a chance to compete in a new world.

I think this sort of present-oriented materialism has sort of caught up with us, even on the national level when you look at the national deficit. A deficit is really spending on today's needs with future money. It's stealing from future generations. We're doing the same thing in North Dakota.

Ronald Reagan has been blamed for generating the anti-public-sector mood. He was sort of the breeze that fanned the flames. It certainly hasn't helped to have a chief policy spokesman in the country who keeps saying that government is incompetent and government is bad, the public sector is bad. All of this at the same time the things we call quality of life like parks and education and scenery are in the public sector. What's government? Government is parks and schools and highways, and when you condemn government you're condemning parks and schools and highways and human programs.

There's a lot of wisdom in Lloyd's perspective, but I didn't see all of that. A right-wing group influenced people negatively at times, as in the referral election, but in the end people appreciated candor and really responded to good things. A classic example was the response of the effort to take underprivileged children from all over North Dakota to the state fair in Minot.[81] In how many states are you going to have whole communities help you gather the kids, provide the buses to bring the kids, have airmen volunteer to be their chaperones around the fairgrounds, and get them all back on the buses and haul them home without any negative incidents of any kind?

I thought Chuck Fleming was crazy when he said he wanted to do it. But I didn't care. Let him try. It was a good idea. He and Janis Cheney pulled the damn thing off. With the help of scores of volunteers including Jaycees organizations and Air Force personnel, they brought 2,300 underprivileged children to Minot. This was in 1987, which we had designated as the "Year of the Child" in North Dakota. I was indelibly touched by the scene of the tall, black airman with a Native American child clutching one hand and a little white child clutching the other as they explored the exhibits and screamed in delight on the Murphy Brothers midway rides.

One of the really edifying things that's happened to me was about three or four years ago. We were in Tucson visiting some friends and went to a country club for lunch. We were standing in line waiting to be seated when somebody tapped me on the shoulder. It was State Senator Dave Nething, a Republican from Jamestown. After hello and all that, Nething said, "You have no idea how we miss you. When you were there we worked together to solve the problems, and now people are more interested in *taking credit* for solving the problems than they are in *solving* the problems. The problems don't get much attention. I don't know what's happened, I don't know why it's that way, but it's pretty frustrating."

One night General Alex Macdonald and I were sitting at a reception having a drink. A prominent man in town came by and said, "You know what, you guys did a hell of a job when you were out there." We both thanked him.

Mac leaned over and said, "You know why we did such a good job?"

"I don't really know that I did, but what do you think?"

"Because you let us run the agencies," Mac said.

Then he reminded me that I told them at every cabinet meeting they had to run the place. I said we couldn't do it out of the Governor's Office because we didn't know enough. But they have to tell us when we could help them. Lloyd Omdahl described this system as follows:

It's a combination of close management style and also a loose management style in some ways in that he [Sinner] has given agencies some latitude in operating and being creative to the needs of the people they're serving. We have these twice-a-month cabinet meetings, which had not been conducted by previous governors with whom I've been involved. He does have a reporting system through which they feel accountable but at the same time they have room to do what needs to be done.

The other thing I was careful about when talking to the agencies was to thank them for the work they did. It's impossible to appreciate adequately the fact that new governors come in and really don't know much. Yet state government goes on, kind of by automatic pilot. The agencies continue operating for a long time before the governor figures out what the problems are and how to help. That's most amazing in a place like North Dakota where few of the governors have had much state government experience. Of course Art Link spent a long time in the legislature and one term in Congress, and Bill Guy was also a legislator. Al Olson certainly had a lot of state government experience, as attorney general and working for the Legislative Council earlier, but many governors do not and yet everything runs during the long learning curve period.

The second thing we always told them: "I don't care what announcements need to be made, you make them. You don't need to clear them with anybody. All I ask is you tell the truth and we'll be there." It hadn't been that way before. Somebody up at the Governor's Office always wanted to look over every press release and put the governor's name in to take credit. My press secretary and I had a few arguments about that too and I remember telling him one day, "Look I don't like that, I don't like taking credit for stuff. The opinion makers will figure it out." Anyway, I was just ecstatic with Mac's comment and I've thought about it a lot.

Producing Solutions

My past involvement in agriculture, even in national policy, led me to conclude pretty early that was one area for me to personally follow as governor. The same was true with petroleum and the energy field. Not so much because of my past but because my regular daily involvement with the State Industrial Commission provided a crash course in those issues. But there were all kinds of areas where I simply relied on members of the staff to tell me how things should go and what course of action should be pursued.

Generally speaking my staff and I wanted to have every issue be sacred and we gave every one of them our best shot without reference to partisan politics. Some things were difficult to get a handle on because there were so many facets to them but there again the ability of the staff was invaluable to me. We were constantly consulting with agency heads and finding people who would tell us what the truth was. Also Earl Strinden[82] and some of the other Republican leaders and I had a pretty good understanding on how things were done. One business group came in and said they'd never had such good access to the governor as they had in our office. That was just the way we thought it should operate.

I took huge satisfaction in achievements on problems we had worked for a long time to resolve. Growing North Dakota included policies and initiatives like the PACE program. Another was the Match program, through which the Bank of North Dakota offers loans at lower-interest rates and attracts financially strong companies in manufacturing, processing, and value-added industries. The 1991 legislature implemented the package by approving a $21 million budget for economic development, four times larger than any previous budget. The funds came from Bank of North Dakota earnings.

Growing North Dakota got started when Wally Beyer was chairman of the Economic Development Commission. The EDC was later renamed Economic Development and Finance and became governed by one appointed executive director. As Chuck Fleming recalls, Wally came to the Governor's Office one day and said that economic development in North Dakota was too fragmented and we needed to get it better organized and focused. He said there were so many competing interests and they had to be brought together. Wally said it would take one tough son of a bitch to get everyone working together. I asked Wally who he had in mind to make it happen and he pointed at Chuck. So I got out of my chair and went to the white board in my office and we started listing organizations involved in economic development. The list went from five to ten to twenty and kept going as Chuck began to panic thinking of trying to ride herd over all these people.

In the 1980s, farm foreclosures had become another knotty situation. If we hadn't found an answer for the banks the drama would have been far more tragic. The answer we came up with saved many farms at least for ten or fifteen years and we didn't lose a bunch of banks.

Numerous meetings took place and so many hours were spent finding an answer to the problem the banks all faced, particularly the farm creditors. They had loaned more money than the land was currently worth and there wasn't any hope of being paid back. Foreclosures left ownership of the farm in the bank's hands but the anti-corporate farming laws limited the banks from keeping the farms more than three years before they had to sell them. There was no way they could win. Banks didn't know how to deal with their own policies, which required them to foreclose. We had worked and worked trying to find an alternative to this scenario. Early one morning, I was lying in bed unable to sleep and suddenly realized that if the lender had a good farmer it should rewrite the loan to a level the farmer could handle and then provide for reclaiming the money at the end of a certain number of years if the value returned.

Right away from the office I called a man named Larry Biegler at the St. Paul Farm Credit Bank and told him. He said I was absolutely right and they put the policy into effect immediately.[83] Somebody later at the local farm credit bank said everyone thought Larry Biegler walked on water because *he'd* come up with the answer, which was fine with me.

The word spread rapidly that that was the best solution, everyone adopted it and as far as I know we didn't lose a bank. Who knows how many farmers had been abandoned and how many banks actually foreclosed, but it was a huge, huge day when we realized there was a solution to the problem. It turned out later that many of the farmers were in trouble when the ten years were up. Many went down the tube in the early and middle nineties, but at least they had that time to make a more sane adjustment in their lives.

One of the economic development leaders that I liked, Bill Patrie, was actually critical of me for being too cautious in economic development. He believed that you should have some failures, that you should give money to help more risky companies. I remember saying, "Bill, listen. Business failures end up leaving many communities with people owed money, people out of a job, the banks disenchanted, and they are double negatives for further economic development." Somewhere between what he believed and what I believed is probably right and the fact is the PACE program over time has proven to be helpful for well-planned, well-managed companies. But it is probably not sufficiently helpful for a little more imaginative entrepreneurial programs.

Some businesses do need a tax exemption for a short time. The time of their need varies widely according to industry. It was widely believed that at least five years were needed to get a sugar beet plant profitable because there are just so many start-up problems. But there are some companies that come into an area and are making big money from the get go, particularly retail types.

I don't know what the proper mix is. Venture capital funds are better positioned to assist them. It's embarrassing that we were unable to help companies like Great Plains Software to any great degree. We were unable to provide Great Plains with the kind of money needed because banks require some equity and the equity Great Plains had was all intellectual. It was pretty hard to put intellectual property on a balance sheet on a loan for credit that would guarantee a return. I remember many discussions with Joe Lamb about that. He didn't know how to handle it either and we didn't handle it well. Gratefully, Great Plains got money from somewhere. I'm sure the family put tons of money in there.[84] They had the faith that we probably had but couldn't articulate in terms of solid loans. There was also another company that had that same situation. Those were difficult choices and we may have been too cautious.

The most amazing was the movement of Marvin Windows and Doors into North Dakota. Marvin has done extremely well here, and Tecton Products, the new company that Marvin is part owner of, has also done extremely well. When the Marvins were originally trying to make a location decision they had already purchased an option in Wisconsin and had met four times with the Wisconsin governor Tommy Thompson to work out the details.

I don't remember who suggested we should go up to Warroad and visit with the Marvins, but I said set it up and we'll do it. We flew to that far-north Minnesota community in the state airplane on a bitterly cold winter day. I've learned since that what happened after we left there was totally unpredictable and unforeseen. We were sitting with the Marvin father, Bill, and the senior operators of the company at that time. Jake and Frank Marvin were the day-to-day operators. We had about four people with us. I can't remember who made the statement but in presenting our tax structure the person from North Dakota said our workmen's compensation premium rate was extremely low, and he quoted a figure.

But we knew the workmen's compensation bureau had already voted to raise the rate significantly. "Wait a minute," I said. "You better tell them the rest of the story—we didn't come here to blow smoke at these guys. We want them to be successful and we want to tell them the truth." He then backed up and, somewhat embarrassed, gave them the changed rate. I didn't know it until a friend told me the story much later, but after we left Bill Marvin said to his colleagues that they were going to North Dakota because we were the kind of people they wanted to work with. They made the decision that day.

Marvin Windows has been extremely successful in North Dakota and loves being here. The company had good offers from both Wahpeton and Fargo, so it had a big decision to make about location. I've since learned that Fargo was chosen because they could rely on a supply of degreed, well-trained scientists—they have mostly North Dakota graduates working in their technical division.

I don't think anybody questioned that this state was way too production oriented. The production economy helped produce the closeness I had with governors from similar states. Four of us were good friends: I and Republicans George Mickelson of South Dakota and Norm Bangerter of Utah and Democrat Mike Sullivan of Wyoming were all elected about the same time and all had exactly the same set of problems, which resulted from having largely a production economy.

Bangerter and I, in particular, spoke out about economic concerns. Norm was a Mormon bishop and an extremely good governor. Utah had quite a bit of agriculture and lots of mining and minerals, along with natural resources. The Great Salt Lake was experiencing decline and Norm needed to do some major projects. He was roundly criticized for spending this money. But like every thinking person he knew that they couldn't ignore the problem.

Norm's major fundraiser in his first campaign was a right-wing Republican who then turned against him and ran as an independent in the fall of 1988 when we were both up for reelection. The Democrats' ran the mayor of Salt Lake, Ted Wilson, who was a good candidate. Bangerter was the only sitting Republican governor that the first President Bush—in deference to the conservative wing of the Republican Party—didn't help campaign. Every political analyst in the country wrote that Norm was one of the governors who wouldn't get back in. I talked to Norm frequently because he thought really well and he understood a whole lot of things. He kept saying, "You know, I think I might win this." Bangerter came from behind and won by a small percentage.

We were in close touch and late on election night we celebrated his victory because we had seen what a good and honest person he was. In the years that followed he and I talked a lot about our states' economies and how they were doing and how the overvalued dollar and deficit spending were hurting them. Both of us were doing a lot of speaking around the country and to some people Norm and I were the two "balance budget boys."

I don't know how to equate the debt in terms of current dollars but it's huge and I'm really worried that the country is sinking into a terrible problem again. It's pretty disappointing that people don't remember how those on both the far left and the far right were upset about the failure to pay our bills. A society can do some things that over time really benefit future generations more than the current one. But that doesn't work when, like now, we don't even come close to paying our bills. It was bad in the Eighties but it's worse now by far than it ever was then.

CHAPTER FOURTEEN: supporting critical industries

Helping Farms

The first year I was in office, the fall of 1985, my son Bob called. "Dad," he said, "there's a terrible scandal brewing at the county ASC "Agricultural Stabilization and Conservation Office." Do you know what PIK "payment-in-kind" certificates are?"

"Tell me again," I said.

So he explained to me what I pretty much understood that a PIK certificate was a certificate to claim money from the government when you sold your grain. It had an established value that went up if the market price fell. The value changed weekly.[85]

"Where's the scandal?" I said.

"The values are announced every Monday but for some strange reason the information on the value for the Monday announcement is sent to the county offices on Friday," he said. "Most of those people in there are farm people—spouses and farmers—and they're trading all weekend. This is going on all over the country."

"Bob, don't tell a soul about this. I will call Keith Bjerke and Milt Hertz of the USDA's Agricultural Stabilization and Conservation Service and I'll call the secretary of agriculture so there are enough people that know to get it fixed."

I talked to Keith first. I told him he didn't need to call me back but just get it fixed because we can't stand a scandal like this in the farm program. And then I told Milt the same thing. I called Agriculture Secretary Richard Lyng, who had been in the

Farm Bureau in California. I introduced myself, and then filled him in. I told him I didn't know how it happened but that there was a bad scandal brewing, and that I had asked the people who told me about it to keep it quiet and let me try to get it fixed.

They corrected it instantly. The scandal was nipped in the bud and it never hit the press. It never got to the extent it might have gotten, as far as I know.

After my first two years in office I became the lead governor on agriculture for the National Governors Association. By the middle of 1987, I followed Governor Terry Branstad of Iowa and became chair of the Governors' Agriculture and Rural Development Committee. The farm programs at the time were not adequate and we were losing a lot of farmers.

A terrible drought started in 1986 and continued through 1987 and into 1988. It almost devastated us.[86] Were it not for the huge helpful response of Secretary Lyng, the work of Kent Conrad, and the head of the House Agriculture Committee, Kika de la Garza from Texas, we would have experienced an even worse disaster than we did.

While talking to other governors at a conference in Idaho it became evident that about eight states were going to be devastated by the drought, which was getting worse and worse and came to be called another "Dirty Thirties" dust bowl. When I got home and back to my office I called Lyng. We had not talked in those intervening years. I had done some work on the farm bill with some of his staff but not directly with him. "Mr. Secretary, I've just come back from a governors' meeting and I think there are about eight states that are going to get blasted by the drought," I said. "With Governor Branstad to help me get some climatologists and some economists together in Chicago, would you come?"

There was a brief pause and he said, "You tell me when and where, Governor, and I'll be there."

That's exactly what happened. We met in late June of 1988.[87] Governors George Mickelson from South Dakota, Rudy Perpich from Minnesota, John Ashcroft from Missouri, and Jim Martin from North Carolina joined Branstad and me there. We had work sessions and briefings on livestock feed, water supplies, and crop and farm income. Climatologists forecasted that the drought would likely extend through '88 and maybe beyond. The economists told us it was going to decimate the farm population if something wasn't done. After agreeing on an approach at that Chicago session, we met in Washington with de la Garza, and Senator Pat Leahy, who chaired the Senate Agriculture Committee. Kent Conrad was probably the foremost brain on that committee and he and the rest of the staff who understood the numbers put the thing together. Earlier that summer, prior to our Chicago meeting, Lyng had been quoted saying drought assistance was premature. But he was now a strong believer and made our case to Congress. North Dakota farmers ended up with $488 million out of the $3.9 billion authorized in the Drought Relief Act, which President Reagan signed in August. The bill had amazingly passed in six weeks and saved a ton of people from bankruptcy.

The other result derived from the Chicago meeting was a trip that fall by Lyng to North Dakota. During his two days here he was unabashed in telling people about my important role in getting this farm relief done. We didn't see a lot of each other but we had a level of trust that few people have and he wanted to do what was right the same as I did. We shared a wonderful level of understanding.

Energy and Environment

In the early years, we were being deluged with environmental issues and it didn't take long to discover that many of the so-called environmental issues really were not about the environment. They were somebody's economic benefit or gain. We didn't ignore them but we were pretty discriminating about how far we went and what approach we took.

Two classic examples involved the Canadian government. The Arctic National Wildlife Refuge (ANWR) discussion was being exploited by the Canadian government and from what I could find out Canada drilled something like eighty-five test holes in 1983 and 1984 top to bottom alongside the ANWR. They found lots of oil. They were heavily into oil development in the lower border provinces, had no pipelines, and did not want competing development. So they started the ballyhoo about endangering caribou. As it turned out the caribou were never in trouble and were repopulating at an incredible rate. Even though I wasn't eager to see the oil deposits exploited, it seemed to me we needed reserves and we needed some place to keep the reserves and that looked to me like a good place. It was pretty obviously being exploited way beyond its significance environmentally. The frozen tundra area is so huge up there I felt certain the environmental significance was not what people were saying it was.

The same was true with the spotted owl in Washington. It became clear pretty early on there was nothing happening to impact the spotted owl population. In fact, the numbers were growing. Again, this was about the Canadian government, which owned the forests in Canada and was getting hurt in the market because American lumbermen received a government-sponsored stumpage removal subsidy. Canadians promoted both these issues for their own economic benefit.

During my first years as governor, with Reagan in the White House, Prime Minister Brian Mulroney of Canada was blasting almost weekly tirades against the United States and our terrible environmental reputation. Our electrical generating industry was under significant pressure to construct much more expensive and complex scrubbers on power plants. Yet industry people here told me that much of the pollution coming into western North Dakota originated in Canada, from two or three generators up near Estevan, Saskatchewan. You could see this layer of yellow coloration coming down at a low elevation around the Missouri River and a little to the west of the Missouri.

Then I learned Canada had no scrubbers of any kind on its coal-fired generators. I was at governors' conference and visiting with John Sununu, governor of New Hampshire, and telling him about this. "Listen," Sununu said. "We're getting flak over here. We're getting a lot of water out of Canada and it's the dirtiest, filthiest, most polluted stuff I've ever seen in my whole life."

So I said, "Let's go on the attack. I'm going home and will do a press release saying I'm tired of it and if Canada wants to be so environmentally holy, let them clean up their own house." Afterward the *Winnipeg Free Press* ran a headline saying Canadians are hypocrites on clean air. It was a damning story.

We then went in to see President Reagan. That was in the summer of 1986. Jim Baker, his chief of staff, was with him that time and I think the secretary of energy was there too. I remember sitting close and Baker was holding Reagan's arm as we spoke. Finally, seeing the confusion on the president's face, Baker said to him, "Mr. President, your friend Mr. Mulroney has been pulling your leg." The president looked so mystified about what we were telling him, almost starry-eyed at times. It was probably one of those bad days early on in his Alzheimer's.

Later a friend in the White House told me that during the last two years in office Reagan had four people working full time to make sure he didn't get lost. She also said in the mornings he could handle the press and do pretty well, but for two and a half years he was pretty sick. Clearly one of the heroes was Baker, who Nancy Reagan rightly trusted. Baker was knowledgeable. He really ran the government and was able to contain Henry Kissinger and Al Haig who were both power hungry.

The matter of deciding what the real problems were in the environmental discussions got a different reaction from me when we reached the conclusion to do something about surface water. Wetlands preservation had lots of things going for it. It helped restore ground water, reduced flooding and the drainage phenomenon that aggravates floods in many parts of the state, and it produces good wildlife habitat. After the policy was put in place we led the nation in wetlands preservation and I received the highest award given by the EPA for our accomplishments. Lloyd Jones, Jeff Weispfenning, and Lisa Novacek really did the work.

By the end of the 1980s I had moved from National Governors Association Agriculture Committee chair to Energy Committee chair because I also had headed the Interstate Oil Compact Commission, an organization of all twenty-nine oil producing states. In fighting some of the oil industry battles and at the same time trying to get the states to do a better job of environmental protection, I proposed a national meeting of all the environmental group leaders and all the energy industry people to find a way to move forward in a more compatible way.

I had challenged the federal government because there was a great effort in Congress and the federal administration to have the Environmental Protection Agency take over regulation of oil and gas exploration and production wastes from the states. The fact was that the EPA couldn't do what it was already trying to do. Most of the states managed their production wastes adequately and did so at less expense than it would cost the EPA. During a visit to Alaska's North Slope I learned a private team under contract with EPA had been up there investigating some of the production sites and had reported finding oil in the water ponds adjacent to the oil wells. I arranged for a meeting with this EPA team and got a copy of their report. Out at the specific sites I ran my hand through the water in these ponds and discovered in all six cases there was algae scum, but no oil. It looked like oil on the surface because it cast that rainbow-like look but it wasn't oil at all. My hand was dry within seconds.

I blasted really hard in a letter to EPA Administrator Bill Reilly questioning how that agency could possibly talk about taking over regulation when it had so little expertise. A lot of people were pretty grateful.[88]

Along with energy industry leaders, two other governors, Mike Sullivan of Wyoming and George Mickelson of South Dakota, shared my interest in finding a way to develop a national energy strategy. We formed the American Energy Assurance Council in 1987 and Apache Oil Company provided one of its executives, John Jenkins, to serve as executive director. I was the first AEAC chairman and learned that nobody was talking to anybody else. Environmentalists were jawboning mainly to themselves about problems they saw and the energy industry was damning the environmentalists for various things that were being said and happening in Congress because of environmental pressure. So we got the idea of trying to bring them together. Dick Gross worked with Jenkins and the staff of other governors, wrote a grant application, and, as I recall, we had about a million and a quarter dollars to hold a national meeting of the leaders in the environmental and energy fields to try get them to talk to each other.

Dick and John Jenkins pretty much organized it. The AEAC asked a renowned public disputes organization on the East Coast (the Harvard-MIT Public Disputes Program) to conduct what was called a National Energy Policy Simulation. That twenty-three-hour event in November 1988 brought together many of the stake-holders involved in the energy policy debate across the country. The whole thing turned out to be a pretty embarrassing episode because highly paid people that the Harvard-MIT organization brought in to facilitate the various group sessions didn't even bother to learn the jargon of the energy industry and probably not even of the environmental field. Half the time had to be spent explaining things, or they were misinterpreting them. Often, they didn't have a clue what people were talking about and they were making it up as they went along. We had raised and spent a lot of money on this effort, but no consensus was achieved.

After that disaster, we eventually started our own dispute resolution program here in North Dakota because we saw so many things that demonstrated the inability of people who were in the early stages of the consensus-building field to understand that to help they must know the issues. The strong feelings and lack of understanding that led to the people's rejection of tax measures in the 1989 referendum demonstrated the need for building consensus in North Dakota. That national energy exercise had demonstrated how *not* to do it. Dick worked with some of our state agency grant-writing people and proposed and received a significant grant from The Northwest Area Foundation to fund what was initially called the North Dakota Consensus Council. Larry Spears, a Quaker lawyer who had been assistant Supreme Court administrator, was chosen to head the staff. The North Dakota Consensus Council, which later became the Consensus Council Inc., has a bipartisan board and has done amazing work around the country and around the world as well as here. It is among the best in the country and remains a model for other consensus-building efforts.

In November of 1990, State Health Officer Bob Wentz wrote me a letter critical of the proposed Echo Mountain municipal solid waste incinerator and landfill near Sawyer. The public hearing on the company's permit application was scheduled for a few days after that. Wentz stated that he was "firmly opposed to permitting the landfill" and his preference would be "to approach the public hearing with an announced intent to deny the permit." He acknowledged that his position differed from his own Environmental Health Section staff members who were reviewing the permit application.

When that letter came I immediately asked Dick Gross to run around and stop its circulation because Wentz was going to be the hearing officer. Dick tried but it was too late, the letter was all over. Attorney General Nick Spaeth came in and said, "You've got to fire him (Wentz). This is ridiculous."

"I'm not going to fire him," I said. "He's a good health officer. He made a mistake." I liked Bob Wentz and his passion for doing things right so I didn't even chastise him. What was ironic was when the Sawyer landfill had first got on my screen I went back to the office and called Fritz Schwindt, who headed the Environmental Health Section. "What's the deal with the landfill? Are these guys meeting our requirements?"

"Absolutely," he said. "They're going far beyond them."

"I have to tell people that if they meet the standards they get approved," I said. "We don't play by changing rules here."

"Well that'll be great if you can do it, Governor," he said.

I doubt Bob Wentz knew he might be disqualifying himself as hearing officer when he wrote the letter. But I assume he knew Fritz was probably the next in line to hold the hearing. Both Fritz and Bob were honest to a fault.

However, it turned out that Wentz did preside over the hearing and he denied the permit in December 1990. Municipal Services Corporation pursued legal action and the Supreme Court ordered the state to reconsider the application. A second hearing was held in November 1992 with Fritz Schwindt as hearing officer. The Health Department eventually approved the permit after we left office and Bob Wentz was no longer state health officer. MSC agreed to increased treatments of some wastes, an onsite inspector, and a slight change in location of the site. The landfill is still operating there today although under different ownership.[89]

On another occasion I was asked to have dinner with waste management people. The only name that comes to mind is a man named Ryan. By then I was one of the senior governors and we were attending a governors' meeting in Washington. Janie and I and Chuck Fleming and Dick Gross went to join this group of Waste Management Inc. leaders from Chicago. They were promoting and looking for my support for huge regional landfills to hold hazardous products like paint cans. After a long presentation something wasn't ringing true because I'd never heard from anybody that this was really a serious problem. About a dozen people from this company sat around a great big round table. Finally Mr. Ryan asked, "Do you have any thoughts about this?"

"No, but I have a question. What's in this for your company?"

It got quiet and he said, "We get to haul it."

It was in my mind all through the discussion that these guys want to haul the waste and they want to set up this huge collection and delivery system. I never heard of it again. It was something that I had seen earlier—issues that weren't real. Economic interests traveled under the guise of an environmental concern, like we saw from the Canadians with their statements about power plant emissions and the spotted owl.

Goal for Coal

I was firm the day I told the coal industry people that if they wanted a bill passed they had to do it my way. As previously mentioned in the Chapter 8 section on Big Decisions, my worst mistake was with the coal severance tax veto the first year. I was embarrassed to have vetoed that tax cut in the first place under pressure from the Democratic Party. However, two years later when a new bill to cut the coal tax was being drafted, I was sure of another idea (Lignite Research Council) and stuck by my guns. The lignite industry's problems were familiar to me because we were involved with buying a lot of coal at American Crystal. The plants were using Montana-Wyoming coal. I had urged Crystal to burn North Dakota coal and they said they couldn't afford to because it cost way too much to transport and you can't get that much heat out of it. So the bill I strongly supported cut the tax even a little bit more than the previously vetoed measure, and it provided a two-cent check-off to the Industrial Commission to fund a Lignite Research Council, which I set up by executive order. The coal industry came in and didn't want two cents taken for research. I said: "I've been involved with a research fund that was started by the sugar beet growers. It wasn't my idea but I know how powerful it is. I will show you who I will put on the executive committee and the management board, and you will see that industry would have control of it. It's not academic, but it will involve academics. It's not labor, although they are involved. Industry will have control of it."

They insisted that they really didn't want it. But I told them if they wanted the tax cut that had to go with it. And that's the way it was passed.

The coal guys came back in three months later and said, boy we had no idea how powerful this could be. We had provided that the attorney general would sit in on all the meetings and keep them out of trouble and I had learned from some of my previous work that that was the way it had to be. It was just one of those state needs and I found out a way to do it.

I've also always been proud of helping save the coal gasification plant at Beulah.[90] The plant was built for $2.1 billion in 1984 as a pilot project in response to the energy crisis of the 1970s. Its purpose was to develop a process for making natural gas from lignite, a low-grade coal abundant in western North Dakota. Shortly after a consortium of energy companies built the plant, it defaulted on $1.5 billion in federal loans.[91] We convinced the federal Energy Department to sell it rather than tear it down. That sale was a huge coup.

I met with two of the final three bidders: Basin Electric Power Cooperative in Bismarck and Coastal Corporation, a Houston-based Fortune 500 energy company. I gave them both the same advice: if you want to make this work, bid it at a price you can afford and promise to share any profits that develop with the federal government. My sense was that Coastal's people were laughing at me telling them how to do their financing. I didn't even try to prejudice the choice by the US Department of Energy. Basin Electric listened and actually bid the way I had suggested and bought the plant from the Energy Department in October 1988. It's in place today and making pretty good money. Basin's newly formed Dakota Gasification Company subsidiary paid $85 million for the plant, and agreed to pass on some tax breaks and share revenues with the federal agency through 2009. They've done a great job with it. I'm proud that their CO^2 byproduct has a huge market now through its use in the enhanced secondary and tertiary processes for recovery of oil in Canada. In 2000 the plant began capturing carbon dioxide and piping it to an oilfield in Canada. A second oilfield was added in 2006.

If Coastal had gotten that bid I've been told it would have torn the plant down. Coastal is a huge company and big in oil and coal and natural gas. It owned American Natural Resources Company, which was part of the original ownership consortium under which the synthetic fuels plant had been such a fiasco. Coastal's bid indicated it wanted to take available tax credits for only three years, which guaranteed it would operate the plant for that long. Allen Wampler, assistant secretary of energy, told me later that the Energy Department had a strong suspicion the only reason Coastal wanted to buy the plant was to close it. Wampler said its failures may have been intentional and the original owners were all a party to it because they were afraid of the long-term competition from synthetic fuels. They didn't want that technology to develop.

The third finalist, California Edison subsidiary Mission Energy, submitted a bid that wasn't competitive.

CHAPTER FIFTEEN: getting wise counsel

What's Up, Doc?

When it came time to actually move to Bismarck after the 1984 election, there were many things to plan for. One of them was my health care. I called a long-time friend and doctor in Fargo, Gerry Kavanaugh, for advice. There was no hesitation on his part. "Ralph Dunnigan," he said.

It turned out that Ralph, who headed the University of North Dakota Family Practice Center, was Governor Olson's doctor, too. I got to see him fairly soon after moving to Bismarck because while we were still in the transition office I had a kidney stone. He also checked out my general health, which was pretty fair. I had been taking some blood pressure medications, which he reviewed, and there was also family history of serious coronary disease on my father's side. Ralph went right to work on both problems. To say we became instant friends would not be an over statement. I certainly liked him and was impressed by him.

In December of 1985, I had a terrible episode of hemorrhaging from an ulcer and Ralph took care of me.[92] I'd been at Minot for something and felt pretty weak. People were telling me I looked pale. I couldn't sleep that night and finally awakened Janie about four o'clock. She called Ralph. He said to bring me in right away. But when I tried to get up I passed out on the floor and she had to call an ambulance. They had to give me three units of plasma right there in the bedroom. The next morning it was on the front page of *The Bismarck Tribune.*

Over the years, Ralph also took care of several broken bones. I broke my pinkie three times playing basketball, fractured my kneecap playing basketball, and broke my tibia playing basketball. I was a little bit of a hard charger on the basketball court and it was a great time. Playing against John Dwyer (President of the North Dakota Lignite Energy Council) was part of the problem, as he isn't exactly the most delicate elephant on the floor. Two specialists at the doctor's office looked at my broken kneecap. One of them wanted to cast the thing. The other doctor said it might be controlled with a bandage. I chose the bandage.

In late 1986 I had a detached retina, which I had discovered while in Washington for the wedding of one of my children. I called the ophthalmologist back home. He said, "You are describing a detached retina to me, leave what you are doing—come immediately. If we don't fix that immediately you may lose your eye."

I went as he advised. He had a plane reservation for me and had scheduled surgery at the University of Minnesota Hospital.[93] The operation was successful and most of my vision came back.

Speaking of vision, outdoors broadcaster Tony Dean, who had become a friend, called one day and asked if he could shoot video of me hunting. I spent all day with several people and couldn't hit a pheasant. I missed even perfect shots. I'd never been a good shot but I couldn't even hit one all day. Finally they threw up a dead bird and I shot at it as it came down.

I didn't figure out what the devil was wrong until many years later when hunting grouse with my sons and sons-in-law. I walked back across the field to get the car when a covey of partridge got up. I didn't get a shot right away but I watched them. Partridge, unlike pheasants or grouse, don't move much. They stay where they land. So I walked right up to them, picked a bird, and shot. The wad from the shell veered about ten degrees to the left. I knew instantly what the trouble was: I was left-eye dominant. People who hunt much shoot with both eyes open. The right eye is supposed to pick up the bird in the sight in line with the barrel. But my left eye was actually picking up the sight so my shot was going to the left, maybe ten or fifteen degrees. So I found a way to shield my left eye. It's fairly simple: I put a cover on the upper left end corner of my glasses and when my head goes down to the barrel that piece of tape will black out my left eye so my right eye is forced to pick up the bird. I actually hit one once in a while now. Not many, usually, but there are exceptions.

I have suffered with almost daily headaches for a long time and occasionally used quite a bit of medication. Those terrible vascular headaches caused one embarrassing experience with a speech. Doctors at the Mayo Clinic explained that some people have very elastic vessels, and when we relax those vessels expand and the nerves get injured and hurt for a long time.

The drugs available couldn't seem to control the headaches. I was staying away from Ibuprofen after almost bleeding to death from that ulcer in 1985. The doctor prescribed a drug called Fioricet and I didn't realize how it was affecting me until I gave a report on commuter airlines at a governor's conference in Hawaii. Afterward Dick Gross told me I'd said *computer* airlines about five times and he thought it was because of too much headache medication. That frightened me terribly so I reduced the dosage in half. The first dose was fine but by the third one it was piled up and made me goofy. I still occasionally take one Fioricet instead of the two they recommend and have success with one pill along with Tylenol on the side.

Later, on a side trip from one of the governors' conferences, Janie and I went to visit her father, Dr. Bernard Baute, who was a highly respected doctor in Kentucky. When he asked about my headaches, I told him that they were still pretty severe at times. He asked what I was taking for my blood-pressure problem. "Lopressor," I told him.

"I think you should switch to an ace inhibitor," he said. "I will send some samples back with you and you should talk to your doctor about it."

When I got home I told Ralph what Dr. Baute had said. Ralph pondered for a minute or two and said, "Your father-in-law is right. I should have thought of that. You should switch right away." That's the kind of man Ralph was, totally objective and analytical, devoid of even a speck of pride or defensiveness. I loved him for that and always tried to emulate him.

Later, when I had heart pains during the Western Governors' Conference in Rapid City and needed bypass surgery, Janie wanted me to go home or to Minneapolis or the Mayo Clinic. "Why don't you call Ralph Dunnigan and have him check out this surgeon [Dr. Wojewski] and let him make the decision," I said.

I don't think Ralph was too surprised when Janie informed him that my anterior descending artery was all but closed up, and that an immediate operation had to be performed. She asked him to attend the surgery. Ralph told her Dr. Wojewski came from Cleveland Clinic so he's got to be good. He also said I couldn't move to do it in Bismarck. He flew down in the state plane immediately, and was a huge comfort both to Janie and to me when he showed up in time to scrub for the operation. (I'll get more off my chest about this in the next section.)

On another occasion, Ralph and I had stood opposite each other for three hours at a St. Alexius Hospital emergency room table in Bismarck, holding another wonderful friend to both of us, Dick Rayl, as he suffered through his first horrific seizure.[94]

I'm forever grateful for Ralph Dunnigan's medical care and more even for his great friendship. I'd had a physical check-up in December of 1990 and failed a stress test but the doctors couldn't find the problem. Ralph was concerned because my diastolic blood pressure would not come down under stress. They did what was called a thallium test where they put dye in the blood and track it. They tried everything they could to find the cause but couldn't. It continued to get worse, apparently, because the eventual blockage was big-time. By the following May some stretching feelings began to flare up right in the middle of my chest. But it wasn't any pain. I kept looking for pain in my shoulder and my arm but could never detect any so I really didn't think anything about it at first.

In July we were at the lake and I was playing tennis with one of my sons when this stretching phenomenon became pretty pronounced so we walked around a bit and it went away. I didn't feel anything after an hour and a half of pretty hard tennis. The next week, on a basketball court, we had just started playing when I again noticed varying degrees of chest discomfort. I slowed up for a few minutes and it went away. During over an hour of full-court basketball, running back and forth and missing shots and running back and forth and missing some more shots I didn't feel it or think of it again.

Three days later brought a trip to Minot to welcome the troops home from Kuwait. We left early on the state plane, did the presentation at the State Fair Grounds, got back in the plane, and flew home to Bismarck. I didn't feel anything. Janie boarded in Bismarck and we went on to the Western Governors' Conference in Rapid City. I don't recall noticing anything all day until we got back to the hotel room about 10:30 PM, after a reception at Mount Rushmore. This feeling in my chest hit again, more pronounced than ever, so I decided to get checked.

I just didn't feel right, kind of clammy, with a clear sense of pain. My assigned driver, a South Dakota highway patrolman, rushed me to the emergency room. There they administered blood thinner and nitro or something. They got everything quieted down and they admitted me to the hospital.

The next morning they did a major angiogram. The cardiologist stood watching the electrocardiogram and the blood flow and he said he didn't think there's anything there. The surgeon came in, a Polish doctor from Krakow, Dr. Paul Wojewski, who was an excitable, energetic man. I talked to him as he was standing over me. All of a sudden he said, "Ah, zerr it is. I'm not a fool." The blood was barely squeezing through that artery.

The cardiologist came in when he saw the blockage. "It's critical so we've got to operate as soon as we can," he said. "It's a very serious blockage, your main artery is 99 percent blocked."

The funny thing is I don't remember any great angst or sense of fear about the open-heart surgery. Not sure why I wasn't more frightened. It just couldn't seem to click at the time that it was a life-and-death situation. I was more eager to get at it before the heart pains hit again. With the blood thinner and everything, the risks of it occurring again weren't great. Lots of people have blockage but the anterior descending artery is the one they call the widow-maker in medical school.

It all happened pretty fast and the surgery was pretty invasive. They cut the breastbone right in half and they used a pulmonary pump. The last thing I remember is coming out of anesthesia and the surgeon sitting beside the bed. "You are a fortunate man," he said. "What saved your life is your basketball—no normal heart would have taken what yours did. It's amazing your heart was strong enough to push blood through there without any damage because it was really blocked."

He also advised me that cigarettes had started the blockage, even though I had quit smoking many years before. The good news was that there had been no heart attack and no damage to the heart.

At the end of a week, feeling pretty weak, I was sent to our lake home to recover there. I did a lot of walking and wasn't allowed near the phone. After that surgery, I appreciated my wife even more. Janie was pretty strict, but we may have overcorrected a little bit on the length of time away from the office. I might have gotten physically stronger faster by going back sooner. I lost a lot of weight, which was good for me. It would have been wonderful to stay at that level.

Among some pretty vivid memories, while in the hospital I was delivered a ridiculous picture from the office of the staff all posing in goofy positions with Lloyd in charge. Lucky I didn't have another cardiac event right there from laughing out of control.

The Rapid City heart surgeon became a fast friend. Dr. Wojewski went to Poland with us that next fall, after which we worked with health care people from both North Dakota and South Dakota to organize a program called Dakota Heart, an effort to help Eastern Europe's cardiovascular specialists and to show them the latest technology. Those Polish physicians were well trained. Paul Wojewski said he too had good training over there before he came to the United States and the Cleveland Clinic. But he said they didn't know modern technology and weren't able to use it. They just never had that hands-on experience. The plan was to get them to understand how to do things in a modern way.

Paul himself became so frustrated because he couldn't get a good job of character screening done on the people that came over here for the program. Eight of them arrived in the fall of 1992 for training in Bismarck, Rapid City, and Fargo.[95] These heart specialists had lived in a communist climate for so long they took advantage of everything they could. Some of them were pestering the nurses. Two of them took a state car one weekend and drove to Texas, believe it or not, from Fargo. Paul felt personally responsible and, boy, he was livid. I don't remember that we personally ended the program, but we quit pushing it and the clinics just quit bringing them. Basically Paul turned it off.

Fifth and sixth graders wrote more than 1,400 poems about my heart situation for a contest sponsored and promoted by the American Heart Association. Juel Anderson, a Turtle Lake sixth-grader, composed the poem chosen overall winner because it was humorous but also conveyed a message concerning immediate response to heart attacks and prevention of heart disease through a healthy lifestyle.

During a luncheon, Juel read the winning poem and presented me with a plaque with his verse engraved on it. Here's his masterpiece:

Signs of the Heart

Calm was the day in late July,
And bright was the sun across the sky.
But inside his chest the calm had broken,
Governor Sinner had started croakin'.
Thanks to the Heart Association for teaching us signs,
He quickly responded in the nick of time.
From the bypass surgery he soon recovered,
He now is amazed at what he discovered.
Each day he now lives his life with more thought,
He exercises and eats more like he ought.
Gov. Sinner your ability to govern is not diminished.
We wish you good luck until you are finished.

Great Advice

The frequency of death occurring among close friends has made me much more aware of death than that heart bypass episode did.

Those lessons from the monk named Smith (God is all love and will make things work out) and Ralph Dunnigan (forgiveness) are by all odds the greatest teachings in my life. I try often to remind people of them.

I was at the hospital with my brother Dick, who was comatose before he died. Hospice of the Red River Valley was helping take care of him. Down the hall about four doors, an old man from Marion, North Dakota, was also dying. I began visiting with the family. "They told us Dad was dying four or five months ago," they said. "But he can't seem to let go."

"You know, let me go and meet him and talk to him." So I went in and we laughed a little bit. I told a couple stories. And I told him those two teachings. "I hope my brother, who has been ready to die and wanting to die, is aware of this," I said. "He and I have talked a lot about these two teachings."

The man died that night, about four hours later.

The other time this happened I was employed at American Crystal. Somebody called one day and told me my friend Peter Hinrichs was dying. He was a Lutheran pastor in Dickinson, and probably the best scripture scholar I've ever known. He smoked a pipe and he had developed throat cancer. We were very close. A brilliant guy, he had been on the State Board of Higher Education with me. Oh God, he helped me in so many things. I grabbed the phone and called the hospital. The nurses told me that his wife, Lois, was in the room. I knew Lois well, too, so they got her on. "I'm so sorry. I just didn't know about Peter's illness, but somehow let him know that I'll pray for him."

She said, "Bud, I want you to talk to him."

"Can he talk?"

She said, "No, but he can hear. I want to hold the phone up to him and you talk to him," she said. "Believe it or not, he can't let go. He should have died three months ago. That's what the doctors said, but he just can't let go."

At that time Ralph hadn't yet told me this story about forgiveness, but I wanted to share the lesson I learned from Father Smith. I said, "Peter, I didn't know you were so sick, I'm so sorry. You taught me a lot about life and death."

When we closed the Ellendale college, I remember Peter saying, "Institutions have a time to die, just like people do. And this Ellendale is one that needs to stop being what it's been." He was one of the board members who helped get us through that terribly difficult period.

Anyway, I said, "Peter, I've got to tell you what happened when I left the seminary. It's so in line with what you always taught me about death." So I told him the story about what the old priest told me. And then I said, "Peter, I'll be praying for you. Just let go and it'll be fine."

His wife was there and she took the phone. I said, "Lois, I hope it ends soon."

He died twenty minutes later, with the realization that it's okay.

I learned another thing, kind of by accident, when we had a death early on during my term in the Governor's Office, of the spouse of an employee I knew fairly well. I found out about it late in the afternoon and thought my God, those poor people. Leaving work I decided to swing by this home. You know it was such a little thing but it meant so much to that family and I realized people in North Dakota really do appreciate kindness. In some places kindness is almost interpreted as oh, what's that about, what's he after? But that's really not true in North Dakota. People really do appreciate honesty and kindness. That's really special.

CHAPTER SIXTEEN: special treatment

Giving It Gas

We invited Manuel Lujan, the secretary of interior, and Mike Hayden, the former governor of Kansas who ran the US Fish and Wildlife Service, to hunt in North Dakota. Lloyd Jones was state Game and Fish commissioner, so it was after 1988.

Hayden was a professional turkey caller and Lujan was a hunter in his own right. I got the schedule that they had sent out for what they wanted to do. I said to Lloyd, "I wonder when Lujan plans to go to Mass. I know he goes to daily Mass and there's nothing on the schedule."

"It's their schedule, not mine," he said.

The plan was to shoot sandhill crane Saturday afternoon. We were out about twenty miles east of Bismarck in a fifty- or sixty-acre field. About four o'clock or four thirty, Lloyd came trudging across the field. He said, "Governor, the secretary wants to fold up and go in."

"Really? Okay," I said. We got in my Chevy Suburban, drove over, and loaded them and all the gear. We hit the road about ten minutes to five, pulled out of the field, and were driving up to the interstate. As we approached the highway the secretary said to me, "George, do you think we can make the five o'clock Mass?"

"We can get close!" So I kicked the accelerator. We were probably doing eighty on the service road. I looked in the mirror. Son of a bitch, red lights were flashing. I stopped and got out. Here was this young deputy sheriff. He was about six foot three and hand-some. "What the hell are you doing patrolling *this* road?"

"Governor, what the hell are *you* doing going eighty-five?"

"You wouldn't believe me if I told you."

"Try me."

Well, I explained about having the secretary of interior there and his wanting to go to Mass at the last minute. "You've got to give me a ticket," I said. "I'm like everybody else. I screwed up. I need a ticket."

"Governor, I'm not giving you a ticket. Get your ass back in that car and take the secretary to church." So I drove like crazy and we got there probably ten minutes late.

I didn't find out who the deputy was until two years later. Brian Berg asked me to visit a law enforcement school. Standing in the line to get tickets for the lunch, I looked at the trooper next to me. "Are you the guy?"

"Yeah, I'm the one."

I should have followed my instincts at the beginning and made some plans with Lujan and asked him because I was sure he'd want to go to mass. But those were the deputy's exact words: "Get your ass back in the car."

Another experience happened more recently on the way to UND for a football game. My son Bob asked me to drive his son Jeremy's rust-adorned car and then ride back with him. Jeremy's old Honda rattled along on I-29 and I got up to, I suppose, about 12th Avenue in Fargo. I speeded up and got stopped. I had an old hat on, an Australian-type hat, with a pretty wide brim. When the patrolman pulled up behind me, I started to get out. He said, "No, sir, you stay right there." He took my driver's license and started back to his cruiser.

He stopped and looked around. Then he said, "Governor, what are you doing driving that old wreck?"

"It's my grandson's and I'm just taking it up to the university for him," I said. "I've got to have a ticket."

"I'm not going to give you a ticket," he said, "you're the best boss I ever had. I will never be able to repay you for some of the things you did."

What goes around comes around, I guess.

Troopers have always been kind to me, going way back to my campaign for governor in 1984. We were headed for an event somewhere in German-Russian territory, southeast of Bismarck. My press secretary was driving my car, we were running a little late, and his big foot got a little heavy on the accelerator.

A trooper pulled us over and I told our driver it would be courteous of him to get out. So he went back to the patrol car. After the officer did the usual license check, he glanced at our car. "Is that Mr. Sinner in there?"

"Yes," he said, "we're headed for a campaign stop and running late."

"You wait here. I'd like to meet him."

The trooper came over to the car and introduced himself. We shook hands and he wished me well. Then he promptly went back to his car and wrote a speeding ticket.

For some reason, my press secretary remembers that incident much better than I do.

Minding Our Manor

Living in the fish bowl wasn't as uncomfortable for me as it was for the family. A hard part for Janie was always having people around in the Governor's Residence. Hardly any days were totally hers. People kept coming and going—staff and events. That became a source of discomfort to her on many occasions. She wanted to get away. I didn't do as much as I should have, but we did get to the lake a few times each summer. After my bypass surgery, patrolmen were there in case I needed help. Although they were wonderful, she still didn't get the privacy she craved. And yet I don't think she ever publicly complained about the situation.

While never having privacy at the residence was hard, the people there were great. Steve Sharkey, residence manager, was God's gift to all of us. Janie was responsible for getting him. He was in the finest sense of the word a professional at what he does. Thankfully the succeeding governors have kept him on and Steve has retained his professionalism to the nth degree. I call him fairly frequently, but he never talks out of school. I was informal and treated him like I treated everyone else: do what you want to do, just do it right. We were good friends.

One chef at the residence let us down, however. Janie actually got him out of jail a couple of times. He was making pretty good progress with his alcoholism problem but didn't show up for a big dinner one day. Janie then realized it wasn't going to help him any to come back, so she let him go. He has recovered and we see him quite often. He's a successful chef.

Janie did a fabulous job with renovating the Governor's Residence.[96] Right out of the chute she banned smoking inside the building and reminded me year after year that I needed to do something to prohibit smoking in state offices. The first thing she did was put up No Smoking signs. I don't know why I was so slow but once I saw it clearly toward the end of my years I realized that it wasn't tough. All we had to do was create an executive order to ban smoking.

When we got there the roof of the residence was leaking. The state was as poor as a church mouse, so I was not about to spend the money to replace it. Quite by coincidence the residence had the same flat-type, built-up roof as my home in Casselton, which we had just re-roofed. Back there, I couldn't find any way to do it that didn't cost a bundle. I wasn't going to go back to pitch and gravel on a built-up roof. I was trying to find some way to put shingles on but it was pretty flat, a two-twelve pitch. The problem was when they put the shingles on a flat roof the wind would come under and it would start flapping. One day somebody told me about a young roofer who was good. He came out and advised that there was a simple way to fix that. "Instead of using a four-inch overlap on the asphalt shingles you use three inches," he said. "They will last 'till hell freezes over and they will not blow." So I had done that in Casselton.

I remember saying to Dick Rayl, "This is the way to do this roof."[97]

Eric, our youngest, lived with us in Bismarck. He was a freshman at nearby St. Mary's High School when he invited two kids over.[98] One of them told a buddy he was going to the Governor's Residence to play pool. The buddy spread the word there was a party at the Governor's Residence. Janie and I were awakened about 11:30 PM and we could hear laughing. Janie got out of bed first and she immediately called the Highway Patrol. I got dressed and went downstairs. There were thirty or forty kids, and cases of beer everywhere.

From the two-step rise looking into the big room I said, "Listen up. Any of you that have open beer cans, go and dump them in the sink. And if you have any unopened beer, leave it right where it is. The Highway Patrol is on the way over right now and you better get your butt out of here and get home."

I said, "As far as I know you weren't invited, and this certainly isn't the place to have a beer party. This is completely out of order. Leave the beer and get out!"

The Highway Patrol officers told me afterward that they actually sat in their car and watched those kids come running out of the house. After they left there were a half-dozen cans sitting there that were half done. I dumped them out. I put the empties in the garbage bag and the unopened beer in the refrigerator. Eric was completely innocent. I think he appreciated having it over with.

I know my wife was upset with my effort to change the constitution so that the governor's term ended and the new one began on the 15th of December.[99] I had seen the tortuously difficult time we had getting a handle on the budget when we came into office. You have a legislative session coming up the first week in January and it just does not make sense—at least it didn't make sense to me—for the governor to have to start out the day the legislature began. What Janie disliked was that we had to leave the Governor's Residence and move into a new home the week before Christmas. But knowing the personal angst that was involved and the turmoil we had when I took office I just had to kind of tough it out. Maybe there's some way that could be improved upon. Maybe future governors will do better planning and get their things moved well ahead of the day. But it was difficult for us and our Christmas was disrupted. It was still from the point of view of the state the right thing to do. We began the constitutional change process in the 1985 session and voters approved the following year.

Not There for the Perks

Although some perks accompany the position of governor, most of them didn't mean much to me. Although I had been able to attend St. John's University, I grew up in a relatively poor family, with almost nothing but hand-me-downs for most of my childhood. So that sort of stuff didn't really turn me on. Service isn't about getting elected, and there aren't enough perks anyway for that alone to motivate getting re-elected. The only way to really serve was to be there for the needs that were there at the time, as well, for the unseen problems.

I'm hopeful that we are drawing readers here to the same conclusion: that the issues are really important and solving the problems is really important. The satisfaction comes from having faced difficult issues, listening to people, and drawing the best conclusion you can draw.

My decision to do away with the official state car and driver was part of my ordinary guy mentality. I was not much different than anybody else and hated the pretense while we didn't have the money to do the things that were really urgent. I didn't need a driver or a Lincoln Town Car. It was a waste, so I eliminated that and the car brought the state $18,500 when auctioned in March of 1990.

Not everyone thought it was a good idea. Some told me I was demeaning the office. It was demeaning only if you thought the office was about pomp and circumstance. I drove my own car and rarely submitted mileage. I had a Dodge van when I got there and then traded it off for a Chevy Suburban.

Dick Rayl came by one day to talk about the old State Office Building, the brick structure on the southeast corner of the Capitol Grounds that originally housed Bismarck Junior College. "We've got to get a new place for the Water Commission," he said. "That whole building over there is such a mess."

"Dick, I don't object to repairing it and putting a face on it, but I don't want a new building."

"Yeah, but everybody thinks it's a horrible mess."

"I just don't think it makes sense," I said. "And it's a bad image."

"Well, I think it'll cost just about as much to remodel it."

"Do it," I said. "I think given the circumstances of what we have to do here with this budget I just don't think we should build a new building. Do it as cheaply as you can but do whatever you do well."

They did a good job. After the remodeling, it is still an attractive building. That was a little bit like the state's luxury sedan. It just didn't fit with all the other stuff we had to cut. And constructing something new was not a good signal to people.

Years later, Janie and I were helping a young woman with some problems and she asked why you have to be famous or something to get great medical care. And it is true, you automatically get preferential treatment and you're always extremely grateful for it. It's one of the perks of the office. It's a really, really special perk.

There were other perks. I hunted a lot better when I was governor. A bird would fall and everyone would yell "Great shot, Governor!" I didn't have to use my gun and could have kept all my shells.

And playing golf I would get a lot of gimmies. Oh yeah, that thirty-footer is a gimme. Of course there were perks involving airplanes. I'll explain in the next section.

Flying Really Fast

General Alex Macdonald called one day and asked if I'd like to go for a ride in a Happy Hooligans F-4D Phantom. I answered, "Would I? Would I!" I came over to Fargo and what an experience that was. During the one-hour flight we flew over Aberdeen and north to Grand Forks at supersonic Mach 2 speeds exceeding 1,000 miles per hour at 45,000 feet.[100] The pilot was Lieutenant Colonel James Reimers, the unit's deputy commander for operations. He turned on the afterburners and man did we fly.

Earlier, I had probably my most fabulous ride with the Blue Angels when Gil Rud was commander and they came to Fargo for the air show.[101] They had two two-seater A-4s. We didn't wear G-suits, which was a little bit scary. Of all the things I have ever done, that was by far the most thrilling.

I got in the back seat and Reimers taxied out to the north end of the north-south runway at Hector Airport. We roared down the runway and the next thing I heard was, "Are you ready?"

"I'm ready!" And he went right straight up to 6,000 feet. He flew that sucker right straight up into the clouds. I was dumb struck.

We got up and he leveled off and he said, "I'm going to go out in the country a ways and show you a few maneuvers." So we flew west, over Amenia or somewhere out there.

"I want you to put your hand on the stick," Reimers said. "Don't press it. Just get the feel of it. Kind of follow me."

The next thing I knew he did a roll. He just flipped that thing around so far and brought it up. I looked up and he had his hands on the handle on the upper part of the canopy. "Now you do yours," he said.

I've been a nut about flying nearly all of my life so I knew you had to keep your eye on the horizon when you did those maneuvers. If you didn't you'd go goofy. I had gotten the feel of it. It was a full-movement stick before they went to the joy stick. I did the move and I kept watching, I kept looking right straight ahead and I rolled it, and then stopped it. I aimed dead flat right toward the horizon.

"Not bad," he said. "You lost about three degrees. There's a little trick there you didn't catch. I put the plane on about a 3 or 4 percent incline before I rolled it. You always lose three or four degrees even if your roll is dead flat."

I was just ecstatic.

"I'm going to do a loop now," he said. "Are you ready for that?"

"Yeah, I'm ready."

He did the loop. "Do you want to try that?"

"Nope. I don't want to try that," I said. "I'll probably drive into the ground."

Then came one of the hard parts. He did a maneuver where he went straight up and turned three quarter and put it into a power dive. We were flying at about 11,500 feet. If you get above 12,000 feet you're supposed to have a G-suit and oxygen, so we were staying below that. My ears were just screaming because he came down so fast. The maneuver of all kinds of stuff went on for about thirty-five minutes.

"Would you like to try simulating an aircraft carrier type of landing? We've got the runway set up and we can do one if you want to. Are you alright?"

"My ears are killing me."

"This won't make them any worse."

The A-4 topped at about 500 or 600 miles an hour. "This is going to probably give you the most Gs you can stand without a G-suit," he said.

"That's fine. I'm okay."

He came screaming in from the north end of the runway. All of a sudden he set the plane on its wingtip and it absolutely took off straight west. Almost like a ninety-degree turn. He turned that sucker on its wingtip and threw the aileron and the flap. I'm sitting in the back seat trying to get my head up with my hands and I just got it up when he did the next one. He did a rectangle with these crazy right turns.

By the time he got around the north again ready to come in for a landing, he asked, "Are you okay?"

"Yaaaah," I slurred, still trying to push my head up.

I wasn't prepared for what happened next. He got over the runway, suddenly pulled the nose up, and the damn thing just stopped flying. It stopped flying because of all that aerodynamic pressure. He dropped the nose at just the right time. We must have been twenty-five, thirty feet off the runway. I thought, holy crap!

I could feel it going down toward the runway and I thought wow, we're going to crash. What I didn't know was they have air-over-hydraulic cylinders, big long struts on that A-4, and when you hit that just all compresses. The plane has the big tail hook on the back to catch the cable that stops it when landing on an aircraft carrier, which we simulated. We went down really easily, settled in. No bounce, nothing.

I just couldn't believe it because when we were going down it felt like we were going to crash. But of course we didn't. This guy knew what he was doing. He'd been flying A-4s for a long time. Janie will tell you I wanted to reenlist in the Air Force on the spot.

Later, the last year in office, I got a ride with the Happy Hooligans in an F-16 fighter.[102] The F-16 was really a hot airplane, though not as quick as the F-15. Alex Macdonald always said it was one of the best airplanes ever made. It was heavily armed and had lots of power. The Air Force sent a B-1 bomber out of Grand Forks and we tracked it down in the clouds and theoretically put the radar guns on the plane. We refueled in the air. That was unbelievable. Here's how it works: this long chute comes out of the C-135 that was up there to refuel us and our fighter pilot flew to the bottom of that into kind of a trough about two feet wide with a sloped bottom. He actually flies this fighter plane into the refilling hose and it locks in.

The pilot does his best to match the speed of the C-135 but actually I think it was pulling us a little bit. All he really had to do was maintain altitude. We refueled, disconnected, and took off and came home. That was one exciting trip! Of all the things I did, those three flights were by far the most exhilarating.

CHAPTER SEVENTEEN: respecting gender and race

Wise and Wonderful Women

One thing that I feel badly about is I don't often give my wife the credit she deserves. She has been a huge help to me. Janie's a brilliant woman and I've always paid close attention to what she thinks and says. So many times during those eight years in the Governor's Office she made some small hint that I needed to pick up on.

Janie wasn't deeply into the history of the abortion discussion herself but she understood what I wrote and trusted my research. When I had to develop the veto message I will never forget her saying you have to write something different, you can't use the same stuff you used in the background paper. It was at that point I decided, with her help, to include background information from the official statements of several prominent American churches. Together we worked on several drafts and prepared the veto message that was so widely reported. And of course the staff did most of the research.

As I said earlier, my wife was clear on banning smoking from the beginning. It took me a lot longer to realize that I not only could do something but that I had to do something. Even before I was governor Janie led me into the mental health field, and probably more because of her activity than my own, I chaired the founding of the Southeast Regional Mental Health Clinic. It was the first in North Dakota.

Ruth Meiers left a legacy for North Dakota people and took the role of women and the role of service to new heights. We learned of Ruth Meiers' cancer in the fall of 1986 and she went awfully fast. We lost her only six months later. I'll always remember that Ruth was still coming into the office after it was pretty clear she wasn't going to recover. Her suffering was a gallant episode. It taught me something about death. Ruth never feared death. She knew it was coming, probably before the rest of us did. Yet she went on and did her job. She was a terrific woman who had a strong background. She came from the farm and she didn't mind doing the things that get your hands dirty and was matter of fact about dealing with lots of problems. She cared about taking care of people. She knew better than most that government is about protecting the rights of people and the rest of us better serve that end or you are badly mistaken about government.

In my eulogy during her memorial service at the little church in Ross, I talked about how much Ruth loved life and how we would miss her hearty laugh in the office. I remembered the delight that showed on her face in the photos taken when she entered a milking contest and lost to another woman, Mandan's mayor. Both of them beat the only male contestant.

I also recalled the time when she rode a circus elephant, for which Ringling Brothers presented her with a certificate of achievement. With wonderfully exaggerated alliteration, it read:

> Whereas, Ruth Meiers, Lieutenant Governor of North Dakota, has perfectly performed perched on a Ponderous Pachyderm of the Greatest Show on Earth, and Whereas, this ride was carried through with disciplined dignity and absolute aplomb. Therefore, Ringling Brothers and Barnum and Bailey Circus hereby confers upon this Regal Rider the celebrated and coveted title of Elephant Equestrian Extraordinaire.

Ruth was loved by legislators. She was president of the Senate, part of her constitutional job, and she was good at it. I never heard a single complaint about Ruth in her work there. She helped keep a rapport with legislators that I wasn't particularly good at. I didn't know how to do it, so I just sort of stayed back with what I did.

After her death some people who really wanted the lieutenant governor's job were disappointed and some others were upset that I didn't appoint a woman. It would have been a good thing to select a woman but we were dealing with so many huge problems with the budget and so many different areas that clearly the easiest thing for me to do was to choose someone I knew extremely well, thought the world of, and trusted implicitly. It was sort of a no-brainer once Lloyd Omdahl's name came up.[103] He overshadowed everyone else even though we were in fact looking for a woman.

Lloyd was so automatically compatible. He was aware of most of the issues, understood them and thought essentially the way I did. It was an easy decision. I agree with Lloyd's characterization of himself and me as "philosophical twins."

As his tenure in office ended, here's how Lloyd Omdahl described his duties in a videotaped interview with historian Tracy Potter:

> I've sort of been the utility player on the baseball team. I have a whole series of routine functions assigned to me in the committees and commissions, which statutorily he's supposed to head. I've been chairing the board of equalization, the emergency commission, the water commission, the Indian Affairs Commission, the Investment Board, the Centennial Trees Commission, the Capitol Grounds Planning Commission, the Investment Board, the Fort Union Missouri Board, the Children Services Coordinating Commission, etc. By my chairing these commissions and committees it's not been necessary for him to put his time into those meetings. These are all important functions of government but there isn't time in the day for his to do all of these by himself, and when critical issues would come up on these boards and commissioners I would see to it that he was aware of what was going on.
>
> There were a number of ad hoc assignments that would come up. For example, when we ran into the fiscal bind back in late 80s and early 90s he asked me to chair a cost reduction commission to sensitize agencies to the fact that we have to watch our money. Then we have a controversy

between the water people and agriculture people so there was a wetlands management committee formed and I was chair of that. And we had a water development task force program, which was a special effort so I became chair of that. When I came they were in the process of reorganizing the highway and transportation department into a single function and I became the chair of that coordinating committee. Even when negotiations became difficult at the Mill and Elevator I became the interim negotiator on the contract between the employees and the Mill and Elevator. When controversy came up over the Western Area Power Association line over near the Badlands I became involved in that on special assignment. I've been available on a continuing basis and a special assignment basis. Many times his schedule would not permit him to attend conventions, welcome groups to North Dakota, make presentations or awards, or otherwise meet all the speaking requirements and I would fill the gap there.

It's important to have a backup person available for the governor so he can have a flexible schedule, and I think that's the proper role for the lieutenant governor.

Although it didn't happen in that case, we *were* pretty conscious of appointing women. During my final months as governor I had the honor of appointing the first woman to serve in the US Senate from North Dakota. Quentin Burdick died September 8, 1992. Many other qualified candidates were interested in the office when I named Quentin's widow, Jocelyn "Jocie" Burdick, only four days later.[104]

My statement to the press declared that, "Events and important issues coming up in Washington make it important for North Dakota to have immediate full representation in the US Senate. Therefore, I am today announcing the appointment of a temporary replacement to fill Senator Burdick's seat until a senator is elected in a special election."

I noted that Jocie had been at Quentin Burdick's side throughout his more than three decades of outstanding, dedicated service to the people of North Dakota and the US Senate. "There are implications for our state in much of the legislation currently under consideration by the Senate," I said. "Important provisions have been authored or influenced by Quentin Burdick. With the help of an experienced, superb staff, Jocelyn will do an outstanding job of representing the interests of North Dakota and the people of our state."

There were so many personal items of Senator Burdick in his Senate office. It just seemed like that was a way to make sure all those things would be taken care of the way Jocie would like them taken care of. That was a major consideration.

Jocie took office September 16, and served about three months, until December 14, 1992, when Kent Conrad took over the Burdick seat after winning a special election on December 4. Kent had pledged that he wouldn't run for re-election to a second term if the federal budget wasn't balanced.[105] Of course, it wasn't balanced when his term expired. I had strongly urged Senator Conrad to reconsider his impending departure from the Senate and run for that Burdick seat. Other people were pressing him too. Kent kept his vow and didn't run for re-election to his original Senate seat. Instead he was elected to the Burdick seat, and Byron Dorgan won the Senate seat Kent was vacating. Earl Pomeroy took Byron's place in the US House.

After Kent was initially elected to the US Senate it was automatic for me to appoint Heidi Heitkamp as tax commissioner. She was later elected attorney general, and ran for governor. Among my other women appointments were Supreme Court Justice Beryl Levine; Jane Lundstrom, banking commissioner; and Jane Robb, state laboratories director. All of them were extremely capable.

Another example was the North Dakota Board of Dental Examiners. We were supposed to take nominees from the North Dakota Dental Association. In the spring of 1988, just into my second term, it turned out that one of their nominating committee members was my former dentist and good friend in Fargo, Fred Lundstrom. The committee sent three male nominations—three male dentists. Although there had been female dental hygienists, there were no women dentists on their board. We'd been supportive of legislation to require that these boards be gender balanced, so we wrote back and said we needed a woman dentist nominee. But that was like pulling teeth. "We have made our list of nominees and we fully expect that you will choose one of them," they answered.

Carol Siegert was pushing for a woman dentist and said she was sure we could find one. I ended up appointing a dentist from up in Bottineau, Lori Witteman, to a five-year term. My friend, Dr. Lundstrom, was not happy with me. I think he kind of understood but he was a little irritated because they thought I had to take one of their nominees. I disagreed, but did appoint one of those men later.

I don't think we ever appointed people we didn't think were qualified. But there were times we had to go on other people's say-so. There weren't enough days in the week to learn to know all these people.

Our First People

I have done a considerable amount of work with people whose ancestors were the first Americans. I have learned from them as I have come to know and love them. In order to be more true to my Christianity, I would like to be more like them, with their completely natural acceptance of humanity and with their profound trust in a personal, omnipotent God who will always care for them.

Historian Thomas Mails in his book *The Mystic Warriors of the Plains*, provides an excellent overview of the history, culture, spirituality, and problems of America's native peoples. In it he quotes a Native American teaching:

"When you arise in the morning, give thanks for the morning light. Give thanks for your life and strength. Give thanks for your joy of living. And if perchance you see no reason for giving thanks, rest assured the fault is in yourself."

Over and over in my work with Native Americans I saw this spirituality and this trust in God. They do not have the passion for material wealth that we have. They trust in God. They do not have the passion for schedules that we have. They enjoy life and its rich, simple pleasures as they go along, day by day.

One of the most moving experiences of my life took place in September of 1987 while waiting my turn to speak at a national Native American powwow, which brought people from all across the country to the United Tribes Technical College complex south of Bismarck. The powwow arena is a quarter of a mile off the end of a runway at the Bismarck airport.

There were nearly a thousand dancers in the arena for the opening ceremony. It was the largest Indian powwow on the North American continent. Twenty-five or twenty-six states were represented, along with half a dozen Canadian provinces. Over half of the approximately 450 North American tribes were represented.

While waiting to deliver my greeting to that huge crowd of people I stood with Dr. David Gipp, a wonderful Native American man whom I have known for more than twenty-five years. He was and still is president of the United Tribes Technical College and has devoted his life to educating Native Americans. The arena was aglow with marvelously colorful costumes overflowing with eagle feathers. I said to him, "David, where on earth do all the eagle feathers come from?"

David smiled. "Now wait a minute, Governor," he said. "It is not what you think. Our people do not kill eagles. Eagles, you see, are a symbol of God to Indian people and even their feathers are handed down from generation to generation. They are sacred. If just one small feather were to drop into the arena during the dance, it would be very ceremoniously retrieved."

Beyond that, he said, "If an eagle should fly over the powwow, it would be seen by everyone here as a sign of blessing from God."

Standing a quarter of a mile off the end of the runway, I peered skyward and there were not one but four golden eagles slowly circling the powwow. I was absolutely awestruck. Eagles are rarely spotted this close to the city and its airport.

David saw the wonderment in my skyward gaze. He looked up, too. Within seconds, the whole arena fell silent. The drums stopped. The dancers stopped. We all stood reverently realizing that these eagles were a sign of God's blessing.

That experience reminded me that we must all continue to learn about all God's people. My six years at St. John's studying philosophy as part of undergraduate preparation for the priesthood taught me that God is a God of all people, a God who cherishes all people, and a God who communicates with all people. But never before had I so forcefully experienced God's presence in another culture's setting. The experience affected me deeply.

Later I learned not only was it significant that one eagle was there, but that four were there was of rare significance indeed. The Indians, you see, believe in the God of the West Wind, of the East Wind, of the South Wind, and of the North Wind. I was deeply moved. I thought about it for days. Beyond doubt God was blessing those people, and it became clear to me how narrow my own experience really was.

I realized how small are the worlds in which we live, how narrow are our cultures, how limited are our perspectives. We rarely see the world, let alone God, from where others see it. Certainly, I had thought all too little about the vision of God that is in the mind and the spirit of others. But here was the vision. Here was God, in undeniable presence. Suddenly it was so clear a message that we must continue to learn about God's people, to pay attention and to realize how ignorant and insensitive we are of their problems.

We know so little. We don't read history. We need to think from other people's perspectives and walk a mile in each other's moccasins. To quote an old African proverb: "Not till you've crossed the river can you say the crocodile has a lump on its jaw."

Some have complained that there are so many politicians in Washington who don't seem to have any principles. They had nothing they were working toward. But to me, the realization that every issue is sacred is probably the corollary if not the primary axiom for man's principle of action, especially in public life. One of the great things I learned during my years as governor is that the truth is like a prism—we each see from a miniscule spot in time and space. Unless we step around and listen to others, read and study their perceptions, we don't see the full beauty of the prism. The hope for finding human compatibility becomes lost. That teaching was of huge importance when I crystallized it from the experience at that Native American powwow.

In the late sixties, as a State Board of Higher Education member, I helped get passed the approval for community colleges on the reservations. Twila Martin, a Chippewa, and Gipp, a Hunkpapa Lakota—both graduate students at UND—asked me to help them start the community colleges. We had just closed the Ellendale campus and I thought, wow, how do we do this now? I talked to Commissioner Ken Raschke about the need. "Bud," he said, "that may be the only way we'll get the Native American kids to college."

These community colleges have had to struggle, but they are doing a tremendous service.[106] Probably the most important thing we on the Board of Higher Education did for them was allowing our state colleges and universities to accept the transfer of certain approved courses from the tribal campuses.

When governor I ran into Ellen Chaffee,[107] then assistant higher education commissioner and later president of Valley City State University, and asked her how the reservation colleges were doing. I'll never forget her answer. "That may be the finest thing you ever did," she said. "They are really doing things. They are making huge progress even though they are way under-funded." North Dakota was the first state with a community college for each reservation and I've been told that North Dakota's initiative has been copied by many other states.

I don't know if others appreciate our exceptionally hard work on getting Indian gaming contracts right. Under the contract negotiated with the North Dakota tribes, a significant percentage of the adjusted gross income must go to the tribes for use of human service programs and economic development, other than gaming. North Dakota was the only state where this was done in this way. I hope the overall quality of life on the reservations has improved as a result of those funds.[108]

Later a tribal attorney told me, "You had a hell of a good idea there. It'll help an awful lot of people who need help." I was grateful for that assurance.

We worked to get good oversight and auditing structure. If the state gets any tax revenue, that comes later. We thought they needed the money for their colleges.

By the 1980s a movement to return the skeletal remains of Native Americans from museums to their descendents for burial gained ground across the country. Ancestral remains have deep spiritual significance to Native Americans, and they ardently sought to get them back. Alice Spotted Bear and Pemina Yellow Bird brought to my attention that the state had such remains in its collections. As far as I knew, after checking with the National Governors Association, no other state had returned remains, but to me it was the respectful thing to do. After we appointed Pemina Yellow Bird to the State Historical Society Board, North Dakota established a means for returning remains for burial, despite initial opposition from institutions like the Smithsonian.[109]

On another matter, one day John Graham came in and I was disgusted with the fact that we had so many Native Americans in the state hospital for alcoholism. John explained that when they got arrested for DUI on the reservation there were only two options: because they didn't have any community-based mental health programs they could either commit themselves to the state hospital, or they could go to the reservation jail. He said once they entered the state hospital we couldn't get them out for ten to fifteen days.

"The cost is just getting insurmountable," John said.

"Is there any place these people can be treated, like mental health centers on the reservations?" I asked.

"No," he said. "Not even close."

"So, let's figure out a way to do that, to get some regional mental health on these reservations."

"We've already had a lot of discussions in the department," he said. "Let us work it through."

They came back with a marvelous plan that was adopted. They bent some rules and through the human service centers worked with tribal agencies, Indian Health Services, and the Bureau of Indian Affairs on a system to bolster on-reservation programs for addiction and mental illness. That state outreach eventually gave way to treatment at the state hospital through special federal funding secured by Senator Byron Dorgan. I came away from the Governor's Office feeling that we didn't do a lot but we did everything we could to help the Native Americans.

In gratitude for these efforts, I was surprised by a wonderful gift in December 1990, at the North Dakota Heritage Center in Bismarck. This took place during the opening of a public educational program put on by Native American leaders on the centennial memorial of the 1890 Wounded Knee Massacre. The Lakota Sioux tribe adopted me in a beautiful spiritual ceremony, and gave me the Indian name Cunku Wanjila, which means "one road."[110] An eagle feather was woven into my hair.

I had no advance knowledge of all of this and was nearly over-come with emotion. I will never forget it. The Associated Press covered the event and distributed the story statewide. The article quoted Isaac Dog Eagle, great-grandson of Sitting Bull, explain-ing that the Lakota people had given me that name "because he will pave the way for two cultures to walk one road together in the future."

I told that audience that Wounded Knee reminds us how di-minished we all are by violence: "Today, especially, in my heart I feel a lot more like praying than speaking. I do not somehow even feel capable of sitting in righteous judgment of all who perpetrated the awful violence at Wounded Knee.

"I feel more in my heart like praying for forgiveness for our own failures in our own day," I said. "So many of us have been left hurt and guilty by violence that we have not yet been able to live as brothers and sisters."

After Sitting Bull's grandson placed that eagle in my hair we smoked a peace pipe of brotherhood and they embraced me as a brother.

We were blessed to have tremendously sensitive people in my cabinet and on my staff who helped accomplish these few things.

CHAPTER EIGHTEEN: Flying High

Keeping Our Guard Up

I was a great advocate of the National Guard even as early as the sixties. It seemed to me that the Guard was better able than the regular branches of service to digest and accommodate militarism to make it work for the citizenry. Many friends were pacifists in World War II and I began to realize that an overt militarism is dangerous. The idea of a citizen soldier in the model of the Minutemen appealed to me because while military people have a preoccupation with fighting wars, the citizen soldier has a more balanced attitude toward war and sees it more in terms of peace keeping.

So I had begun way back to advocate a much more active role for the Guard in American defense. I had discussed this concept extensively with David Montplaisir, an Air Force fighter pilot and good friend who was in the legislature with me in the sixties. David, who was originally from around Horace, became head of reserve training for all military branches in Washington at the Pentagon and had a huge influence on people's thinking about the importance of the Guard. He has written a lot about that. He was integral in building up the strength and role of the Guard and the reserves in our military. When I became governor, the Army Guard was over half of the US Army strength. The Air Guard was about 37 percent of the Air Force strength. So, the Guard was important and I was proud and pleased with the ascending role of the Guard in national defense because it was both cheaper and, from my perspective, in many ways better. The Guard units have stood out in every war that we have been involved in. During WWII, on Guadalcanal, and places like that, the National Guard did heroic work.[111]

In 1988, President Reagan had sent several units of the Army Guard into Honduras. I knew our Guard members there were building schools and roads. They were doing many good things for the Honduran people. But a couple of governors—Rudy Perpich of Minnesota and Mike Dukakis of Massachusetts, who was running for president—began a public outcry about the president sending Guard units into foreign countries without the approval of the governor, who is the commanding officer of the state Guard. It was a bad idea to think fifty governors could run the training program. We had to respect the president's role as commander in chief of all US forces, though we may not agree with him. I challenged them both by phone but they persisted.

The matter arose as a National Governors Association meeting was about to start. Bill Clinton had just taken over the chairmanship. He was standing a couple feet from the lectern and ready to call the opening plenary session to order when Rudy told me he was going to bring this to the floor and insist that the governors retain control of the Guard. I was sure he was wrong so I jumped up to alert Clinton, and quickly told him what the problem was. "Bill, I'm ready to fight like hell because they're dead wrong."

He looked at me. "I understand and I agree," he said. "You go talk to Rudy and I'll talk to Dukakis and tell them we can't do that—there's going to be a big fight."

The meeting sat waiting while we did that. To make a long story short, it never came up. National Guard representatives were watching in the back of the room and somehow found out what went on, so they thought I walked on water.

The next major Guard issue arose when Bush senior was elected president. The day after the election, I called Alex Mcdonald, our state adjutant general. I said, "Alex, would you consider being the head of the National Guard in Washington, DC, because I have a pretty good shot at getting you there."

"No," he said. "I am getting too old."

"So who is the right person?"

"General John Conaway," he said, "from Kentucky."

"Well let's get right on this and try for him because we must have a good guy in there," I said. "There are a lot of people that just are not capable of handling that big a responsibility. You start working on the adjutant generals and I'll start working on the governors."

My letter to all the governors told them I had done a small amount of research and had also consulted with people whose judgment I respected completely and they had advised that Conaway was the best candidate. The other governors then wrote their own letters of support for Conaway to the president. Conaway was the only one nominated, and he was immediately appointed.[112] It became a fascinating episode because everyone respected him. He did a superb job. Some members of Congress were well aware of my work with the Guard and with this. So, as a result of that I was again pretty popular with the Guard.

We helped our Guard any way we could. The engineer units captured innumerable awards and the Air National Guard Happy Hooligans won the William Tell competition several times. It is an extraordinary unit. In part that's because our people are much more focused and much more down to earth and try harder. It was also the first Air Guard unit to serve on active duty with North Atlantic Treaty Organization (NATO). Along with them, there were other Guard units involved with the defense around the Capitol, but the Happy Hooligans were the ones who would have had to shoot down that hijacked United Airlines Flight 93, which crashed in a Pennsylvania field during the September 11, 2001, terrorist attacks. The Army Guard units also won trophy after trophy in many different kinds of competition among all the military forces.

Mac fought bitterly at the national level to have the Air Guard keep the F-16 aircraft rather than build the new F-20 Tigershark. When that fight was going on in Congress he wanted F-15 fly-by-wire technology put into the F-16. He said it would be a better plane and cost about a fifth of the money. Mac lost that argument. I was only on the periphery but was so impressed by Macdonald at that time if he said rabbit I'd jump. I just trusted him implicitly. Later, I was at the Pentagon on some Guard matter and noticed the name on the door of the general who had been head of North American Aerospace

Defense Command (NORAD). I knew him some and stopped in his office—this was a couple of years after they lost the fight over the F-16. I asked him who was right about the F-20 or the F-16. "Mac was so right it just made a lot of us sick because we all knew what he knew, that the F-16 was a hell of an airplane," he told me.

Looking way back, there was only one time when I got upset with the Happy Hooligans. That was way back in 1952, not too long after we came home from the Air Force when the Korean War ended. I was working with the last team of horses at our farm (yes, I reigned over the horses at times), which we used in the feedlot because it was often too muddy for a tractor. I had tied the reigns over a pole on the wagon as I shoveled feed from the wagon into the feed bunkers. Just then four Air Guard F-94 Starfires roared over the shelterbelt with their afterburners blasting. It almost blew me over. The horses took off with the wagon and the cattle were frantic. After getting the horses back under control I went to a phone and angrily called Marsh Johnson, the Fargo Air Guard commander, and told him to keep those damn jets out of here.

Got It Made In China

Clinton—and the first George Bush to a much lesser extent—aren't the only former "presidents" I call friends.

Another close relationship began during a trip to the Republic of China with the late John Odegaard of the University of North Dakota Center for Aerospace Sciences. There I met General Wu and General Shan. Wu was the president of China Airlines and Chan was past president. We were there several days. During that time they took me to meet Taiwan President Lee Teng-hui, who was a Cornell University graduate with a PhD in agricultural economics.[113] I learned a lot of things on that trip. I began to understand that the polemics that occur between mainland China and Taipei are more engendered by political campaigns than they are by public policy. They told me often the trade between the two countries was huge. Just like the huge trade between North Korea and South Korea, it became a blessing because it makes it difficult to jeopardize all that for the sake of a political identity.

I liked several things Lee told me. He said they tried to limit corporate leadership compensation to ten times the lowest-paid person in the company. "You look at this country with all these people who have nothing," he said. "We just can't let people come in here and take advantage of them."

I found a new respect for the Taiwanese, particularly for Lee. He understood the same things I did about what his job was. I was amazed by this culture that I thought was pretty crass and power hungry, and yet they had all these democratic principles and these free-enterprise activities. Lee and I became fast friends.

The next trip to Taiwan we probably spent an hour and a half talking about the philosophy of government. I began to realize American openness was huge to those people. I celebrated my sixtieth birthday with Wu and Chan at a big party. We drank whatever they drank, had this wonderful Kobe beef, and a great big birthday cake.

Janie wrote about the visit in 1987 when we signed a sister-state relationship with Taiwan. I wanted to do my part by speaking in their language. So I had a young Taiwanese man come to our room and translate my short speech into Chinese syllables that I could pronounce. I practiced it for hours and the next day astounded them in the middle of my speech by switching from English to Chinese.

Later, I got Lee into the United States, or at least helped accomplish that. In 1995 he was invited to give a commencement address at Cornell and went through the formality of applying for a visa. However, in deference to mainland China, the United States had never permitted a Taiwanese head of state to visit. I was just shocked even though I had read about that. I came home, went into my office in Casselton, picked up the phone, and called the White House. "This is Governor Sinner, may I speak to Bill Clinton? I'll be brief."

He came on the line. "Bill, this is by far the most progressive economy and government in Asia and we're not going to let the president of the most progressive nation in Asia come to the United States? That's crazy. Just defy the tradition."

"Okay, I'll do that," he said. And he did. I don't know how Lee found out I had intervened but not long after the announcement that he was coming he called John Odegaard and asked John if he could bring me up to Cornell to visit. So I flew to Cornell with John in their Citation and sat with Lee for another hour and a half, along with a couple of his staff. We renewed our growing friendship.[114]

Saber rattling started again a year or two later during an election campaign in mainland China, as it does every election over there. Taiwan asked for some airplanes. So I called the White House again. "I don't get this. Here we have the best free society and they don't want much," I said. "Give them some fighter planes." I don't remember who I talked to at the White House but I advised getting Taiwan some F-4s or F-16s. And by God they did give them seventeen F-16s. They were extremely grateful and they knew again who the source had been.

My son Bob travels to the Republic of China frequently and hears their praise. Finally Bob said, "You need to go back and see these people one more time." So I accompanied him for a week a couple years ago. It was only then I found out those really weren't good F-16s we gave them. Those aircraft had underpowered engines. But they're still flying them.

I began to understand the political nature, the campaign nature of the saber rattling that periodically went on. I found that in Korea, too. When I was there trade was growing at an incredible rate. Boats would go right around the demilitarized zone and down into Seoul, and go back up north with another load of cargo.

Sharing a Heart

Miracles do happen. Here's one amazing example. The Governor's Residence phone rang in the middle of the night just before Christmas in 1986, and Dr. Tom Witt, husband of our daughter Betsy, answered it. A Dr. Stinson from Stanford University was calling from Valley Aviation in Fargo. "I have an infant dying in California, and our jet plane broke," he told Tom.

They were flying the heart of another baby, Mike McCann of Fargo (a name we didn't know until twenty years later), which had been recovered at Fargo's St. Luke's Hospital (now Sanford Health) for a transplant in California. "One of our engines can't be started. I need a fast plane to go from Fargo to Stanford. Can you help me?"

"I'll go up and talk to my father-in-law and see what we can do," he said. He came up and told me what was going on and gave me the doctor's number.

I called the doctor back. "I'm pretty sure I can get you a Citation [from the University of North Dakota] in about forty minutes," I said.

"That's not fast enough," he almost yelled into the phone. "We've got to get that heart out there faster than that."

"Let me think a minute." Then I suddenly realized we had pilots with F-4s sitting there on standby right in Fargo, right beside him. So I said, "Just hold the line." I flipped over to the next line and called Adjutant General Alex Macdonald, got him out of bed.

"Mac, do we dare commandeer an F-4?"

Yes, we dared. "Stay on the line," he said, "I'll call NORAD!" Two minutes later he came back to me. "It's a go. I'll order the plane rolled out."

We called the doctor back. I told him to, "Get ready immediately!"

"We'll take it," Dr. Stinson said. "Where should we go?"

"You're right there. Go across the field to command headquarters."

And the race was on.

The Stanford doctors were greeted at the Air Guard headquarters by Colonel Wally Hegg, the unit commander, whom Mac had called. The doctor was pleasantly surprised to learn that the mission was already in motion. Time was of the essence because they had never had a heart recovered from a donor and transplanted more than four hours later. We were already at four hours. The child, Andrew De La Pena, was dying in California from a rare hereditary heart defect that had claimed his older sister.

Ultimately pilot Bob Becklund Jr., then a lieutenant and later a colonel and commander of the Happy Hooligans, flew the heart to Hill Air Force Base in Utah and then on to Moffet Field in California, after which the precious cargo was successfully transplanted into Andrew, who was able to return home to his parents a few weeks later.

Along the way there were a couple glitches. The F-4s fly with a copilot in the back seat and the crew decided to attach a belly canister. But the heart would have frozen. They put the cooler with the heart in the back seat and Becklund whispered to his copilot that he was sorry but he would have to stay home. That added a great deal of tension to the trip.

A second glitch crossed Becklund's mind: his F-4 was "hot"—armed with live machine guns, cannons, and rockets. *There's just no time to disarm*, Becklund had to realize, and he jumped into the cockpit and raced off down the runway and turned his speedy craft toward California.

A problem came up at Hill Air Force Base. We assumed NORAD had called and told them who Becklund was and that he was supposed to meet a Lear jet from Stanford there. But the tower told him, "We don't know you and we've heard nothing about a Lear jet."

"Call NORAD and get a tanker ready," Becklund replied. "I'm coming in." As he hit the runway I have always imagined Becklund peering into the night darkness praying to see a waiting tanker. Then suddenly the truck's lights came on. Excitedly Becklund braked to a stop. In minutes he was again tearing down the runway with a full load of fuel, headed again for California. It had been a fairly long time frame when he got the infant heart to a waiting ambulance at Moffet, but the mission was successful. It almost suggests a divine guidance in what got done that night.

Several months afterward, *The New York Times Magazine* ran a huge feature article spread titled, "Racing for Life," about the incident. Later, it got even wider exposure in a *Reader's Digest* article headlined, "A New Heart for Andrew," and subtitled "In a race against the clock, two surgical teams and the Air National Guard struggle to get a healthy heart to a dying five-month-old boy."[115]

In May of 2007, a group of us—mostly people from the Air National Guard and MeritCare—brought Andrew and his parents, Stephen and Deborah, to a reunion in Fargo where they met with Mike McCann's parents, Steve and Karen, and Mike's two siblings. As the backdrop for a news conference at the Fargo Air Museum, the Guard had an F-4 with "Lt. Becklund" painted beneath the front cockpit, and "Andrew De La Pena/Mike McCann" lettered below the rear cockpit.

Andrew overcame two bouts of cancer and requires only a minimal dosage of rejection medication. He beat all the odds. He has grown into a handsome and talented young man, and at the time of the reunion he was president of his high school class, a varsity swimmer, and then later a student at Loyola University in New Orleans.[116]

Tears filled a lot of eyes that day, not only the two families but all who were involved with the miraculous episode and the emotional reunion.

CHAPTER NINETEEN: outside traditional decorum

Thumbs Up

I knew that I would be in trouble if anybody ever found out that I was a governor who picked up hitchhikers. I was driving to Fargo in my Suburban and gave a ride to two men, about thirty-five to forty years old. I can't remember where I picked them up but I took them into Fargo. They were decently dressed. I asked them where they were going and they said, "Well, we don't know. We haven't got any money."

"Here's fifty bucks," I said. "You guys take care of yourselves."

Brian Berg, Highway Patrol superintendent, confronted me about it some time later. I don't know to this day how he found out—whether I told somebody or what. But he was suspicious they were running from something. "Governor," he said, "use a little sense!"

"Sometimes I don't have much of that," I said. My own experience many years earlier taught me that when you need a ride you learn to hate people who drive on by and look the other way. I didn't enjoy that feeling as a hitchhiker and I didn't want to be looked at that way.

An earlier hitchhiker episode occurred maybe ten years before my election as governor. I was driving from Fargo to Casselton and a young man was standing there on the I-94 curve around West Fargo. He was a college student, I later learned. He was wearing all dark colors and I came within inches of hitting him. He got too close to the driving lane and I was making that curve and didn't see him quickly enough. I had my low-beam lights on. I stopped and went back and picked him up. "God, I had no way to see you," I said. "You have all these dark clothes on. Do you know how close you came to being hit?"

I figured I had to give him something white or he could be hit and killed. Wearing a suit, I took my coat and my shirt off and gave him my white T-shirt from under my shirt. "Listen to me," I told him, "put this on over your clothes so people can see you or you're going to get killed out here." Then I got back on the highway and eventually let him off at Casselton. I forgot all about it.

But a few years ago at a reception, this young man of about forty came up and said, "Remember that time you gave that young guy a T-shirt when he was hitchhiking?"

"Yeah, I was so frightened that night I would have given whatever I had," I said.

"I'm the guy."

It turns out that he's a professional, an architect or something.

"I will never forget that as long as I live," he said.

"I won't either." It was a cool thing for him to remind me of it because it was just one of those heartfelt things. I was frightened and scared. At home they all asked, why is your shirt pulled out?

Funny Things Happened

There were so many wonderful experiences during my time as governor. Wherever I went at the Capitol people were working away and they'd all look up and smile. Early on it was apparent something really wonderful had happened. It was fun to come to work. The Governor's Suite is a small complex of offices and work cubicles on both the ground floor and first floor of the Capitol, connected by a private internal stairway. Often I would arrive singing and would usually make the rounds on my way in, greeting the staff individually. I sang because I was happy to get there and see everyone and it was always so pleasant.

One of my songs sung so often was "Old Man River." Another was called "Good Morning Sun," or something like that.

Even when we were dealing with difficult problems, people knew it wasn't so much that we might get beat up or abused, but rather that we had to try to do it right. That sense of trying to *do it right* seemed to help make everyone happy. It certainly made me more relaxed and comfortable with criticism. There were lots of bright people in the office who helped me reach intelligent conclusions. It was just a great time. It was all about trying to be a good servant. The happy part of it was almost everyone in the office was that way. Even the staff members that I didn't see often were always happy. I only know of one or two instances of unhappy people. They even laughed at my corny jokes when I told them for the first time. And sometimes the second time, or third or...

The other thing I think was probably the most pivotal part of all this was our Thursday staff lunches. Chuck Fleming originated the gatherings. Those were the most uplifting events of the whole time and I always looked forward to them. We celebrated birthdays and anniversaries. My press secretary's regular wit was usually embodied in a written piece. Sometimes Chuck would sing, albeit badly, but he was entertaining and it was great fun. I had gotten into writing limericks and occasionally shared one.

I don't know what provoked one memorable event that happened at one of those lunches. On my birthday in 1986, some prominent women in the community came in modeling T-shirts colorfully emblazoned with Georgie's Girls on the front. We laughed that day. Oh my God, we had such a great time. It was a Pat Ness production. They gave me a handmade card crafted from a manila folder with their signatures and original lyrics of the song they serenaded me with. We had a birthday cake. I remember four women along with Pat, but the card contained six signatures: Fran Gronberg, Lois Erdmann, Joni and Laura Leifur, Bonnie Rothenberger, and Barb Evenson.

The almost weekly staff lunches were usually in the Governor's Conference Room, a rectangular carpeted cavern on the ground floor with access to both office area and to the outside hallway. We sat around a long table that dominated the center of the room. A portable wooden lectern, adorned by the state seal, is moved against the end of the table to accommodate news conferences.

I wasn't aware of what was happening at the time, but one humorous incident is legendary among some in our Governor's Office. They refer to it as simply, "The bowl story."

Janie and I had purchased a quantity of glazed ceramic bowls by Casselton native and renowned St. John's University potter, Richard Bresnahan. His navy bean straw ash bowls are unique works of art. We used them as special gifts. We gave one to each member of the staff at Christmas that year and kept some in the office for dignitaries.

A while later came a day heavily scheduled with appointments. Although we didn't realize it right away, one of them involved a rather important representative of some foreign country. Rita, my scheduler, asked Dick Gross to staff the meeting at the last minute. Neither he nor I knew much about this courtesy visit. After getting acquainted and talking a while, we realized our guest was indeed a dignitary of significant stature. It dawned on Dick and me that according to protocol we should present this man with something. Just then receptionist Renee Ulmer happened to look in the open door. Motioning and making a circular indication with his hands, Dick signaled to her silently that we needed a bowl.

A bowl, Renee silently mouthed? She mimed the same circular gesture.

Dick nodded his head yes. Our visitor was seated with his back to the door, unaware.

Renee immediately went into the small utility room across from my office where we kept the coffee pot and snacks and various supplies. She came back quickly holding in her two hands a small white disposable Styrofoam soup bowl.

Dick shook his head. No, no, not that!

Realizing the mix-up, Renee sheepishly backed out the door and then couldn't stop herself from laughing. Kathy Dwyer, our office manager, happened along and Renee told her what had happened. Renee and Kathy ended up laughing so hard they had to tumble out of the Governor's Office suite and into the Capitol's Great Hall. Like many others in the office, both Renee and Kathy had a particularly wonderful sense of humor and an ability to not take everything too seriously. Inside my office, Dick was also laughing pretty hard while trying not to show it.

I don't remember whether our distinguished visitor ever did get one of those nice Bresnahan pottery pieces. But we will never forget the cheap little bowl.

One day I walked out of the office, going up to the Office of Management and Budget or some place, and I headed to the elevator. There was a lady standing with about eight books stacked up high on top of both arms. She was waiting for the elevator doors to open. Being sort of a smart ass I said, "You got a match?"

She looked at me and said, "Not since Wonder Woman died."

I loved that priceless rebuttal. No hesitation—just wham! She was so clever.

More recently the nuns in Fargo were putting on a tea that they do every year. We had an early morning meeting of us volunteer butlers. The butlers are a pretty humorous bunch of guys who wear tuxes and serve the tea. There was a lot of kidding around and clever jokes being told. My son George told me as we walked out that one of the sisters said, "You know, I heard more laughter here this morning than I heard in a month of Sundays."

Humor sometimes came in handy in responding to criticism or controversy. For example, I don't know where my quip about Bryce Streibel came from. Bryce and other ultraconservative legislators like Pete Naaden had criticized me after a newspaper ran a photo of a radar detector in my Suburban, parked in the lot at the Capitol. Along with focusing on the radar detector, the photo showed a large smudge on the windshield. When asked by a reporter about the smudge I suggested that it "was Bryce Streibel's nose print." I had few of those classic retorts and didn't particularly work at them, but when one of them came out it certainly was fun. I admire the people who come up with them routinely.

In that case, we found a way to diffuse the controversy with some humor and have a little fun while also helping a worthy cause at the same time. I donated the radar detector to the annual auction of the North Dakota Mental Health Association. "It grieves me greatly to depart with this precious family heirloom, but I am willing to make this sacrifice in the interest of promoting mental tranquility for Bryce Streibel and Pete Naaden," we said in a statement to the press.

"It is my hope that this one-owner, seldom-used, not-quite-state-of-the-art sentimental artifact will attract the same amount of local, statewide, and national prominence for the North Dakota Mental Health Association as it has for me," we continued. "In fact, Bryce and Pete are welcome to attend the auction and bid on it or take more pictures for their collection if they wish."

They didn't, but the chairman of the state Republican Party did. Kevin Cramer won a bidding war and claimed it for two hundred dollars.[117]

Another opportunity came up when a proposal for a new centennial license plate was blasted by Republicans in the legislature and their leader, Earl Strinden, because the estimated cost was about $1.6 million. Clearly it wasn't going to fly, so we announced at a press conference that Motor Vehicle Registrar Bruce Larson had been directed to withdraw the legislation. "The license plates are an issue that shouldn't remain an irritant in these critical times," I explained, pointing out ten additional reasons for taking this action. Looking back, they do somewhat reflect the political times. *The Bismarck Tribune* published the list.[118] Some of those reasons were:

—The current license has about 100 things on it, so it is already an appropriate centennial license.

—Our inmates don't need the money.

—Instead of licensing plates, we are thinking about licensing political rhetoric. That would raise a lot more money.

—In 1988, Byron Dorgan and Quentin Burdick bumper stickers will take up all the space and there won't be room for state license plates anyway.

—The only way to solve our state's revenue problem is to have the inmates print money, not license plates.

—It is just too hard to keep tabs on the license plate issue.

—The most compelling reason for abandoning the centennial license plate proposal is the ever-present fear of a referral, which would stop the making of the plates…it would be embarrassing for all of us to run around with bare bumpers.

Despite that dispute over an appropriation, the Department of Transportation developed an attractive and uncluttered new version of the plate later that year anyway. First Lady Janie is proud to have selected the winning design for the centennial license plate from among five or six designs.

Sometimes attempted humor can backfire. An incident I will always remember happened one day in the pool area at the Holiday Inn in Fargo. The sugar beet growers were enjoying their annual bash. Everyone was in a pretty spirited mood. Some big dude about six-six came up and grabbed my hand. "Hi, Governor," he gushed, "I bet you don't remember where you met me, do you?"

I didn't have a clue, but I looked at him and quipped: "The hell I don't. I met you in a massage parlor in Minneapolis." The guy's wife was standing with her back toward me. She whirled around. He had a drink in his hand. She knocked it about fifteen feet and it took thirty minutes to quiet that poor lady down. It was just a joke, but apparently not to her.

Some of the stories I told were by my judgment bawdy but I did try to avoid those that were just inappropriate. I maybe crossed the line a few times. People have a kind of a double standard. They act as if something that's a little risqué is just awful because that seems to make them feel or appear more proper or something. I always resented that. Humor is extremely important. We take ourselves way too seriously. Actually, life gets pretty silly sometimes.

I told a series of Norwegian jokes, and had a whole file of puns that I loved. A lot of people don't appreciate puns, but I'm sort of nutty about them. One came down the line from my son George, the banker. He told the story about the frog that came into the bank one day to get a loan and was assigned to Patty Black, who was a loan officer for frogs. "Mr. Frog, do you have any collateral?" she asked.

"Yes, well I have this," and he pulls out of his pocket a beautiful ceramic.

She said, "Sir, if you'll excuse me, I need to speak to my superior about this." So she took the ceramic and went in and told her supervisor the story.

He said, "Miss Black, does the frog have any collateral?"

"He has this, but what is it?"

He said, "That's a knickknack, Patty Black, give the frog a loan."

In Others' Words

There's something about clever expression of ideas that everyone strives for. If you're doing any public speaking or writing, you try to find a clever, memorable expression of a thought. I love alliteration and use it a lot.

I studied English literature and American literature, and still have original hardcover editions of classics: O. Henry stories, The Modern Library, poems by Elizabeth Barrett Browning, Tolstoy's *War and Peace* (which I *have* read), classic poems of Walt Whitman, work by Daniel Defoe, *Les Miserables* by Victor Hugo, *Conquest of Mexico* by William H. Prescott. I also have several Bibles.

It's been so long since I did a lot of reading, though. When my cataracts were bad it was difficult and I just got out of practice. I've always been able to read a legislative bill, understand it, and recognize implied meanings, and at times I found errors that needed to be corrected. But I'm a rather slow reader and also had to review so many journals and memos and reports to get the work done that I didn't read a lot of literature as such.

Without question my favorite American author is Louis L'Amour. Nobody moves a story like L'Amour does. He's probably the greatest American storyteller.[119] Janie and I had lunch with him and his wife in Denver about a year before he died.

Janie is a great fan of James Michener. Michener and his wife were at our home in Casselton for almost a full day. Janie is a much better reader, much more prolific than I. She reads constantly. I've often wondered if I'm not a better experience learner and a hearing learner than a reading learner. However, as long as I can remember I was able to read a legal document and understand it and see many of the nuances.

I suppose my appreciation for poetry came from my college and high school years. I've always loved poetry and have quite a few books of it, although I've never really tried to write anything serious. I've always loved Rudyard Kipling. His *Gunga Din* was always a favorite of mine. Kipling was a little bit like Louis L'Amour with poetry. He could make a scene live with a few words.

At one time I read quite a bit of Shakespeare, took a course in Shakespeare, and played the ghost of King Hamlet in *Hamlet*. I've always had a fairly good memory for verse.

Hankinson fourth graders sent me a bunch of cards, pictures, and poems one time. It was probably a class project. I was thinking about the years of drought with this brief limerick in my thank-you letter to them:

> There once was a Gov'nor named Bud,
> Whose grandchildren never saw mud.
> Cuz it just wouldn't rain,
> Which caused so much pain,
> That he'd much rather deal with a flood.

CHAPTER TWENTY: the right time

Third Term Not a Charm

A series of incidents and events in the fall of 1991 preceded my decision whether to run for a third term as governor. Consciously or at least subconsciously, they probably helped influence that decision.

I remember my passion giving way to anger only a couple of times that fall. They were after my heart surgery when I was suffering a bit from what was then called a pulmonary pump syndrome. The classic episode, of course, was an incident where I punched a legislator, which made me realize that something had happened.

The confrontation was with Gordon Berg, a Devils Lake Democrat and member of the North Dakota House of Representatives. Everyone in Bismarck knew at the time that Gordon was deeply concerned about the sinking water level of Devils Lake. Gordon was a frequent and often pestering advocate, always pitching for several different projects to resolve or ameliorate the problems of the low water. A major fish kill was imminent if the lake level couldn't come up. One of the recurring phenomena of Devils Lake is that it's either too low or too high. Although we have more recently been worried about too much water, Devils Lake at that time was the reverse of what it is now. We had begun working on the proposal to build a two-way drain, one that had a ridge in the middle with big pumps to move water in or out.

I had been away resting and recovering from my heart surgery for a few weeks. When I came back I had worked about four days the first week and on Saturday I had taken a bunch of letters home to the Governor's Residence and I was tape recording my replies. I had just put that material back into my briefcase when the door-bell rang. I stupidly went to the door and there was Gordon. He immediately began talking and asking questions. Before I could answer he would go on talking. After what seemed like about thirty minutes, I was getting more and more irritated.

I finally gently but firmly forced him back over to the door. As we approached the exit he asked another question. I began to give him an answer and he started babbling again. I reached the point of no return and grabbed him by the shirt. Using an exple-tive, I told Gordon to shut his mouth, and then I hit him. I pulled the punch some and struck him below the chin, in the neck. He left then. I was shocked that I had done it because I had never hit anybody in my life. Gordon didn't mention the incident afterward and nothing ever came of it.

I was shocked by my anger. So I immediately called my doc-tor and asked what in the world was happening. "Oh, we forgot to tell you the fact that with heart pumps there's often severe mood changes for a short time," he said. "Remember we told you about depression?"

"Yes," I said, "I've been careful of that." If I sensed any evi-dence of depression, I tried to overcorrect.

"Well, we should have told you about anger too because it's typi-cal of heart pumps," he said. "I hope there's no permanent damage."

"I don't think so," I said.

Gordon never brought it up. He may have been slightly inebri-ated. Something about him was different that day. He often talked a lot but that day he was totally out of control. A little fruit of the vine may have facilitated his loquacity.

This was followed by an episode in Dickinson and one in Grand Forks. I recall them both vividly. I was angry with cause but my usual tactful way of saying things kind of disappeared. Both events related to water. The setting in Grand Forks involved the state chamber of commerce, the GNDA. The water people at the gathering had been part of a previous meeting where we all agreed on a half-cent sales tax to help us pay for water projects. We had spent tons of money to solve the greatest need and bring Missouri River water to the southwest part of the state and we'd spent a lot of money on the West Fargo Sheyenne River bypass.[120] Plenty of other projects out there were needed not only for economic reasons but to also help people have decent lives. When I arrived, GNDA President Dale Anderson told me the board had voted to withdraw support for the sales tax idea and the strongest opposition to the tax had come from Dickinson where we were about to open the southwest pipeline. I was under control at the beginning of my speech, but then all of a sudden got angry. I said I couldn't imagine the ingratitude of people who benefited from huge public expenditures to get clean water to their region and now oppose doing the same kinds of projects for others. I was furious and people looked at me in astonishment. I couldn't help myself. My emotions were out of control.

Not long afterward, the same thing happened during a speech in Dickinson for the dedication of that southwest pipeline. I was breathing fire in my remarks, again about the dastardly ingratitude of people. Didn't mention names in either case but everyone knew damn well who I was talking about.[121]

Then, on a late October Saturday morning in a goose blind, I remembered Governor Schwinden's advice to not even consider running for a third term. "I've seen several people do it and they all end up in ruin," he warned. "They're spent and people get tired of them and they want a change. Just don't ever think about it… and it's too darn hard on your children."

He told me exactly why I shouldn't run again. "You will be risking arrogance, because you do get power as things go along and you learn how to use it," he said. "There's lot of dangers in going beyond two terms. You risk doing things that you probably should not do and probably more important than that are the dangers that come to your family. You've got to devote a lot of attention to your family. A lot of families get hurt by being in the shadow."

The episode in the goose blind happened when my son George and I were up at Underwood with Dave Kjelstrup, a local banker. It was his land, his goose pit. Rough guy, he swears almost as well as I do—or more. It was about 9:30 AM when the sun got bright and the geese weren't flying anymore and we were waiting for Dave to come and pick us up. That's when the conversation took place. It was pretty brief. "We don't want you to run again," my son said. "We're proud of what you do but nobody ever treats us like ourselves. We're all treated like the governor's kids."

I said, "Oh my God, I knew this could be a problem and I know what I must do." So I left that goose pit and become a lame duck.[122]

I stayed home the next morning and before we got out of bed I said to Janie, "I made a decision yesterday."

"Really?" she said. "So did I. What did you decide?"

"I decided I am not going to run again."

"That's a good thing," she said, "because that's what I decided too."

I had a press conference the next morning. About once every month before that the reporters would ask whether I had made a decision about a third term. I knew what I had to do. I didn't want a lot of people assuming I was going to run again when I had decided not to. It was clear to both Janie and me what we had to do so we let everybody know right away.

I reflected on that decision in a letter I sent two weeks later to Jeanne and Ellery Bresnahan, indicating that while I didn't know what the future held for me I knew that God would make it work out all right. I wrote: "It was a difficult call because I do love my work. But I found myself running out of patience. That can't work here, or anywhere else, for that matter. I hope we can continue to serve others in some way."

I also observed the worth of Schwinden's advice another time with another governor. I tried to tell Iowa Governor Terry Branstad not to run for a fourth term. But he did and apparently it took a toll. Ultimately his son was on drugs and killed somebody in a car accident and went to jail. That was a lovely family and Terry was a decent guy. He was popular and a good governor and wonderful to work with. His family didn't deserve that suffering.

Worth Remembering

A period of eight years in the Governor's Office generates a variety of highlights and also some lowlights.

The Republican candidate for the Senate in Montana provided the idea for the Prairie Rose State Games. I was on my way to a governors' conference in Idaho when we stopped in Billings to refuel the state plane. I called a former St. John's friend, Bill Osborne, and asked him to have lunch. He came out and we had a great time.[123] He had been a successful coach at Billings High School and later went back to coaching. As we were leaving he said, "Bud, you know what you ought to do, you ought to go home and start a state games. My son is running it here and they are wonderful." He described the program to me.

I got home and called Alex Macdonald, asked if he would lead our effort. "Yeah, I'll do it." That was Mac. No baloney, just I'll do it. And he did all the rest, with the help of a wonderful steering committee working with Tim Mueller and Karen Aasel and others from the State Parks and Recreation Department. They made a decision that has helped our games be so uniquely successful when so many of the other state games programs no longer exist. That was to move city to city—rotate between Bismarck, Fargo, Grand Forks, and Minot. This program requires quite a bit of money and much of it is contributed. But these communities only have to do it every four years. It also takes a lot of volunteer work and by moving the games around they don't wear out the same people year after year after year. When their turn comes they remember the games fondly.

Look what's happened. It started out with seventeen events in 1987 and we're now with many, many more. Karen and Tim and Mac and that committee did it. Two legends in North Dakota sports, Sid Cichy and Jack Brown, were also on that original committee.

I participated in the tennis competition a couple times. The most memorable was the first year. I hadn't been playing and wasn't playing well, but lo and behold there were so few in my bracket I got to the finals, where I met Warner McNair, a Republican activist who had been the state open champion sometime in the thirties when I was a teenager. We were playing what's called a pro set. The winner has to have eight points and win by two. Trailing 6-2, I realized he couldn't retreat into his backhand. He was in his late seventies. I hit every single shot to his left side and beat him 8-6 and he was absolutely beside himself. Later I became good friends with him and his wife, Esther. Tennis courts in Fargo were named in his honor and I was there for the dedication. He was a good tennis player but a little bit handicapped by health and age.

After he was governor, Ed Schafer explained why the games were so important. He participated in the first games as a runner. He said, "Think of the people who have a wonderful weekend doing something they dearly love to do and they don't have to travel far." Bismarck has been the leader in number of participants because that city is quite reachable by everyone. People come from Minot and Fargo and Dickinson and all corners of the state. With high fuel prices, it's important to have those kinds of events within the state.

The North American Regatta was also a huge success, though it is no longer in existence. I can't remember where the idea came from. We got kicking around the discussion of how we were going to finance it because we didn't have any money. Somehow or other the name North American Regatta came up and of course North American Coal. I called Augie Keller, who was always a good friend, told him what the idea was, and asked whether North American would help us pay for it. He went to Cliff Miercort, the company CEO. I think they gave us ten grand to help us put it on, and then subsidized it every year. State Parks and Recreation organized the event. At that time only thirty-five or thirty-six Hobie Class regattas in the United States existed for which you could get points to qualify for the Olympic Games. In the second or third year the North American Regatta achieved that Olympic-qualifying status.[124]

Our great event succeeded because it differed from most of the regattas around the country, which were run at fancy yacht clubs where only the rich and famous could compete. Lake Sakakawea has no expensive hotels. People camped in tents. We had food and other necessities in the field—that was important. The big lake always had wind, which was the most critical. They never worried about the boats being becalmed. I was a landlubber, not a good sailor, so my participation went poorly.

In February of 1991 I signed a bill repealing the state's 100-year-old blue laws, which limited the sale of goods and services sold on Sundays. As the last state in the country to prohibit Sunday shopping, we were kind of an island. That was evident in Fargo-Moorhead with tons of people shopping in Moorhead on Sundays. I think philosophically it would be a good thing if the whole society would block marketing on Sunday. But the blue law was really built on a religious principle. As much as I believe in the principle of worshiping God and resting from the run of the mill activities on Sunday, I didn't think the state should be imposing it unless it was done nationwide. The Sunday opening law was referred to the voters and upheld in the June 1991 primary election.[125]

For obvious reasons—obvious to me, anyway—I've always opposed capital punishment. If it's so wrong to take a person's life, why does society do it as a punishment? If it's wrong, it's wrong. The intrinsic evil of it is compounded by the fact that so many people put to death have later been proven to be innocent. That alone should give pause. What kind of society will forgive the most outrageous crimes, yet some people do other certain things and they require the death penalty?

Early on in the campaign I let it be known if I were elected it would be over my dead body that a capital punishment bill ever became law. It's become more and more obvious that that's not a good solution. I spoke to one of the principals in the Alfonso Rodriguez murder case and said "Don't do it, don't go there. It'll come back to haunt the society that engages in that."[126]

I vetoed a mandatory sentencing requirement for lots of reasons. First of all, why do we have judges if sentences are automatic? Regardless of the circumstances, regardless of the curability of the perpetrator, regardless of everything individual about a case, it just imposes a sentence according to some distant and abstract law. In addition, as we've seen with drug and alcohol addiction, the state did nothing about treatment after mandatory sentences were established. Instead, addicts were just sent to prison where they *really* learned about crime. There are a lot of violent criminals in prison. We were told for several years that there's no cure for methamphetamine addiction. But even meth use has now been proven treatable with a months-long process.

The conclusion is absolutely false that everyone who is a drunk driver is evil and a criminal. Most of them are sick people. Admittedly they've done things that need to be dealt with but nobody was willing to find an answer. The attorney general from South Dakota, Larry Long, told us in a public policy discussion about a sheriff who works with a county court that waves the sentence provided the convicted person shows up every morning and every night for testing. He said it is unbelievable how many people have been cured, how few have violated their alternate sentence, and how many have come back and thanked them for helping get over their alcoholism. The concept is now being tried in several North Dakota counties. But there's so little of that being done, even though incarceration is more expensive than treatment. It's a sad comment on a society that wants to send everyone to jail, which leads frequently to terrible mistakes.

Two years prior to my election, the landmark decision by federal Judge Bruce Van Sickle in the lawsuit brought against the state by the Association of Retarded Citizens (ARC) found that the care, treatment, and facilities at the Grafton State School and San Haven Hospital violated the constitutional rights of the residents.[127] The court ordered the state to begin moving people with developmental disabilities from the institutions into community programs. It was a major undertaking and it had caused a lot of public angst before we got to the Governor's Office. We worked darned hard to pay attention to what the court ordered, and to do it within the limits of our ability.

I recall being acutely aware of the court order and strongly determined to move past the lawsuit. We worked to improve the services delivery system so it wasn't quite as stereotyped as it had been. With the leadership of Dick Gross and Dick Rayl we did get out from under the court order. Dick Gross and I met with Judge Van Sickle twice. I don't even know if that was kosher. I also vaguely remember meeting with the ARC attorney, Mike Williams, and one other ARC lawyer. Whether we did the best that could be done is uncertain, but we did the best we were able to do.

More recently I read in the newspaper about a federal educator who criticized what he saw as an excessive number of children identified as requiring special education. He said we're over correcting. That tends to be the philosophy of those in government service who don't appropriately prioritize the human factor. They don't see that in a real way the priority is people and their rights. I've always been proud that when we left office we were listed as number one in the nation in providing care for our handicapped.

However, we weren't that successful at promoting school re-organization in the state. It required vast amounts of legislative courage and foresight. Everyone was aware that if we didn't plan for school reorganization it was going to happen after lots of mistakes. Many, many schools had been built that never should have been, and others were still being built. It was particularly obvious to me that lots of children were short the academic work they needed, particularly in the last two years of high school. There were just too many upper-level courses that the small high schools couldn't offer. Some of them were providing a few of the science courses by using a rotating teacher, but lots of times there weren't adequate lab facilities. Lots of things weren't working well, but reorganization was like pulling teeth.

I had tried it when I was in the legislature. Clearly the section of law called the Joint Powers Act was responsible for many school reorganizations. It gave school districts the ability to try joint efforts by contract. It probably wasn't as dramatic as some of us would have liked to have seen in bringing about reorganization, but it's a wonderful section of law and it was used often in putting joint efforts together.

Grades ten through twelve should be unified high schools. Freshman year students get used to the regimen of moving from class to class in different rooms. The upper-level kids are better able to handle traveling in buses. It's not as good to have little children traveling a long way. I was pretty sure from my own kids that until they got to tenth grade they didn't need the science labs and the expensive facilities that they could only get with centralized schools. One or two of our children took courses at North Dakota State University while still in high school. It was a huge benefit to them. A couple of our children went on to sophisticated schools and did well. Several of the kids were way brighter than I was, more like their mother.

The other area of frustration where reorganization was so badly needed was in many of the county functions. I was determined to get extension programs regionalized, not just because it would probably be more efficient but because we could provide specialists in the region that we couldn't afford in every county. We actually cut the budget one time and said we wouldn't raise it unless there's a commitment to get these county offices central-ized. Oh yeah, they said, we'll do that, just give us the money. It never happened. I've always been upset about that, and about weakening to giving them the money without a plan or certitude that it was going to happen. The issue is really the same as with schools—quality of service.

Looking at continuing disappointments, the history of Garrison Diversion is really a complex tale of broken promises.[128] Pardon the cliché, but North Dakota came out on the short end of that stick. The states on the Missouri River below us are big water users. Everybody below South Dakota was fighting tooth and nail to keep the water for their barges in the spring. A whole lot of things were devious and we weren't able to fight them off because they had more votes in Congress. They still do. However, if the nation became short of food, which would happen if we had a national war, even that attitude might change.

Inadequate water in the Red River basin means every place in the Red River Valley up to Winnipeg will be short of water in the near future. The Canadians are talking about running a pipeline from the Assiniboine River down to the northern US border to get water to people in that area. I think the cost is over $50 million to do that, and yet a solution of bringing Garrison Reservoir and Missouri River water to the valley would help everyone above and below the Canadian border. There comes a time when you have to move regardless of the cries of protest, as with the Devils Lake outlet. Nobody knows how successful that will be, but Governor Hoeven was in a position where to fulfill the responsibility of his job he had to do something and he did. He built the outlet on the west end of the lake despite Canadian objections.

Random Observations

Every talk I gave in my initial campaign for governor revolved around what was happening in the state. I had the good for-tune to be involved in an economics crash course through the Federal Reserve Bank in Minneapolis. A man named Gerald Corrigan headed up the Minneapolis Federal Reserve Bank and

Gary Stern was his major assistant. Corrigan and Stern—along with a man named Jim Hammill, who remains a close friend to this day—helped me understand that a production-oriented economy like North Dakota's is going to take a lethal blow from a strong or bloated dollar. We certainly had a bloated dollar. Everything we sold was in dollar terms, so every potential foreign buyer had to pay huge amounts of their own money to get the dollar to buy our products, and we were getting killed in the market worldwide. It had an immediate effect on the US market. As if that weren't enough, the other terrible thing that happened was *real* interest rates. The real interest rate is the difference between inflation and the value of your product in terms of its growth. For example, some at that time were probably paying 12 to 16 percent, and our product value was going down, our asset values were going down, which meant we probably had a 20 percent *real* rate. All kinds of business people—more so in the agricultural sector—were getting killed by that phenomenon and many of them didn't understand it. They didn't realize that when they were borrowing at 10 percent and the value of the product they were selling was actually going down, they were paying huge interest rates. Everything in the economy dealing with products of any kind got hurt. I warned all through the campaign we were riding into a big canyon and the only way to deal with it was to cut spending.

When I was young we thought that Fargo, only twenty miles away, was a really big city and a different place. Now there's no question that our neighbors are not just in Bismarck, but they are in Louisiana and Ethiopia and Pakistan and Asia. It's an inescapable reality we are becoming, in a sense, the neighbors that Christ spoke of in the gospel when the man asked, "Who is my neighbor?"

It's all too often about whether or not the global market is working or the dollar is in good shape worldwide. It's about America's interests and whether America's economy is doing well. We have an awful time comprehending that when the casualties are reported out of Iraq, the death of a hundred Iraqi citizens is really the death of our neighbors. There were only two Americans killed yesterday so we think that's not so bad, never mind the two hundred Iraqis that are dead. We tend to get provincial in our attitudes toward life, forgetting we do have an effect one way or another on the people of the world.

We've really come into an age of communication and interdependence. It's really a global society, both by transportation and by trade. That's why it's so difficult to determine how legitimate trade agreements are that don't go beyond just the trade, that don't go into seeing to the benefit of the lives of the people in your trading partner.

Energy and food are so critical to human existence that to try to include them in free trade is absolutely not going to work. I saw too many times even in my public career where countries would talk about free trade and yet when their energy supply or their food supply was at stake it was all forgotten. Doublespeak becomes almost common language because no country with any sense is going to abandon their own people to hunger or cold. The Middle East crisis has been all about petroleum products. Even before the military adventure we had our Seventh Fleet over there all the time, protecting our oil butts. Something like 40 percent of our refined product comes from there. That's crazy.

Hillary Clinton, before she became First Lady, made a landmark statement when she said the world is a village. We can no longer ignore or pretend we don't know about the suffering in Africa, about the turmoil in the Middle East, about the economic upsurge in China, about the whole world, which is the village where we live now. I'm not an expert on world happenings but it's impossible in this time to forget that those are our neighbors in Africa dying by the hundreds of thousands in poverty and famine. Tsunami floods on the other side of the world aren't meaningless, they are all over our TV sets and we all experience some of the horror. The sufferings from hurricane Katrina weren't thousands of miles away because we watched the devastation over the airwaves.

You see people like Father Jack Davis giving his whole life helping to resurrect the poorest of the poor in Peru and you gain an understanding of someone like Mother Teresa and many others who have lived those lives. A friend, Dellis Schrock, who died while he was in New Orleans helping rebuild homes, constantly lived in the global society. He reminded us that we must be neighbors to all the people of the world to the best of our ability.

In November 2001, I spoke at the North Dakota Heritage Center with Governor John Hoeven and former Governors Bill Guy, Art Link, Ed Schafer, and Allen Olson. The event kicked off a campaign to support the Heritage Center expansion.[129] I suggested that maybe even more important than the building project might be hiring a staff historian who would record significant events. Democracy grows and gets stronger by its testing, and we as a nation are being tested. But unless that growth and the results of that testing are recorded for future generations, growth isn't as fast as it should be. Unless we single out and spotlight those significant periods of growth in democracy, our democracy will become stagnant and will not continue to grow and be appealing to the rest of the world.

CHAPTER TWENTY-ONE: good shall come of it

Rewards and Gratification

I've been blessed in countless ways. In return, sometimes I get called upon to help with something and for reasons that are never really clear or thought out I say yes or no. That's kind of the way my life has gone and that's the way it will go, whether I set plans or not. At one point a few years ago, I even tried to help a group of independent truckers who were literally going broke because of high fuel prices. It's hard for me because I'm trying to not get involved with problems like that, but I found these people who came to me almost in tears are so appreciative and so in need of someone to just listen and maybe make some phone calls. It is extremely rewarding and I find myself unable to say no to people who have needs like that. I can see that maybe it's just a way for me to continue to fulfill what seems to be the mission of my life—to serve.

I met the father of an old friend, and in visiting with him discovered he had lost his wife a couple months before and was extremely lonely. I had the opportunity to invite him to lunch with some other friends and saw from him that day sheer delight at being included and being listened to and being talked to. It was just a little thing but it was the kind of thing that one, it seemed to me, must do if you're able when you are committed to service. And it's also satisfying for that reason.

However, I'm embarrassed by my failure to help someone on one occasion. An elderly lady who had been a neighbor went into a nursing home about ten years earlier. I was talking with her at a gathering of some kind and she said, "Come and visit me, will ya?" That was the last time I saw here before she died some time later. I was distressed by my failure to get over and visit with her, to help her pass her day, and maybe add a bit of happiness. It would have meant quite a bit to her and would have been easy for me to do if I had just focused on it.

Helping people is more than feeling good, but there's no question that it does feel good. Much of the Christianity I espouse is in Christ's constant reminder that we must be good neighbors to all the people who enter our lives. In many ways it's the source of my dictum and disgust about the bureaucratic church, which is interested in rules and regulations and edifices and doesn't do enough to help the poor and the other needs of society. It is as far as I can see the essential message of the Gospel to do good to those who hurt you.

The fact that I like people can have its negatives. My wife complains that wherever we go I am always visiting with the guy next to me or the guy on the plane. But I find there's something intriguing in every person, even ones who are offensive to me at times. There are a lot of really good people in the world who are really different from us. I found that the quilt-like pattern of the people in our lives were worth listening to and admiring and paying attention to.

Early in my political career, in the sixties, I came in contact with Torfin Teigen, a political activist who was something of a gadfly.[130] Torfin could be a pain with his strange and loquacious style of discussing politics and all these wonderful ideas. He had his agriculture programs, and many theories about many subjects. Both Torfin and his brother Ingmar, who was a battery collector, used to stop at the farm frequently. They seemed to know when we were having coffee because that's when they appeared. They were fabulously interesting people, both quite eccentric. Ingmar was a scripture scholar of sorts. He would stretch out on a lounge chair, put his head back, and the scriptures would just roll out. Some of us were so intrigued by this man that we spent an hour straight listening to him carry on. Torfin elicited somewhat the same reaction from us. We knew he was terribly eccentric like his brother, but a fascinating characteristic they both had was a concern about people. They were compassionate to others and interested in big issues as well as small. Maybe we all learn from these kinds of people.

In thinking about the rewards my life has generated, I am more and more aware of the blessings of a spouse who has been with me and put up with me and all of my mistakes and activities for all of these years, who forgives me and hangs in there with me. That's probably the greatest reward I'll ever get on this earth. Growing old together has brought a new sense of happiness derived from the more peaceful existence than the sometimes over-energized activity of public life. We've both found that learning new things in terms of human relations is a non-ending experience and produces non-ending rewards. But knowing how to share the blessings we've received with so many in need is difficult. We get so many requests, non-stop calls for help in many areas, not the least of which is financial. That's complicated by the fact that we don't know what our own needs are because we don't know how long we're going to live. I'm not sure we do a good enough job of giving to the poor. I'm probably not doing well enough in financial gifts but I try to make up for it in service.

I used to hear some kidding about the size of our family. Ten kids. Janie and I didn't know we would eventually need all the fingers on two hands to tally our brood, but those kids are our greatest accomplishment and a wonderful source of continuing pride. We have been blessed to be the parents of these unique individuals. Each of them is successful in life. A father's perspective is certainly not objective, but I see all of them as special people. They are universally sensitive to other people and universally truthful. They are in many ways a reminder how important all that is. They've become my closest friends.

It's difficult to adequately explain the rewards of grandparents that come with loving grandchildren who sometimes dote on you and sometimes come with something that needs to be fixed. I wish they both would happen more often. Just to be able to fix some little thing and hand it back to a grandson or granddaughter is very rewarding when one gets to be eighty. For example, during a visit to the Twin Cities I fixed two chairs for a granddaughter and

I fixed a shovel for my grandson. For me, whom my wife calls a feedlot carpenter, these little abilities I learned along the way are wonderfully satisfying.

Somebody asked me once what part of my life I have enjoyed the most, and found most rewarding. God, I loved everything, including my time in the seminary and my experience in the service. The Guard produced many great friends. My brother-in-law Ellery and his wife, my sister Jeanne, were there. My cousin Tom Sinner, a close friend, was there with his wife Lois.

Being a Catholic is rewarding in that to me the Eucharist is fundamental to Christianity and to the gift of forgiveness that Christ gave us. The Eucharist has always been extremely important to me and should be available to everyone, regardless of their loyalty in faith. Sometimes we hear the priest say something like: "Well, if you aren't an active Catholic don't come to share the Eucharist." That's simply incompatible with Christ's message at the Last Supper, and with his whole life of welcoming and embracing the friendship of others that he came across whether they were the tax collector, the woman at the well, Mary Magdalene, or all the people who came into his life. I have always thought that the most soul-searching verse in scripture is Christ's distribution of the bread and the wine at the Last Supper, when he said it's for the forgiveness of sins that I'm leaving you this as a gift.

The church has maintained a small concentration of good things in spite of all the deviation that is often so irritating to us members. I'm pretty loyal to regular worship though not stupidly, irrationally loyal to it. There is a reward in the frequency and regularity of worship because you get not only the Eucharist but also the message of the Gospel and the writings of the apostles in the readings. Unfortunately, probably a greater percentage of the homilies are bland and lack instruction, but on rare occasions you find priests who actually preach the Gospel. That is hugely important on a regular basis to remind you who you are and what this is all about.

As I've mentioned, it does get irritating at times to see the preoccupation with bureaucracy and rules and falderal. I read a column in the *High Plains Reader* by Ed Raymond about the 2008 visit of Pope Benedict XVI to the United States.[131] It was a poignant critique of the pomp and circumstance that the Pope brought into his visit. That's so characteristic of many of the hierarchy in the church. It's pretty hard to take when you know what's important is the message of forgiveness, the message of feeding or caring for the poor. The church is active in humanitarian circles, but it's hard to deal with its desire for huge buildings and elegant surroundings in the face of so much need.

It's rewarding to be a Democrat because of that strong tradition of attention to people and people's needs. At times every Democrat probably loses sight of that, but the tradition is clear. It's almost axiomatic that the preoccupation of the Democratic Party has for the most part been on protecting and securing the rights of people. It was the Democrat leadership in the thirties that finally brought a focus on stopping major corporations from running roughshod over small entrepreneurial business, and that helped individual people with food and shelter during the Great Depression.

You would be hard pressed to find that consistent a trend in the Republican Party. Certainly Abraham Lincoln's life and work stand out in a way that's a wonderful testimony to America's goal of securing the rights of all people. We still struggle with race issues and with equal rights for women, but the tradition is pretty clear that what Lincoln did was a landmark. He was a Republican but traditionally Democrats have held more tightly to his beliefs and his attitude of serving all the people and protecting their rights with government.

Summing This Up

I've never forgotten that Trappist monk's teaching in 1950 about God making things work out. It had such an effect on my learning to make decisions, sometimes praying they would work out or they would be right. With a whole lot of uncertainty we all have in our lives, we need to do the best we can and not be afraid because there's still time to go back and make a change. I had many instances of that in Bismarck. I'll never forget the day Chuck Fleming said to me, "How the hell do you make decisions anyway? We usually know all that you know and sometimes more and yet we don't know what the action should be and you always seem to make the decision."

Well, it was that assurance that it was going to work out. You read in a lot of the psychological columns that one of the most important things to learn is to forgive yourself. If you don't learn that you are going to have trouble. That monk taught me I couldn't go back and change the stupidity of some things I did. We all make stupid mistakes in our lives and need the ability to say it will work out and to go on and not kick ourselves into the dumpster because of a stupid thing we did. The forgiveness advice from Ralph Dunnigan and the realization that salvation would come anyway despite my stupidity were also huge lessons to me.

In the late 1970s, long before becoming governor, I was chairman of the sugar beet growers and went with a group of farmers who testified in Washington at a hearing held by the Environmental Protection Agency. The EPA wanted to ban a particular farm chemical from use on wild oats and we were opposed. After we gave our side, the hearing was stopped and the EPA cancellation process didn't proceed. The same thing had happened on an earlier occasion.

At the airport the next morning I ran into the chairman of the scientific advisory panel committee that had conducted the hearing. "You know," he said. "There's something different about you North Dakota people. You don't know what you're not supposed to do." He explained they had never before heard from farmers. I think that's reflected in the attitude of many North Dakotans when they face daunting challenges. They don't shy away from a struggle just because somebody sitting six inches higher might not like it.

We've suffered through two or three really difficult economic times in the farm economy and yet the state has done well. Watch the extraordinary numbers of North Dakota high school graduates and the percentage of the graduates that go on to our colleges and universities and you have to remember that this is a pretty young culture and the people in the age group that were parents and becoming grandparents when we were in office were people who'd come through some hard times. They wanted something better for their kids.

We've experienced in North Dakota a unique simplicity in our lives where an awful lot of people are extremely friendly and out-going and have an understanding that people are people regardless of where they come from and who they are. The warm hospitality of the West River people for someone from the eastern part of the state is striking. You can go on to almost any farm or ranch out in western North Dakota and you are invited in for coffee. "Come on in and sit down." No matter whether you're selling yourself or a product, you're treated as a human being. That's true also but to a lesser degree here in the east. There's something straightforward about this society. One thing I've always admired and inherited to some extent is the belief that we can do things. The confidence in our own thinking and in our ability to make change is truly unique in North Dakota. For example, the development of food processing and the manufacturing industry in our own times has been truly remarkable.

When it comes to politics, in North Dakota you frequently see unknown people come out of the woodwork to run for office. Nobody knows them but they have a passion to make a change and to make things better. They don't often need a lot of coaching. Those are really the great people who have kept the state from getting drowned out by the urban society. While we are moving more toward an urban society with the demise of the small farms, the heritage of our small-farm independence and self-confidence is still here. That helps make North Dakota a wonderful place to live and work.

In addition, the success record of people in high school getting beyond that and going to college and succeeding after college is pretty exciting stuff. A vice president with 3M told me one day, "Bud, you people don't understand how good your universities are." He said, "3M would hire every engineer that comes out of those two universities if we could. They're that good, and they're con-sistently good."

Another friend, John Jambois, who as the head of Tecton Products came here to open the new wing of the Marvin Window Company group, also just can't say enough good things about North Dakota graduates and North Dakota people in general.

At one of the Tri-College symposiums we had on alcohol and alcohol abuse, Fargo Chief of Police Chris Magnus made a startling comment, and it was something we all need to understand. He was talking about the new job he was taking in California, in a city twice as big as Fargo. He said they have one of the highest proportions of gang membership in the country and they have a lot of violent crime. "And yet, you know something," Magnus said, "the people there think they live in the greatest place on earth. They all will tell you they love it there. Most of the people aren't affected by the crime. They live comfortably in the suburbs, and life is good. They're untouched directly for the most part by the crime.

"There's some of that going on," Magnus said. "The alcohol abuse rate here is the highest in the country at the college level and nearly the highest among the adult population. People here don't realize that. They think this is the most wonderful place on the face of the earth."

For most people I suppose it is. But not for all those who suffer, either directly or indirectly, because of alcoholism or other addictions. A higher percentage of car accidents are resulting from the use of alcohol, and those crashes devastate families. Yet we tend to like it here and we like the friendliness of the people. We like their directness and their honesty. We overlook the blemishes that are in some areas of life all around us.

That observation notwithstanding, I've always said there were two places in the world where I'd like to retire. One was Fargo, and the other was probably Minneapolis. But it's difficult to think about leaving here. As you get older the ties of family become all the more binding. More than that, life here is good, with ample access to the arts and creative thinking.

One thing I regret while governor was not fighting for a higher minimum wage. It's beyond frustrating that people negatively connect morality with those earning a low wage and birth control. But a lot of them work three and four jobs, have no health benefits, and scrape together barely enough income to keep body and soul together, in addition to raising children.

At the same time, what's happened with our health care is an outrage. So many companies have gone to part-time employment to evade giving employees the same health benefits the management team has. Under current law, if you hire somebody for less than thirty hours or some magical irrational figure you don't have to provide them with benefits. That has always upset me. I think if push came to shove, if the constitutionality of separate treatment for part-time employees was ever tested, it would be thrown out.

Benefits in many ways are more important than take-home salary. On the farm, we didn't have benefits for our employees in the sixties. They weren't that common then. But one day it became obvious that we had to take better care of our workers long term. And we started providing good benefits.

As I sum this all up, and look back at all the challenges we faced in the Governor's Office, clearly I was worried about the tax referrals in 1989. Even so, the work of the Finance and Taxation Committee I chaired in 1983 before I was elected governor had lasting value. The *U. S. News & World Report* article I mentioned earlier credited North Dakota for having the fairest, most even-handed tax structure in the United States. It didn't go into detail but recognized the work of a group of legislators in both parties who toiled night and day to try to make sense of things that needed changing in the tax code. There are lots of episodes from that period that I won't ever forget. But I don't think I'd change a whole lot we did in that committee or that I did on tax issues when I was governor.

I'm proud of the fact that Dick Rayl, who was absolutely a genius at budgeting and the management of that office, helped me spend hours and hours going through the budget with his analysts. Major changes that we made in the budget were always well discussed, well thought through. Chuck Fleming was a huge help with that. He understood the budget better than I did. I think the two of us, along with the OMB staff, spent way, way more time on the budget than any other governor had ever done. We had to. We had to get the priorities covered and make the best sense possible out of the short-funded budget.

I'm also extremely proud of the work of the Lignite Research Council I established in the early period. The council has done a great deal of good. Also, we did the best we could for higher education under the circumstances, and for all of the "people" service agencies.

How would I like to be remembered as governor? I wasn't perfect, but was open and honestly trying to be a good servant.

I didn't put a lot of stock in prestige. I wanted people to know that I was just like they were, somebody who laughed at his own mistakes, and someone who understood human need and human suffering and had a good sense of humor.

I guarded against offending people, even those who offended me. But it did happen, as illustrated by a more recent mistake that I'm sorry for. Some legislators criticized me for talking about high property taxes. It fortunately didn't come across as harsh but I responded by asking where the hell they had been. *The Forum* quoted me, leaving out the "hell." It's a difficult issue and legislators get sucked in by people beating the drum of *no new taxes*. That's understandable, but what it really means is *let them raise property taxes*. I regret my tone and do recognize the problems legislators face.

I'm hoping for some understanding that the things I've experienced can help others avoid mistakes, that readers will remember that doing what's right is important. It's not just about having a long career. But nobody ever did a good job that didn't have good people around them. In the Governor's Office, over and over again we said this is what's right and it is what we're going to do. The whole staff was dedicated to that. The agency heads also became wonderful advocates of that motivation. I had the best staff of any governor in North Dakota's history. Anyone who doubts that needs to take a look at who was there, at how bright they were, and how dedicated they were to keeping me doing good things and the right things. While they were actually pretty small in number, they were loyal to me and loyal to doing what was right.

In 1999 I was inspired to write this poem and send it to those friends from my former staff:

> I'm just a man who is growing old,
> With friends, worth way more than gold,
> Who carried a light
> To do what was right.
> It's a memory I will forever hold.
> For leadership falls to those who are weak,
> Yet humble enough to dare to speak
> And risk being wrong

Or despised by the throng
For bringing human rights to a bit higher peak.
But friends like you make the weak stand tall
You help hear and answer each human call.
You strengthen the frailty
With your noble fidelity
And together tear down each tyrannical wall.
Age has a way of highlighting each flaw,
And our many neglects of God's loving law.
But friends keep lifting our tired eyes
To the preeminent human service prize.
My love for those friends advances in awe.
Thank you so much for all you have been.
And most especially for being there when
Pride and fear made others retire,
Or good peoples' dreams were under fire,
For God rewards your kind of women and men.

Art Link and Bill Guy both really wanted to serve. They weren't swelled up with pomp and circumstance. They wanted to be good servants and help make things better. I think most of the governors have been.

Bill had Lloyd Omdahl and some other good people on his staff. Lloyd was a genius. You can just read it in his newspaper columns. He's about as perceptive a man you will ever find. Ruth Meiers, who preceded Lloyd as lieutenant governor, possessed huge qualities that were compatible with all the things I was trying to do. She gave her whole life to public service.

The failure of the Democratic Party candidate to succeed me as governor is something I didn't see coming. I gave the nominating speech for Attorney General Nick Spaeth at the 1992 state convention, but the delegates favored Bill Heigaard. People urged me to support the party nominee. I reminded Democrats that the open primary is an important part of our political system. Nick beat Bill in that primary election and lost to Ed Schafer in the fall.[132] That campaign was a huge disappointment to me. I was responsible, in part, and felt terrible in realizing Bill might well have won, and certainly would have been a great governor.

There are a lot of good politicians in this state. Neither party has a corner on good people. The trick is to work with those who are sincere and willing to tackle the tough issues for the long-range good of the state. I'm strongly encouraged by seeing young people politically active, because there's always more idealism among the young than among the old. They seem to understand that it's not who gets the credit, but that the issues that are important. And the most difficult to face are often the ones that most need to be addressed.

I've always told people, too, don't run negative campaigns, because they prove nothing. That's what was done to Tom Daschle in South Dakota in 2004 and it was so disgusting.[133] Some Republican friends say he was one of the best members of Congress they've ever known. People who were in the middle of the battle in Washington told me there was no one as fair minded as Tom. I've advised everyone who has ever asked to run a positive campaign. Know what you stand for and don't be afraid to take stands.

What more is there to accomplish? It's like what I've said all along through this discussion of what's transpired, I just kind of walk along. I don't have any plans. The one thing I want to do and must do is be a loyal and supportive husband, doing everything possible to make my spouse happy and to take care of the things she needs.

I do want to actually expand my understanding of eternity and where I'm going after this life. At this point in time I can't escape thinking of death—it's all around me. Friends are dying. Every day it seems like there's another funeral. The fact that death is imminent is impossible to escape. In moments of thoughtfulness I recognize the need to increase my awareness of God and eternity and adjust to it.

My philosophy has always been to keep on going and not be immobilized by fear. For example, a horribly ruptured disc in my lower back in 1970 eventually required surgery in late 1971. It was killing me all that fall but I had to keep going. That winter, five or six days after the surgery, I went to the Constitutional Convention in Bismarck and got along fine.

If you are going to stop and mope over life or health issues you will die there. You have to trust that it is going to work out and that good will come of it. Both in psychology and activity you have to keep going because the most common cause of death is dying. If you consciously give up and quit trucking, the truck isn't going to run. The truck gets old, the cylinders set and won't move, and you can't get them started again.

Age continues to take its toll. But I still want to keep on going.

APPENDIX

State of North Dakota
OFFICE OF THE GOVERNOR
BISMARCK, NORTH DAKOTA 58505
(701) 224-2200

April 1, 1991

The Honorable Ronald Anderson
Speaker of the House
House Chamber
State Capitol
Bismarck, North Dakota 58505

Dear Mr. Speaker:

While each of us has strong beliefs, the heart of the controversy over HB 1515 is women's rights during pregnancy and the question of when the separate human person, with immortal intellect and will, is present. Is it at conception, sometime later, or at birth?

No one knows.

The opinions of thoughtful people, religious and secular, on this issue, differ widely throughout history and in the present day.

Given that unknown, government's role must clearly be restrained. History is full of accounts of the misuse of governmental power, often for a "good" cause. On this issue abuse can exist on both sides. Some even suggest legally requiring abortions for cases of AIDS and to curtail overpopulation. Such abuse must be resisted vigorously on both sides. Government must not overstep its bounds. It must not play God.

I am a Catholic and, although throughout history Catholic writings on when life begins vary widely, I agree with the current Catholic judgment that abortion is wrong.

The issue here, however, is the role of law.

I do not agree with those churchmen who urge government to impose extremely restrictive laws. In that regard, I am in far greater agreement with the many Christians of all faiths who rely heavily on Christ's admonition to cling to "faith, hope and love," not "faith, hope and law," remembering that not once did Jesus say, "There ought to be a law."

The fact that so many thoughtful people today and throughout history have differed in their beliefs on this issue is perhaps why a great many caring faith communities, Jewish, Christian and otherwise, have admonished public officials to tread carefully in public policy in this area.

Let me quote some individual statements which indicate the heartfelt differences of opinion (realizing that, in some cases, there may have been varying statements by these organizations):

The Lutheran Church in America, in its 1970 social statement on "Sex, Marriage and Family," stated:

> On the basis of the Evangelical ethic, a woman or couple may decide responsibly to seek an abortion. Ernest consideration should be given to the life and total health of the mother, her responsibilities to others in her family, the state of development of the fetus, the economic and psychological stability of the home, the laws of the land, and the consequences for society as a whole.

The National Council of Catholic Bishops, on November 7, 1989, adopted the following statement:

> Our long—and short-range public policy goals include: (1) constitutional protection for the right to life of unborn children to the maximum degree possible; (2) federal and state laws and administrative policies that restrict support for and the practice of abortion; (3) continual refinement and ultimate reversal of Supreme Court and other court decisions that deny the inalienable right to life; (4) supportive legislation to provide morally acceptable alternatives to

abortion, and social policy initiatives which provide support to pregnant women for prenatal care and extended support for low income women and their children. We urge public officials, especially Catholics, to advance these goals in recognition of their moral responsibility to protect the weak and defenseless among us.

The United Methodist Church, in General Conference in 1988, adopted the following resolution:

We support the legal right to abortion as established by the 1973 Supreme Court decision. We encourage women in counsel with husbands, doctors, and pastors to make their own responsible decisions concerning the personal and moral questions surrounding the issue of abortion.

The American Jewish Congress, at its Biennial Convention in 1989, said the following:

The American Jewish Congress has long recognized that reproductive freedom is a fundamental right, grounded in the most basic notions of personal privacy, individual integrity and religious liberty. Jewish religious traditions hold that a woman must be left to her own conscience and God to decide for herself what is morally correct.

The policy of the Presbyterian Church, adopted in the General Assembly 1983, and reaffirmed in 1985, 1987, and 1989 reads:

...The church's position on public policy concerning abortion should reflect respect for other religion's traditions and advocacy for full exercise of religious liberty. The Presbyterian Church exists within a very pluralistic environment. Its own members hold a variety of views. It is exactly this pluralism of beliefs which lead us to the conviction that the decision regarding abortion must remain with the individual, to be made on the basis of conscience and personal religious principles, and free from governmental interference.

Consequently, we have a responsibility to work to maintain a public policy of elective abortion, regulated by the health code, not the criminal code. The legal right to have an abortion is a necessary prerequisite to the exercise of conscience in abortion decision. Legally speaking, abortion should be a woman's right because, theologically speaking, making a decision about abortion is, above all, her responsibility.

The United Church of Christ, in its General Synod 16, wrote the following:

(The Synod) Upholds the right of men and women to have access to adequately funded family planning services, and to safe, legal abortions as one option among others....

The Reorganized Church of Jesus Christ of Latter Day Saints in 1974 (reaffirmed in 1980) adopted the following:

We affirm the inadequacy of simplistic answers that regard all abortions as murder, or, on the other hand, regard abortion only as a medical procedure without moral significance.

We affirm the right of the woman to make her own decision regarding the continuation or termination of problem pregnancies. Preferably, this decision should be made in cooperation with her companion and in consultation with a physician, qualified minister, or professional counselor....

The Episcopal Church, in its General Convention in 1988, adopted the following:

We believe that legislation concerning abortions will not address the root of the problem. We therefore express our deep conviction that any proposed legislation on the part of national or state governments regarding abortions must take special care to see that individual conscience is respected and that the responsibility of individuals to reach informed decisions in this matter is acknowledged and honored.

These are the varied conclusions of thinking, caring religious Americans.

There are many other historical writings as well which have led me to conclude that, since neither I nor anyone else can prove the presence of a separate human person at the moment of conception, women's consciences must be respected.

Government policy must find a balanced way which respects the freedom of women in this difficult area. The bill does not do so.

This is why I have vetoed HB 1515.

Sincerely,

George A. Sinner
Governor

Abortion in Public Policy
George A. Sinner

Edited December 1991

The morality of abortion and the more basic question of when human life begins have been a controversy throughout Judeo-Christian history. For students of Christian history and theology, disparity of thought between leading thinkers throughout history is well known. In recent years, the abortion issue has become both a matter of Church conflict, and a matter of conflict in the public policy arena. In any attempt to deal with this important issue, we must not lose sight of several perspectives:

1. In light of history, even within the religious communi-
    ty, few "absolutes" exist. Certainly even fewer can be
    legislated and are more helpful if recognized as ideals.

2. For many of us, morally, abortion is abhorrent. Teaching
    and preaching against abortion and the conditions and
    mentalities that cause and promote it is not only appro-
    priate, but obligatory, if our consciences so guide us.

3. The legal question, in the public arena, is a different one
    –and must be based on historical analysis of what this
    society can legitimately develop (without absolutes)
    about the beginning of human life. That is the essen-
    tial issue in public policy. "When do a woman's rights
    come into conflict with the rights of a new person?"

In making personal decisions, we will have to deal honestly with our own convictions and emotions. We also have a responsibility to educate ourselves. It is not a given that our personal conviction will be identical to the posture we take on public policy. It seems appropriate to add here that even an "I don't know" is an accept-able position, or "I cannot prove what I believe," since these may be the most honest for many in the absence of absolute or even apparent scientific conclusions.

Faith and public law bring forth the constitutional question of separation of church and state that is quite clearly at the heart of much of our present controversy. It is not surprising that otherwise disparate religions and denominations have become bedfellows on both sides of this issue. It is also not surprising that abortion continues to divide otherwise united religions groups. The Christian position changed substantially since the early thinkers tackled the question of when human life begins. It varies widely even today. The difficulty is essentially to determine when the human soul exists. Since our constitution is pledged to protect human beings, we cannot risk setting policies based solely on current religious thoughts of a portion of the people. Clearly an historical perspective is imperative.

The facts of Christian history, (to say nothing of the pre-Christian era and to say nothing of other than Christian thought) display a wide divergence of thought. St. Augustine talked very clearly about the time of quickening as the time when human life began. St. Thomas talked about vegetable life, animal life, and human life. Some people think you could probably go to the seventh or eighth month as the time when St. Thomas talked about human life. It is fairly clear that for those leading thinkers in Christian history, the time of the presence of human life was not at all clear. And there are many other writings displaying similar conclusions.

In addition, for years after Saint Thomas wrote, the Christian church actually prohibited baptism to a prematurely born fetus precisely because the fetus was not a human person. To this day there generally are not burial services for fetuses. So we begin to see that even the practices of the church have not exhibited a very uniform attitude toward the identical nature of a deceased child and a deceased fetus.

Probably more importantly, the church has generally taught that human beings are unique and are even like God because of their intellect and will: that makes them human. The question then becomes, when can intellect and will be demonstrated? Many of the advocates of constitutional amendments (that would equate abortion to murder and subsequently to the punishments of capital punishment or life imprisonment) allege they can demonstrate response stimuli of several kinds in the fetus at an early age. I'm sure that's true. You can demonstrate the same kinds of response in the animal fetus, too. The question of humanity, however, is the question of intellect and will and the unique emotional and social characteristics that flow from them.

Some have also alleged that modern science has removed all question of when human life begins. The problem is, however, that much of the modern scientific community denies even the uniqueness of the human spirit. As a result those of us who believe in immortality and the uniqueness of the human soul can put little reliance on modern scientific conclusions in this area.

It is safe to say that the court in its recent decision should clearly have established some time certain for legal abortions rather than leave this whole argument up to the states. We should press the court to ascertain a workable compromise because it is quite obviously a judgment subject to all sorts of uncertainty. The basic lesson here is that throughout the Judeo-Christian tradition, there have been all kinds of different theories as to when human life begins. To righteously conclude that what current Christians or other groups think is final and absolute is unfortunate especially when the conclusion would impose legal penalties on those who disagree.

It is reasonable, however, to expect some compromise in this very contentious area. It would be intelligent for the court to declare that there should be no abortions after a certain month of pregnancy and that there is no obligation on the part of the general public to support abortions. Clearly, we must be careful to support the poor generally, however. It is the establishment of a punishable prohibition in those early months that is the most offensive and that honest Christians especially should avoid. Public policy people absolutely must avoid such impositions.

A compromise abortion policy should address each of those areas.

No matter what one's present personal position is on abortion, it seems safe to assume that everyone is interested in protecting human life. This is a good place to start. Agreement about the beginning of life, and therefore when it is protected, however is unlikely. Compromise will be the only valid approach in public policy.

All of us who truly care about human life have much to do. We must embrace all who are pregnant. We must help and support them.

We must not make them social outcasts as even so many religious groups have done. We must help society care for dependent children, handicapped, ill, and elderly. We must work for the causes of peace and against capital punishment.

COMMENCEMENT ADDRESS OF
GEORGE A. SINNER, GOVERNOR OF NORTH DAKOTA
BEFORE THE 1992 GRADUATING CLASS OF
ST. JOHN'S UNIVERSITY, COLLEGEVILLE, MN

My remarks to you today will be somewhat somber, but I have governed some of the most wonderful people on earth for seven and one-half strenuous, difficult years. We've had to get along with severely restricted budgets and income decline, but we have together survived.

Today I will trust you to understand what is in my gut and in my heart.

I, frankly, am very worried about America.

We have lived in an eat, drink and be merry society for a long time. We are a society that consumes and does not save; spends and does not pay; we are a society that pursues personal profit and pleasure and ignores the poverty and pain of most of the world's people. Our society goes from crisis to crisis without ever learning from the last crisis to plan for avoidance of future crises.

We are, indeed, a nation at risk and not just in education as the now famous national report on education found. Already, we are the largest debtor nation in the world, and by the lights of most people, the *budget deficit* this year may hit well over $400 billion. That's 7 or 8 percent of our total national earnings.

The interest payments alone this year will grow by $50 billion and the total interest payments portion of the budget will amount to almost 1/3 of the budget and will exceed the defense budget.

And we still do not have a safe, assured energy or food supply for today's people, let alone tomorrow's.

In spite of all the ballyhoo, we really are not handling environmental concerns well, either. We have let blind laissez-faire economics and laissez-faire government ignore long range needs, and we have failed to address the human needs in energy and food and water, as well as earth and air.

Yesterday's polls and the quarterly report syndrome and the next election have controlled all we have done in the body politic and there are plenty of indications that the "just in time" planning instant gratification mentality pervades the voters of the nation, as well. Turned on by sensationalism, pandered not only by tabloids but by political campaigns as well, real human issues never reach the voter screen.

There has been, at most, a tenuous consensus only when disaster strikes the financial world or the trade world or comes through drought or threat of energy shortage, or food or water shortage. In fact, food shortage, a reality to over half the world's people, is scarcely a memory to most of us. Even after the Middle East war, a clear derivative of our neglect in planning in energy, we still have no consensus. We've not yet learned. Despite the war and the cost of 200,000 plus lives and $100 billion dollars—the President's people still contend the market is working.

And, of course, even the more avid flag wavers opposed the taxes to pay for the war. They applauded and cheered the battle, but denied the budget budget…as they denied even the cause of the war.

Amazingly, some avid free traders ignore the folly of failed energy planning that's made us all so vulnerable to oil tyranny.

Alas, even environmentalists, who want a cleaner and greener America, show little concern about government-imposed costs upon American producers, even while they glibly applaud the cheap, foreign unencumbered products which invade our shores and aggravate our trade deficit, even while foreign environments are spoiled.

And consumers argue for greater and greater liability burdens on our producers again while they glibly welcome foreign products for which there is no consumer protection.

Immersed in a global economy ourselves, we have lost any sense of real unity, any sense of vision for tomorrow for our nation. The quarterly report and the next election are all that matters.

So what are you commencing to—a mess? Yes, I am afraid, a mess. But a mess that is also a challenge. There is still hope if we learn from our failings. The good news is that there seems to be an awakened sense of concern among people

But, there will be no hope without sacrifice. There will be no hope without a renewed sense of community and a renewed dedication to America's promise to secure human rights.

You see, Democracy, at least American Democracy, was born of the belief that the cacophony of conflicting causes can be converted into a kaleidoscope of calm compatibility. Philosophically, our forefathers believed all the things good for humans are compatible.

American Democracy believes human rights and human needs have a commonality. They are not in conflict.

American Democracy believes this commonality of human goods is discoverable and governable by a government of the people. And that search for commonality of human need is what I want to talk about today.

As the search for solutions to human problems involves more and more global trade and global environmental conservation, recycling, clean earth and clean water and a safe, assured access to essential food and energy, there are several salient, fundamental points to remember.

Let me tell you a story to explain the first point.

Three years ago last September, I stood on the stage of an Indian powwow ground at the United Tribes Center in the southeast corner of Bismarck, North Dakota's capital. The Powwow Arena is a quarter of a mile off the end of the northeast–southwest runway at Bismarck Airport.

There were nearly a thousand dancers in the arena for the opening dance. It was the largest Indian powwow on the North American continent. Twenty-five or twenty-six states were represented; half a dozen Canadian provinces, and over half of the approximately 450 North American Tribes were represented.

I stood with a wonderful man, a Native American, a PhD. whom I have known for 25 years. His name is David Gipp–he is a man who has given his life to the educational efforts of Native Americans and to enriching the world's appreciation for Native American culture. I was waiting to be introduced by David to give a greeting to the people.

As we waited I said to him, "David, where on earth do all the eagle feathers come from?" The arena was aglow with marvelously colorful costumes overflowing with eagle feathers.

David smiled and said, "Now wait a minute, Governor, it is not what you think. Our people do not kill eagles. Eagles, you see, are a symbol of God to Indian people and even their feathers are handed down from generation to generation. They are very sacred. If just one small feather were to drop into the arena during the dance, it would be very ceremoniously retrieved," he said.

"Beyond that, if an eagle should fly over the powwow, it would be seen by everyone here as a sign of blessing from God."

Involuntarily, standing as I said a quarter of a mile off the end of the runway, I looked skyward and there I saw not one, but four golden eagles slowly circling the powwow. I was awestruck.

Eagles are rarely seen this close to the city and its airport. David saw the wonderment in my skyward gaze. He looked up, too.

Within seconds, the whole arena fell silent. The drums stopped; the dancers stopped; and we all stood reverently realizing of course, these eagles were a sign of God's blessing.

Now, I spent six years here at St. John's studying philosophy in the undergraduate preparation for the priesthood, and I learned that God is a God of all people, a God who cherishes all people and a God who communicates with all people, but never before had I so forcefully experienced God's presence in another culture setting. The experience affected me deeply.

It was only later that I learned not only was it significant that one eagle was there, but that four were there in the center of this aeronautical flight pattern, was of very rare significance indeed.

The Indians, you see, believe in the God of the west wind, of the east wind, of the south wind and of the north wind. As I said, I was deeply moved – and I thought for days about what I had seen. I realized beyond doubt that God was blessing those people. But I also realized how narrow my experience really was.

I realized how small are the worlds in which we live, how narrow are our cultures, how small are our perspectives. We rarely see the world, let alone God, from where others see it. We rarely think about the world and its problems and its grandeur from other people's point of view.

Certainly, I had thought all too little about the vision of God that is in the mind and the spirit of others. But here was the vision. Here was God, in undeniable presence.

Suddenly, I saw again, that we must continue to learn about God's people–to pay attention and to realize how ignorant and insensitive we are of their problems. An educator friend of mine used to say "Education is the transition from cocksure ignorance to knowledgeable uncertainty."

This "unforgettable experience" at that powwow taught me again how true that teaching is. Ever since that spiritual experience, I have tried much harder to think from other people's vantage points. I have also tried much harder to teach people to understand that truth is like a beautiful prism that has many, many facets and each of us sees that beautiful prism from only a little tiny place...just a narrow minuscule spot in time and space and cultural setting.

We do not often enough step around to see the prism from where others see it. We have no sense of history. Most of us have read little literature. We travel little and barely know about the people of our own communities. We have a narrow, selfish, "now" focus, and we never see the world in the way others see it.

We rarely listen to the American Indian plea: "Walk a mile in my moccasins." And there's an old African proverb that I've always loved that says, "Not until you've crossed the river can you say the crocodile has a lump on his jaw."

That's the first point I want to make today, that we have failed so badly to take a holistic point of view and build a holistic community consensus to bolster our law and legal determinations in order to share our world's goods with today's people everywhere... and to preserve a the world for tomorrow's people so they, too, may have secure rights.

Democracy will fail if we do not listen to all of the stakeholders–to get them to listen to each other and to share the good things of the earth.

There's a second story I want to tell you that adds an additional needed dimension to all of this.

A few years ago, Dick Lamm, former Governor of Colorado, asked me: if he were able to gather the think tanks of Western United States together, if I would come and speak to them–I was very honored and said I would, of course. A year ago last summer, he did get them together in Vail.

There were 20 of the major think tanks in the western United States. Some of the brightest people in the West were there. There were about 60 people in the room. They sat around a large quadrangle of tables.

In opening the conference, I spoke about the macro problems and the vision and about the uniqueness of the West. The discussion had gone on for some three hours about waste, water, the history of the West, about wetlands and economics and trade and environmental concerns and military bases. It was a serious, enlightening discussion by serious, thoughtful people.

But, suddenly a man, who was sitting sullenly across the square of tables from me—a man who had not spoken—literally exploded on the meeting. His name was Arturo Madrid. He was from Claremont, California. He led a think tank in Claremont that works to help the burgeoning brown population of the southwestern part of the United States.

His voice was angry, yet pleading. He said, "Doesn't anyone care about people? No one has mentioned people. I represent millions of brown people who have no hope. Whose lives are desperate. Their children grow up in poverty and drugs and crime and violence. All they want is a chance to have children, who can be educated, and have some hope.

They don't give a damn about environmental issues. They don't give a damn about economics. They don't give a damn about military power and that's all you've talked about. Does not anybody here care about people? No one has mentioned people—not once, in all these macro discussions." He went on passionately about the festering fury that filled the people with whom he worked.

It was a shocking statement and we were all stunned and duly chastised. We all knew that he know all of these forces of economics and environment affect people. But we had not said so…nor had we even hinted at the awareness of the frightening human problems of which he spoke at length–the homeless, the hungry, the helpless.

He was right, of course. We had spoken, as if there was some sacredness to economic theories–to environmentalism—to many macro issues. No one had mentioned any relevance to people. We sat in stunned silence and then betraying the truth of his allegations, we clumsily went back to the same sanitized subjects—safe from human implication.

But I remained deeply troubled long after. I realized what he had reminded us all of was the philosophical fact that has to be fundamental to all governmental activities—indeed perhaps all societal actions. Every issue is a human issue—or it is not an issue. Every issue is a human issue–or it is not an issue at all. Certainly in the American governmental scheme it is people who matter. Even from a theological point of view, God is served when we serve the creatures God created.

The American Constitution says nothing about capitalism or free trade, says nothing about environmentalism or spotted owls. The relevance of all of these issues is human—short term and long term—or there is no relevance.

Mr. Madrid knew economics has a basis and bearing, and a benefit or harm to human beings, and he knew environmentalism has a basis and a bearing, and a benefit or harm to human beings, but most of the time we forget. Most of the time they are ends in themselves…we act as if they are laws with some divine sanctity.

He wanted us who are environmentalists to remember we are not neopantheists–we do not worship God in nature. We do not serve environmental causes for their own sake, but for people's sake.

Neither are we blind capitalists who worship development and profit.

We are, constitutionally (if not philosophically and morally) bound to serve human beings. Arturo Madrid drove that home in a way I have never heard before, when he asked the very simple question, "Doesn't anybody care about people?" But my God, how we have given in to isms and slogans and have forgotten it is people that matter.

We've forgotten that American government is committed to work for the people—all people.

Many of us have become so preoccupied with narrow causes and quarterly reports and winning elections and grand economic dicta that we have forgotten people and the democracy that serves them.

Disaster–in some areas, among some people has brought only brief awakenings. But even after the Los Angeles explosion, I predict we will see little lasting dedication to deal with the problems there, and in the other major cities in the United States, just as we ignored the implications of the war in Iraq.

The third fundamental point I want to make is less ideological, but every bit as important as we face the future.

The federal government is virtually bankrupt. For anyone to suggest that the federal government, without major change, can micro-manage the nation's problems is, quite frankly, utterly naïve. There is no money.

The only solution is for the states to act and they must seriously face people issues.

The states can no longer pass the buck to the feds, because the feds can do less and less. In many areas, the feds can't manage their appropriate role of rational global relations and essential inter-state relations, let alone micro-manage the states.

Here's why: the Federal debt–deficit problem will soon render the government bankrupt.

Ronald Reagan arrived in 1980 and never before did the nation have a federal deficit in excess of 2 percent of the GNP. Ever since Reagan took over, the deficit has been 5, then 6, then 7 percent. The accrued debt is indescribable.

The national debt, under the Bush budget is $4.5 trillion. That's:
$75,999 for every family of four in the U.S.
$18,000 for every man, woman and child.

The federal deficit this year will be over $400 billion. That equals nearly one and a half times the combined general fund budgets of all the states.

Adding the interest portion of the budget makes it nearly two and a half times the combined general fund budgets of all the states.

A $400 billion deficit is 7.3 percent of the GNP.

Interest costs will increase…$32 billion this year and amount to between 25 percent and 30 percent of the federal budget.

So you see, as I said earlier this is the mess we all face.

There are many things we must do:

1. We must cut spending.

2. We must raise taxes considerably to pay off the debt.

3. Unfortunately, we must also let the economy inflate
   and keep the dollar value down to pay off the debt
   with cheap dollars.

4. We must do a much better job of distributing jobs
   and income. Inner city crises will take significant,
   dramatic, action.

5. This will mean a decline in the standard of living of some of us…but we cannot continue the extravagance of our consumption or the extravagance of the disparity of income in a world with over half its people hungry.

We must change or democracy may fail just as Communism has.

Communism failed in the first place because the theory is wrong. The theory is that there is a combative, inherent conflict in human needs and human desires and human goods…and conflict is inherent in the human struggle for happiness. That's why Communism denies human freedom. That's the opposite of what we believe. We believe in freedom.

We believe those things which are good for human beings are compatible. *But, more specifically, Communism has failed because it has not solved the practical needs of people for safe, assured access to the basics of human life–land, air, water, energy and food.*

There's little comfort to us in Communism's failure if we do not solve the problems for our people and for other people who seek freedom. Democracy may fail, too, given where we are. Given the outcry of people like Arturo Madrid, given the conflict which pervades our society today, and given our short-sighted failure to make government responsible and workable.

The failures are not the fault of politicians alone. There has been, among the people, a pervading philosophy of instant gratification and selfishness. A philosophy that ignores other suffering people of today and the needs of the people of tomorrow. So, it is the people's fault, too. They like hearing "no new taxes." Read my lips–and we are now so in debt–some suggest we will not survive.

A great Scotsman and jurist historian of considerable renown, Sir Alex Fraser Tytler, wrote in 1801 the following:

"A Democracy cannot exist as a permanent form of government. It can exist only until voters discover that they can vote themselves largesse from the public treasury. From that time on, the majority always vote for the candidates promising the most benefits from the public treasury with the result that a Democracy always collapses over loose fiscal policy, always followed by a dictatorship."

The average age of the world's great civilizations has been 200 years. These nations have progressed through this sequence: from bondage to spiritual faith; from spiritual faith to great courage: from courage to liberty; from liberty to abundance; from abundance to selfishness; from selfishness to complacency; from complacency to apathy; from apathy to dependency; from dependency back again to bondage.

It is, I think, our great challenge to speak clearly to the people, to tell them the truth even if it is difficult.

It is time for realism, for our children's sake, as well as for our own.

We must be Americans concerned about people and our nation before we are politicians.

We must be Americans concerned about Democracy and freedom before we are Republicans or Democrats, before we are capitalists or environmentalists or militarists.

The only lasting legacy any of us will leave is a legacy of helping to make this society work for people through a government of the people. And we must believe in government.

After all, when Jefferson wrote the Declaration of Independence, everyone remembered the great line that "We hold these truths to be self evident, that all men are created equal, that they are endowed by their creator with certain unalienable rights, that among these are life, liberty and the pursuit of happiness." But almost everyone forgets the next line in which Jefferson wrote: "And to secure these rights, governments are instituted among men."

We must press on to make certain America's body politic is not steered by greed and by blind adherence to causes and theories and isms which ignore people. We must elect people who have a commitment to service of people—who have seen the displaced workers and the elderly poor and the racially and physically and gender discriminated against.

We must look out to others who are poor and suffering. We must see the truth prism from their many places. We must all heed the cry of Arturo Madrid: "For God's sake, doesn't anyone care about people?"

It's late–very late, but we've made it past 200 years. And it is not too late.

We've made it through the Civil War, World War I, the Great Depression and World War II. We can still make it. You can make it. You can prove Sir Alex Fraser Tytler wrong.

We look to you, most of all to you who commence from this special place—where learning about others and serving others has always been foremost.

I congratulate you. I wish you Godspeed.

ACKNOWLEDGMENTS

For their specific assistance with producing this book, my co-author Bob Jansen and I want to thank, in alphabetical order: American Crystal Sugar Company for its major financial support, David Borlaug, Ellery and Jeanne Bresnahan, Jackie Brodshaug, Janis Cheney, Kathy Davison, Kathy Dwyer, Peter Dwyer, Chuck Fleming, Jim Fuglie, David Gipp, Dick Gross. Jake Gust, Lisa Novacek Hertel, John Jambois, Clay Jenkinson, Alex Macdonald, Gerald Newborg, the NDSU Library and Institute for Regional Studies, Tracy Potter, the State Historical Society of North Dakota, Jane Sinner and Sinner family members, Wendy Spencer, Steve Tillotson, Sarah Trandahl, and Jolynn Zeller.

—George Sinner

NOTES

1. The Democratic National Convention took place in Atlantic City, New Jersey, August 24–27, 1964. The convention endorsed Lyndon Johnson for re-election, and chose Hubert Humphrey as its nominee for vice president. The racially integrated Mississippi Freedom Democratic Party (MFDP) claimed the seats for delegates for Mississippi, claiming that the official Mississippi delegation had been elected by a Jim Crow primary. The party's liberal leaders supported an even division of the seats between the two delegations. President Johnson was concerned that seating the MFDP delegates would jeopardize his re-election. Eventually, Hubert Humphrey, Walter Reuther, and the black civil rights leaders including Roy Wilkins, Martin Luther King Jr., and Bayard Rustin worked out a compromise: the MFDP took two of Mississippi's seats; the regular Mississippi delegation was required to pledge to support the party ticket; and no future Democratic convention would accept a delegation chosen by a discriminatory poll. Joseph Rauh, the MFDP's lawyer, initially refused this deal, but they eventually took their seats. Many white delegates from Mississippi and Alabama refused to sign any pledge and left the convention; and many young civil rights workers were offended by any compromise. In the end, President Johnson was re-elected by one of the largest landslides in American history. Johnson received 486 electoral votes to Goldwater's 52, which included all 7 of Mississippi's electoral votes. Goldwater carried 6 states: his home state Arizona, plus Mississippi, Louisiana, Georgia, Alabama, and South Carolina.

2. Frank McGee interview quotes are from television file footage.

3. The Red River Flood of 1997 which occurred in April and May, was the result of abundant snowfall and extreme temperatures. It was the most severe flood of the Red River since 1826. The flood inundated the entire Red River Valley, affecting Fargo and Winnipeg, but was much more devastating in Grand Forks and East Grand Forks. There floodwaters spread more than three miles from the banks of the Red River in both directions, inundating virtually everything in the two communities. Much of the flooding occurred not only from the rising river itself, but from overland flooding, as the Red River was unable to drain melt water away, necessitating dikes on both along riverfront and around the edges of towns. Total damages for the Red River region were estimated at $3.5 billion. The Sinner home

was in an area of southwest Fargo that required construction of temporary dikes to protect from overland flooding and overflowing of the nearby Rose Creek, which drains into the Red.

4. A citizens committee filed petitions and placed the issue on the June 13, 2006, Fargo election ballot. By extending a half-cent city sales tax that was due to expire, the initiative would have generated $8.4 million annually to cut property taxes that go to fund schools. Vote totals were: 8,568 or 50.7 percent yes; 8,330 or 49.3 percent no. Because a majority of 60 percent was needed, the initiative failed.

5. A native of New Mexico with deep roots in the southwestern United States, Arturo Madrid was a scholar, public servant, and advocate for the advancement of the Latina and Latino community in the United States. Madrid's social and cultural perspectives were shaped by the intense social activism of the Chicano/a movement of the 1960s. In addition to encouraging the Hispanic community to excel in education, Madrid advocated for the reform of public education, including higher education, to serve better the needs of this community. This concern was furthered by Madrid's appointment as the director of the Fund for the Improvement of Postsecondary Education (FIPSE) in 1980.

6. The District 10 convention was held March 11, 1962, in Casselton.

7. Republican Don Otos of Mapleton represented District 10 in the North Dakota House during the 1961 legislature.

8. In 1963, Mark Andrews was elected a member of the US House of Representatives from North Dakota's 1st congressional district following the death of Hjalmar Nygaard. Andrews ran for re-election in 1964. The 1964 congressional race vote totals were Andrews 69,575; Sinner 63,208.

9. Alexandre Ledru-Rollin: French lawyer and politician, 1807–1874.

10. The 1968 Democratic National Convention was held August 26–28, 1968 in Chicago. Due in large part to the unpopularity of the Vietnam War,

Democratic President Lyndon Johnson had announced he would not seek a second full term, so the chief purpose of the convention was to select a new presidential nominee. Prior to LBJ's withdrawal, Senator Eugene McCarthy of Minnesota had entered Democratic primaries against Johnson and polled impressively. With the assassination of New York Senator Robert Kennedy on June 6, the Democratic Party's divisions grew. On one side stood supporters of Eugene McCarthy, who ran an anti-war campaign and was seen as the peace candidate. On the other side was Vice President Hubert Humphrey, who was considered a surrogate for President Johnson's point of view. Although Humphrey had not entered a single primary, the Democratic Party convention nominated him by a vote of 1759.25 to 601. Even though 80 percent of the primary voters had been for anti-war candidates, the delegates defeated a proposed peace plank in the party's platform by 1,567.75 to 1,041.25. Most members of the peace coalition believed that Mayor of Chicago Richard Daley and President Johnson were pulling strings behind the scenes. Humphrey lost the general election to Republican Richard Nixon. Nixon won the popular vote with a plurality of 512,000 votes, or a victory margin of about one percentage point. In the Electoral College, Nixon's victory was larger, as he carried 32 states with 301 electoral votes, to Humphrey's 13 states and 191 electoral votes. Segregationist candidate George Wallace won 5 states and 46 electoral votes running under the banner of the American Independent Party.

11. The twenty-five-member North Dakota delegation voted 19-6 against the peace plank minority report. *The Forum* article on the 1968 platform ran August 30, 1968.

12. Baseball Hall-of-Famer Ralph Kiner was among baseball's top sluggers during his major league career, 1946–1954. A back injury forced the all-star outfielder to retire at age thirty-two. In 1961 he launched a long career as a baseball broadcaster.

13. The Notre Dame Box was a variation of the single-wing formation used with great success by University of Notre Dame football teams of the 1920s. It differed from the traditional single-wing offense in that the line was balanced and the halfback who normally played the "wing" in the single-wing was brought in more tightly, with the option of shifting out

to the wing. These two changes made the backs' formation resemble a square (hence the "box") and made the formation less predictable, allowing offenses to run more easily to the weak side.

14. Author Robert K. Greenleaf (1904–1990) argued that leaders achieve results for their organizations by giving priority attention to the needs of their colleagues and those they serve. Greenleaf's most important work is titled *Servant Leadership*.

15. Uranium was spilled August 27, 1985, when a truck carrying fifty-three barrels of the substance collided with a Burlington Northern train about three miles east of Bowdon, in central North Dakota. The truck's driver was killed. No harmful levels of uranium were found in urine samples of thirty-six people exposed to the ore at the scene of the accident.

16. On March 4, 1933, Governor Bill Langer declared a state bank holiday and a moratorium on all debts in North Dakota. On April 17th, he issued a moratorium prohibiting mortgage foreclosures on all locally operated farms in the state.

17. Korean War truce talks began July 10, 1951. Although the talks started slowly, the two sides on November 27, 1951 agreed on the 38th Parallel as the line of demarcation and almost immediately military operations slowed down.

18. The Second Ecumenical Council of the Vatican opened under Pope John XXIII on October 11, 1962 and closed under Pope Paul VI on December 8, 1965. It resulted in a modernizing of the Catholic Church in a number of ways, including a movement away from the use of Latin in the Catholic Mass.

19. The Catholic Latin Mass officially was changed from Latin to the vernacular when Pope Paul VI approved the New Order of the Mass in the vernacular in April 1969. The changes were carried out the following year, in 1970.

20. In 1972, the bishop dismissed Father Dick Sinner from his pastoral duties at two churches after he allowed a suspended married priest to speak

and administer communion in his parish. That same year Father Sinner was arrested for driving with a suspended license. In 1987, Father Sinner twice had a car confiscated when he tried to transport Central American refugees into Canada. He wasn't charged with criminal violations. Federal authorities declined prosecution and released the cars after Father Sinner signed an agreement in which he forfeited a posted bond, paid a settlement, and promised to not violate immigration laws.

21. Governor Sinner was on hand when in 1987, Melroe introduced the world's largest skid-steer loader—the Bobcat 980.

22. A graduate degree in theology and taking higher orders was required to become a priest. The steps toward priesthood included the offices of sub-deacon, deacon, and priest. After ordination, a sub-deacon assisted the deacon or the priest with the Mass and was allowed to wear a cassock and collar. The office of sub-deacon was abolished in 1972.

23. Jane Sinner's comments are from her book, *Of Days Gone By*, which she self-published in 2009.

24. Malcolm Moos joined President Eisenhower's staff as a special assistant in 1957 and became his chief speech writer in 1958. The famous phrase was part of President Dwight Eisenhower's farewell speech, January 17, 1961.

25. The 1969 legislature provided for a constitutional convention. Voters authorized the convention on September 2, 1970. Voters elected ninety-eight delegates to the convention in the November 3, 1970 general election. Governor Bill Guy called the convention to order April 6, 1971, for an organizational session. On January 3, 1972, the convention convened for a 30-day plenary session. The final draft was adopted February 17, 1972. An opposition campaign was successful and the new constitution was defeated in a special election on April 28, 1972, by a lopsided vote of 107,643 to 64,973.

26. Quotations are from the *Journal of the Constitutional Convention*.

27. P. O. Sathre served on the North Dakota Supreme Court from 1937 to 1938 and 1951 to 1962.

28. The Pharmacy Permits bill, with Senator George Sinner as prime sponsor and Senators William Reichert of Dickinson and Harry George of Steele as co-sponsors, was approved by the legislature on March 11, 1963.

29. The Outdoor Advertising Act passed by the 1963 legislature was vetoed by Governor Bill Guy on March 19, 1963.

30. Local Mental Health and Retardation Units were authorized on March 15, 1965, with the approval of legislation sponsored by Senator George Longmire of Grand Forks and Senator William Reichert of Dickinson.

31. The first Board of Higher Education meeting for new member George Sinner was August 24–25, 1967, at the Prince Hotel in downtown Bismarck.

32. *The Dakota Student* is the campus newspaper produced by University of North Dakota students.

33. Walter R. Hjelle served as North Dakota Highway Commissioner longer than any other commissioner in state history—from 1961 to 1981 and again from 1985 until he resigned effective December 31, 1988. He was arrested and convicted for drunk driving in November 1988.

34. During the 1971 legislature the House Appropriations Committee eliminated the operating budget for the University of North Dakota-Ellendale Branch in anticipation of eliminating it as an institution of higher learning effective July 1, 1971.

35. The constitutional amendment was submitted to the voters by the 1971 legislature when it approved a concurrent resolution that was submitted by the House Appropriations Committee. On the Board of Higher Education, George Sinner moved in January 1972 that chairman Peter Hinrichs lease the Ellendale college facilities to the city of Ellendale. Trinity Bible College would then lease the facilities from the city. The vote in the September 5, 1972 primary election to remove the college from the State Constitution was 68,575 to 41,350.

36. Commencement speech coverage: *The Fargo Forum*, June 2, 1968.

37. The North Dakota/Minnesota reciprocity program is a program of student exchange instituted in 1975. Students generally pay the higher of the two states in-state tuition rates. Thus, North Dakota students attending Minnesota campuses pay the rate that Minnesota residents pay, while Minnesota students attending North Dakota campuses also pay the Minnesota rate, which is generally higher than the North Dakota rate but lower than what other non-resident students pay.

38. The inaugural Governor George Sinner Public Policy Symposium held at North Dakota State University on December 9, 2004; followed by a second symposium on December 1, 1995 at Minnesota State University Moorhead; and third forum, November 28, 2006 at Concordia College.

39. The Red River Valley Sugarbeet Growers Association was formed in 1926 to represent growers for the American Beet Sugar Company, later the American Crystal Sugar Company. In 1973 the association members purchased American Crystal and formed a cooperative. George Sinner served as president of the Red River Valley Sugarbeet Growers Association Board from 1975 to 1979.

40. Ruth Meiers and Dick Backes were both members of the North Dakota House of Representatives at the time of the 1984 convention.

41. Allen Olson acknowledged the weekend before the election that he may have been delinquent in paying his federal income taxes. He had received a four-month extension to file a late return and applied for a second four-month extension. However, the tax code allowed only a total of six months, which expired October 15th. The election results were: Sinner-Meiers, 173,922; Olson-Sands, 149,460.

42. In 1988, the vote totals were George Sinner-Lloyd Omdahl, 179,094; Leon Mallberg-Donna Nalewaja, 119,986.

43. Governor Sinner vetoed the severance tax bill on April 16, 1985.

44. Declaration of Emergency Storm Closing was issued on February 1, 1989, and applied to the following two days, February 2nd—3rd. Because the closure was ordered at the state level the two days weren't counted as storm days and schools didn't have to make them up.

45. Ferdinand Marcos was president of the Philippines for two decades. He was declared re-elected on February 7, 1986, but the results were contested and a citizen-supported rebellion led by Corazon Aquino ended his authoritarian regime and ousted him from office. In late February, he and his wife, Imelda, abandoned the presidential palace and flew to Hawaii in exile. He died there in 1989.

46. The Eighth US Circuit Court of Appeals in 1972 ruled that an area of 360,000 acres of land called the "northeast quadrant" was part of the Fort Berthold Indian Reservation. That area had been settled between 1910 and 1920 when homestead tracts on the reservation were sold by the federal government. The court determined that the homesteading didn't remove the property from the reservation. The majority of the people living in the quadrant were non-tribal members and most of the land there was owned by whites.

47. The prisoners in the October 9, 1992 escape were William R. Holland Jr., a transfer from Alaska; Randal Heitsch, Rugby; and Richard Lee McNair, Minot. Holland was the first apprehended, followed by Heitsch. McNair was on the loose until July 1993 when he was captured in Grand Island, Nebraska, and subsequently moved to the federal prison system. He escaped from federal prison in 2006 and was recaptured a year later.

48. The Japanese operation had been projected to employ up to 236 workers. *The Fargo Forum* reported on January 14, 1992, that Seibulite Corporation pulled out because of health problems of its principal owner, adverse economic conditions, and tightening loan policies by the Japanese minister of finance.

49. President George H. W. Bush visited North Dakota, April 24, 1989

50. Democrat Thomas Moodie (1878–1948) was elected in 1934, removed from office February 16, 1935. Republican Bill Langer (1886–1859) was elected in 1932, removed from office July 17, 1934, then elected in 1936. Langer and did not seek re-election in 1938.

51. According to a summary prepared by the Office of Management and Budget in 1992, Governor George Sinner's first budget message, on February 5, 1985, cut $73 million from the executive budget recommenda-

tions of Governor Allen Olson. The 1985 legislature put back nearly $20 million, thus reducing available reserves. The agriculture and oil industries continued to decline, forcing a $45 million allotment (spending cut) during the 1985–1987 biennium. Governor Sinner's 1987–1989 recommendations were $20 million less than the appropriation for 1985–1987; the 1987 legislature appropriated nearly $57 million less than the governor's already spare recommendations. After an expansion of the sales tax by the 1987 legislature was referred to the people and rejected (by a 81,662 to 23,497 vote), Governor Sinner decreased general fund budgets by $3,175,000. With the state's economy continuing to suffer, Governor Sinner ordered another 2 percent or $21 million budget cut in August 1988 and submitted a 1989–1991 base budget recommendation that was $38 million less than the 1987–1989 biennium. The 1989–1991 budget recommendations also included an enhancement package of $60 million tied to specific tax increases. The legislature increased taxes and appropriated $4.9 million more than the enhanced level of spending, but voters rejected all of those tax increases in the December 1989 referral election. The budget recommendation for 1991–1993 called for spending 4 percent more than the level approved by the 1989 legislature.

52. State income tax increases were upheld by a vote of 62,635 to 59,340 in a special election on March 3, 1987.

53. Citizens who use the referral process circulate and file petitions to place a new law on the ballot where voters will decide whether to accept or reject the proposal.

54. Those presentations around the state started November 1, 1989, in Langdon.

55. In the December 1989 special election, the sales tax increase was defeated 118,108 to 135,833; the income tax increase was defeated 99,866 to 153,457; and the motor fuels tax was defeated 102,786 to 151,499.

56. The Bank of North Dakota (BND) is the only state-owned bank in the United States. During the early 1900s, North Dakota's economy was based on agriculture. Serious in-state problems prevented cohesive efforts in buying and selling crops and financing farm operations. Grain dealers outside the state suppressed grain prices. Farm suppliers increased

their prices; and interest rates on farm loans climbed. By 1919, popular consensus wanted state ownership and control of marketing and credit agencies. Thus, the state legislature established Bank of North Dakota and the North Dakota Mill and Elevator Association. BND was charged with the mission of "promoting agriculture, commerce, and industry" in North Dakota. It was never intended for BND to compete with or replace existing banks. Instead, BND was created to partner with other financial institutions and assist them in meeting the needs of the citizens of North Dakota. BND opened July 28, 1919, with $2 million of capital. Today, the bank operates with more than $230 million in capital. The state of North Dakota began using bank profits in 1945 when money was first transferred into the general fund. Since that time, capital transfers have become the norm to augment state budgets.

57. Governor Sinner vetoed the Abortion Ban bill on April 1, 1991. The House upheld the veto the following day, coming up eight votes short of override.

58. The guest commentary on the topic of abortion was published in *The Forum* on March 6, 2005. It was followed by other commentaries and responding letters throughout that month expressing varying perspectives and points of disagreement or agreement.

59. George Sinner has honorary doctorate degrees from North Dakota State University, the University of North Dakota, and his alma mater, St. John's University.

60. The Theodore Roosevelt Rough Rider Award recognizes present or former North Dakotans who have been influenced by this state in achieving national recognition in their fields of endeavor, thereby reflecting credit and honor upon North Dakota and its citizens. Governor George Sinner's Rough Rider inductions were Ronald Davies, June 11, 1987; Phil Jackson, July 30, 1992; Larry Woiwode, October 23, 1992; and Angie Dickinson, December 2, 1992.

61. Federal Judge Ronald Davies of Fargo ordered the integration of Little Rock Central High School in September 1957. *The New York Times* called Judge Davies' ruling the "landmark decision on racial integration in our nation." While filling a temporary vacancy, he faced down Governor

Orval Faubas and the Arkansas National Guard with the simple principle that "integration must begin forthwith."

62. In a 1959 interview, Angie Dickinson was asked whether she planned to return to her home state and she said no. When asked why, she replied, "Have you ever been to North Dakota?" When the interviewer said yes, she countered with, "Well?" She apologized later for that remark. In May 1988 she joined the Sinners at campaign fundraiser birthday parties in Grand Forks, Minot, West Fargo, and Mandan.

63. The ad hoc International Flood Mitigation Initiative held meetings for a few months following the 1997 Red River flood, but is now inactive.

64. Governor George Sinner was appointed to the Federal Advisory Commission on Intergovernmental Relations and the Intergovernmental Policy Advisory Committee to the US Trade Representative.

65. Jane Sinner's letter appeared in *The Forum* November 16, 2004, with the headline "The hypocrisy of the church disturbing."

66. An executive order on April 17, 1990 prohibited smoking after October 1, 1990 in buildings under the control of the governor or gubernatorial appointees.

67. The meeting with the president-elect occurred on December 23, 1992.

68. The 1996 bill, intended to gradually move farmers off federal support payments, came to be known as "Freedom to Farm Bill." The bill marked a seismic shift in government's role in agriculture and was as loudly criticized by its opponents as it was praised by its supporters. In spite of these efforts, federal farm support has continued to be an important prop to North Dakota family farms.

69. President Bill Clinton established the controversial "don't ask-don't tell" compromise policy through executive order in 1993. The policy prohibits any homosexual or bisexual person from disclosing his or her sexual orientation or from speaking about any homosexual relationships, including marriages or other familial attributes, while serving in the military. The "don't ask" part of the policy indicates that superiors

should not initiate investigation of a service member's orientation in the absence of disallowed behaviors.

70. September 23, 1989.

71. North Dakota's rankings vary year to year, but at that time the litany included the state's leadership in producing several agricultural commodities and standing tall in many other areas such as clean air and clean water and low rate of violent crime and being the first state to complete its interstate highway system.

72. The speech to 371 seniors and 13 School of Theology graduates was delivered on May 24, 1992.

73. Comedian Rodney Dangerfield (1921-2004) was famous for saying "I get no respect, I tell ya."

74. Mario Cuono (1932-) was governor of New York from 1983 to 1994.

75. Fred Haeffner was appointed director July 9, 1990 and resigned March 13, 1991.

76. Zander were first experimentally stocked into Spiritwood Lake in 1987. The Game and Fish Department's Whopper Club directory shows a Jamestown man pulling a record-sized eight-pound plus zander from the lake in 2007.

77. The securities commissioner resigned January 15, 1989.

78. In the fall of 1986, Governor George Sinner and the Greater North Dakota Association (since then renamed the North Dakota Chamber of Commerce) collaborated in creating the Committee of 100, also called the New Wealth Creation Task Force, a group of citizens that studied the state's economy to seek ways to create new jobs and new wealth in the state.

79. The first Lignite Research Council executive order was issued on April 16, 1987, and was later superceded by executive orders when the council was expanded beyond the original twenty-five members.

80. The Lloyd Omdahl interview was in the fall of 1992.

81. Underprivileged children were brought to the North Dakota State Fair in July 1987.

82. Representative Earl Strinden, R-Grand Forks, was State House of Representatives majority leader.

83. Following that conversation with Larry Biegler, a preliminary agreement with Farm Credit Services to renegotiate farm loans was announced in early March 1986.

84. Investment by relatives helped founder Doug Burgum start and develop Fargo-based Great Plains Software, which was acquired by Microsoft Corporation in 2001 and now operates as Microsoft Dynamics GP. He is the son of Joe and Katherine "Kay" Kilbourne Burgum with family owned agricultural enterprises in Arthur, North Dakota.

85. Under the federal PIK (payment-in-kind) program, farmers who voluntarily controlled planting and set aside an additional percentage of acreage specified by the government received certificates that could be redeemed for government-owned stocks of grain. The stated purpose of PIK was to reduce production through a further cutback in planting. The intent was to decrease surplus stocks, bring supply more in line with demand, and strengthen farm income in future years.

86. Governor George Sinner first proclaimed agricultural emergency in July of 1985 and that scenario continued in subsequent years. Following a gubernatorial declaration of drought emergency in May 1988, US Secretary of Agriculture Richard Lyng in August 1988 declared all fifty-three North Dakota counties a disaster area, qualifying many businesses, farmers, and ranchers for low-interest emergency assistance loans. Drought conditions and problems continued through the 1980s.

87. The Chicago drought meeting was June 23, 1988.

88. Although Governor George Sinner was also concerned about achieving a balanced national energy policy and about governance over wetlands, the

primary and more specific issue was states' authority to regulate oil and gas exploration and production wastes. The EPA wanted that authority. The visit to the North Slope was made in conjunction with an invitation to deliver a speech to the International Arctic Technology Conference sponsored by the Society of Petroleum Engineers on May 30, 1991. Jim Yeager, a friend of son Joe Sinner, helped arrange the separate North Slope trip. The letter to EPA Administrator Reilly was sent after returning home to the Governor's Office.

89. The Health Department maintained a public comment period on the permit application from November 3–December 10, 1990. The department held a public hearing on the application in Sawyer on November 28–29, 1990. Dr. Bob Wentz presided as the department's hearing officer. Approximately 85 witnesses testified and approximately 270 exhibits were received in evidence. On December 20, 1990, Wentz issued findings of fact, conclusions of law, and an order denying MSC's application. Second Hearing: Public comment November 4, 1992–January 15, 1993. Public Hearing on November 17–18, 1992, with Francis Schwindt, Chief of the Environmental Health Section of the Department as the hearing officer. The findings of fact were dated August 5, 1993 signed by Fritz Schwindt. The permit was signed on August 16, 1993, by the director of the Division of Waste Management, Neil Knatterud.

90. The Great Plains synfuels plant, located near Beulah, is the only commercial-scale coal gasification plant in the United States that manufactures natural gas. It produces about 160 million cubic feet of natural gas per day. Under an agreement established in 1988 when the plant was purchased from the US Department of Energy (DOE), Dakota Gas shared natural gas sales revenue with the DOE. Gas prices were low during the 1980s and 1990s, so the plants revenues and payments were minimal. Natural gas prices trended upward beginning in 2001, contributing to multi-million annual revenue-sharing payments. A payment of $7.1 million was made in January 2010 based on 2009 revenues. The total amount paid to the DOE under the revenue-sharing agreement since the sale of the plant to Basin Electric was $388.8 million.

91. Five energy companies built the plant as a consortium called Great Plains Gasification Associates (CGPA). Those partners were American Natural

Gas Company (later called American Natural Resources or ANR), Peoples Gas Company, Columbia Gas Transmission System, Tennessee Gas Pipeline Company, and Transcontinental Pipe Line Company. The five energy companies defaulted on $1.5 billion in federal loan guarantees used to build the plant. It began gasifying lignite in July 1984 but CGPA abandoned it about a year later and the Department of Energy operated the plant until selling it to Basin Electric in 1988. Basin's subsidiary Dakota Gasification Company assumed ownership of the plant on October 31, 1988. This history and perspective is documented in Stan Stelter's book, *The New Synfuels Energy Pioneers: A History of Dakota Gasification Company and the Great Plains Synfuels Plant* (Dakota Gasification Co., 2001).

92. The hemorrhaging incident occurred on December 4, 1985

93. Hospitalization for detached retina occurred on November 12, 1986.

94. Dick Rayl's seizure occurred on February 6, 1991.

95. Medical professionals from Poland arrived in the Dakotas on September 1, 1992, to learn advanced cardiac care techniques.

96. Jane Sinner formed a non-partisan, non-profit foundation called Friends of the North Dakota Governor's Residence in 1987. The foundation's purpose is to raise the funds needed to offset the on-going costs of updating and maintaining the official residence.

97. The legislature appropriated about $40,000 for the roof work, which was done in 1988.

98. The incident took place during the 1988–1989 school year.

99. The constitutional change was approved in the November 1986 general election by a vote of 171,766 to 93,220.

100. The supersonic flight occurred on January 16, 1990.

101. The Blue Angels ride occurred on June 20, 1986.

102. Governor Sinner's F-16 flight occurred on January 16, 1990.

103. Lloyd Omdahl was appointed lieutenant governor April 22, 1987, and sworn in May 15, 1987.

104. Jocelyn Birch Burdick, Fargo, is the only woman to have represented North Dakota in the US Senate and the only woman from North Dakota to serve in Congress. She lives in Fargo.

105. During the 1986 campaign, Kent Conrad pledged that he would not run for re-election if the federal budget deficit had not fallen by the end of his term. By 1992 it became obvious that that would not be the case and Conrad did not run for re-election. He then received an opportunity to run for North Dakota's other Senate seat upon the death (in office) of Quentin Burdick (1908-1992).

106. Tribal colleges in North Dakota are Cankdeska Cikana Community College, Fort Totten; Fort Berthold Community College, New Town; Sitting Bull College, Fort Yates; Turtle Mountain Community College, Belcourt; and United Tribes Technical College, Bismarck.

107. Ellen Chaffee retired as president of Valley City State University in 2008.

108. Agreements with tribal chairmen were signed October 7, 1992. They required the tribes to reserve a quarter of their gross gambling proceeds for health, human services, and non-gambling economic development programs on the reservations.

109. The collection was turned over to the Intertribal Re-internment Committee on January 19, 1990.

110. C-u-n-k-u is sometimes spelled c-a-n-k-u in Lakota language.

111. In the fall of 1940, the nation's first peacetime draft was enacted and the National Guard was called to active duty. All eighteen National Guard divisions saw combat in World War II, and were split between the Pacific and European theatres. When the US Marines needed reinforcements for the Guadalcanal campaign in the autumn of 1942, North Dakota's 164th

Infantry became the first large body of US Army troops to fight offensively in World War II.

112. Lieutenant General John B. Conaway served as the chief of the National Guard Bureau from 1990 to 1993. He is now retired from the Air Force.

113. Lee Teng-hui was president of Taiwan from 1988–2000. This visit occured in late May 1989.

114. The visit with Lee Teng-hui at Cornell occured in June 1995.

115. "Racing for Life" article, *The New York Times*, September 20, 1987; "A New Heart for Andrew" article, *Readers Digest*, February 1988.

116. Andrew de la Pena was a student at Loyola University in New Orleans when the family came to Fargo in May 2007 for a twenty-year reunion of the heart flight.

117. Bryce Streibel and Pete Naaden raised the issue in September 1990. The Mental Health Association auctioned the radar detector later that month.

118. The license plate story was published in *The Bismarck Tribune*, January 10, 1987.

119. An award-winning western author and screenwriter, Jamestown native Louis L'Amour published more than 400 short stories and over 100 novels, most of them westerns. He wrote 65 TV scripts, and sold over 30 stories to the motion picture industry. He was inducted into the North Dakota Hall of Fame (the Rough Rider Award) on May 26, 1972.

120. The Southwest Pipeline transports water from Lake Sakakawea to Dickinson, where it is treated and then delivered to communities in the southwestern section of North Dakota, an area sometimes referred to as the West River region or the Slope. The Sheyenne River Bypass Project includes 6.8 miles of flood diversion channel and 12.7 miles of levee to provide flood protection for West Fargo.

121. Governor Sinner's heart bypass surgery was July 23, 1991. On August 15, 1991, a blue-ribbon task force recommended tax increases to finance

a state water program. Governor Sinner returned to work in his office on September 3, 1991. GNDA annual business conference was held on October 16th—17th in Grand Forks. The Southwest Pipeline was dedicated October 22, 1991, in Dickinson.

122. The decision to not run for a third term was made October 31, 1991.

123. The meeting with Bill Osborne occurred during a trip to Boise, Idaho, for the 1985 National Governors Association annual meeting, August 4th–6th.

124. The first North American Regatta was held in July 1987.

125. Voters upheld Sunday opening law by a vote of 94,725 to 43,988.

126. On August 30, 2006, Alfonso Rodriguez was convicted in federal court of the murder of University of North Dakota student Dru Sjodin. On September 22, 2006, he was sentenced to death. It was the first death penalty case in a century to take place in North Dakota.

127. On August 31, 1982, the landmark US District Court decision by Judge Bruce Van Sickle in *The ARC of North Dakota vs. the State of North Dakota* found that the care, treatment, and facilities at the Grafton State School and San Haven violated the constitutional rights of the residents. North Dakota was ordered by the court to begin moving people with developmental disabilities from the state-operated institution into community programs. The state closed San Haven and reduced the Grafton Developmental Center (former State School) population level to below the court-ordered level of 250.

128. The Garrison Diversion Project was initially authorized by Congress in the Flood Control Act of 1944. The state agreed to a permanent inundation of 550,000 acres of rich Missouri River bottomland and the creation of Lake Sakakawea behind the Garrison Dam in exchange for a water distribution system for agricultural, industrial, and municipal uses. North Dakota was initially promised 1 million acres of irrigation along with recreation, flood control, water supply, and hydroelectric power. The Garrison Dam Unit was authorized by Congress in 1965. Although a number of features of the Garrison Diversion plan were built, the irrigation component has never been realized and Missouri River water has not yet reached the Red River basin.

129. Expansion plans began when North Dakota's six living governors met at a North Dakota Heritage Center forum in November 2001 to celebrate the building's twentieth anniversary. The governors—William Guy, Arthur Link, Allen Olson, George Sinner, and Edward Schafer—signed a resolution asking Governor John Hoeven to appoint a commission to study a possible expansion.

130. In 1974 the North Dakota Supreme Court ruled that Torfin Teigen was ineligible to run for a seat on that court. An activist independent, Torfin Teigen polled 928 votes in a 1980 North Dakota race for Congress against Democrat Byron Dorgan and Republican Jim Smykowski. He ran for Congress several others times in North Dakota and Minnesota, and also a candidate for Cass County superintendent of schools. He died September 30, 1985 at age eighty-four.

131. Ed Raymond's column titled "If Jesus Was at the Pope's White House Dinner, Did He Like the Food and Wine?," appeared in the *High Plains Reader*, April 24, 2008.

132. Nick Spaeth served eight years as North Dakota Attorney General. After defeating Democratic-NPL candidate Bill Heigaard in the 1992 primary election, Spaeth blew a lead in the polls and lost to Republican Ed Schafer in the race for governor, 58.2%–40.9%.

133. South Dakota Democrat Tom Daschle served four terms in the US House, was elected to the Senate in 1986, and became Senate Democratic leader in 1994. In 2004 he was targeted by the national Republican Party and lost his Senate seat to Republican John Thune by a margin of 4,508 votes.

INDEX

A

Aasel, Karen, 133, 285
abortion, ix, 143-
150, 249, 310-314,
315-317, 341n.
Air National Guard, see
National Guard and
Happy Hooligans
agriculture, i, iv, ix, 1,
25, 103, 166, 166-168,
203, 208, 212, 215-
217, 219, 252, 296,
340n.-342n., 344n.
Albrecht, Herb, 90
Allan, Bob, 124, 125
Allen, Warren, 203
American Crystal
Sugar Company, 94,
168, 223, 234, 338n.
American Energy
Assurance
Council, 220
Anderson, Albert,
90, 91
Anderson, Dale, 283
Anderson, Juel, 233
Anderson, Ron, 96, 310
Andrews, Mark, iii, vi,
xiv, 10, 172, 333n.
appointments (by
Governor Sinner), 21-
22, 104, 107, 108, 109,
139, 202, 252, 253
Aquino, Mrs.
Corazon, 120
ARC lawsuit, 288, 349n.
Arctic National
Wildlife Refuge, 217
Ariyoshi, George,
119, 120
Aubol, Clare, 96

B

Babbitt, Bruce, 167
Backes, Dick, 100, 103,
126, 183 (photo), 338n.
Backes, Norman, 106
Baker, Jim, 219
Bakken, A. C., 106
Bangerter, Norm,
212-213
Bank of North Dakota,
24, 25, 104, 127, 139,
202, 209, 340n.-341n.
Barney, Bill, 48
Basin Electric, 224,
345n., 346n.
Baute, Bernard, 229
Baute, Elizabeth Jane,
see Sinner, Jane
Becklund, Bob,
Jr., 267-268
Beithon, Paul, 94
Berg, Brian, 22,
121, 183 (photo),
204, 238, 271
Berg, Gordon, 281, 282
Beyer, Wally, 25, 209
Biegler, Larry,
210, 344n.
Bismarck Tribune,
131, 145, 172 (photo
credit), 176-178
(photo credits), 180-
182 (photo credits),
227, 276, 348n.
Blanchard, Jim, 167
Board of Higher
Education, vi, xiv,
83, 87, 90, 138, 234,
256, 257, 337n.
Bohn, Mick, 183
(photo)

Bond, Julian, 1
Bowdon (North
Dakota), 22, 335n.
Branstad, Terry,
216, 284
Bresnahan, Ellery, 17,
18, 28, 30, 34-37, 47,
51, 59, 170 (photo
credit), 171 (photo
credit), 284, 298
Bresnahan, Jeanne,
28, 34-37, 59, 169
(photos), 170 (photo
credit), 171 (photo
credit), 284, 298
Bresnahan, Richard,
184, 274, 275
Brooks, Lee, 76,
77, 80-82
Brown, Jack, 285
Brown, Malcolm, 106
budget, state, iv, vii,
viii, 20, 21, 40,
66, 88, 96, 102,
134, 137, 139, 180,
209, 213, 241, 242,
251, 289, 303, 319,
337n, 339n.-341n;
federal, 253, 319,
320 , 326, 347n.
Burdick, Jocelyn
"Jocie", 67, 252,
253, 347n.
Burdick, Quentin, iii,
66, 67, 182 (photo),
252, 253, 276, 347n.
Bush, George H.
W., ii, iii, 131-
133, 160-162, 213,
262, 264, 339n.
Bush, George W., 326

North Dakota State
University, vi, viii, 28,
84, 89-91, 95, 96, 102,
194, 289, 338n., 341n.
Northern Crops
Institute, viii, 95, 96
(Novacek) Hertel, Lisa,
118, 119, 202, 219

O

Odegaard, John,
264, 266
oil, iii, 134, 161,
217-220, 225, 292,
320, 340n., 345n.
Olson, Allen, iv, vi, vii,
viii, xv, 66, 96, 100,
101, 103-107, 109,
132, 134, 137, 180
(photo), 200, 201,
202, 208, 227, 293,
338n., 340n., 350n.
Omdahl, Lloyd, xv,
xviii, 102, 137,
179 (photo), 183
(photos), 205, 206,
207, 232, 251, 305,
338n., 344n., 347n.
Orth, Fred, 83, 85
Osborne, Bill,
285, 349n.
Otos, Don, 9, 29, 333n.
Otto Bremer
Foundation, 92, 93
Oxford on the
Prairie, 89

P

PACE program, 24, 25,
139, 202, 209, 210
Painte, Deborah,
183 (photo)
Party of the Century,
ii, 132, 133, 180

Patrie, Bill, 210
Pederson, Vernon, 104
Pena, Frederico, 167
Perpich, Rudy, 216, 262
Peterson, Martin, 49
Peterson, Sheila, 102
pharmacy legislation,
52, 77, 78-80, 337n.
poetry, 279
Polycarp, the
Reverend, 52
Pomeroy, Earl, 139, 253
Pomeroy, Glenn,
96, 183 (photo)
Pope Benedict XVI
(and Cardinal
Ratzinger), 71, 298,
299, 335n., 350n.
Port, Laura, 51
Potter, Tracy, xviii, 251
Prairie Rose State
Games, 284
Pressler, Gary,
183 (photo)
property taxes, 6, 111,
112, 116, 135, 136,
138, 304, 333n.
Pryor, Mark, 168
Pyle, Ernie, 83, 84

R

Raschke, Ken, 85, 256
Rayl, Dick, 20, 21,
40, 66, 102, 137,
139, 230, 240, 242,
288, 303, 346n.
Raymond, Ed,
298, 350n.
Reader's Digest, 268
Reagan, Nancy,
162, 219
Reagan, Ronald, iii,
160-162, 194, 206,
217-219, 262, 326

Redlin, Earl, 79
Redmann, Garry
(photo credits),
175, 179, 180, 183
referred measures, i,
viii, 131, 134-136,
140, 180, 205, 206,
277, 287, 303, 340n.
Richardson, Bill, 167
Riehl, Emil, 96
Reilly, Bill, 220
Reimers, Bob, 87, 88
Reimers, James,
243, 244
Rendahl, Jim, 91
Rohde, Chuck, 18
Roosevelt, Theodore,
131, 153
Rothenberger,
Bonnie, 273
Rough Rider Award,
viii, 153-156, 184,
341n., 348n.
Rubin, Bob, 163
Russell, Seth, 89

S

Sailer, Ella, 51
Sand, Paul, 104
San Haven, 288, 349n.
Sanstead, Wayne, 135
Sathre, P. O., 77, 336n.
Satrom, Joe, 111
Sawyer landfill,
221, 222, 345n.
Schafer, Ed, iv, viii, 202,
286, 293, 305, 350n.
Schmeltzer, Martin, 49
Schneider, John, 96
Schneider, Lois, 103
Schrock, Dellis, 292
Schroeder, Darrell, 199
Schroeder, Hank, 94
Schuchart, Jack, 165